Killer Apps

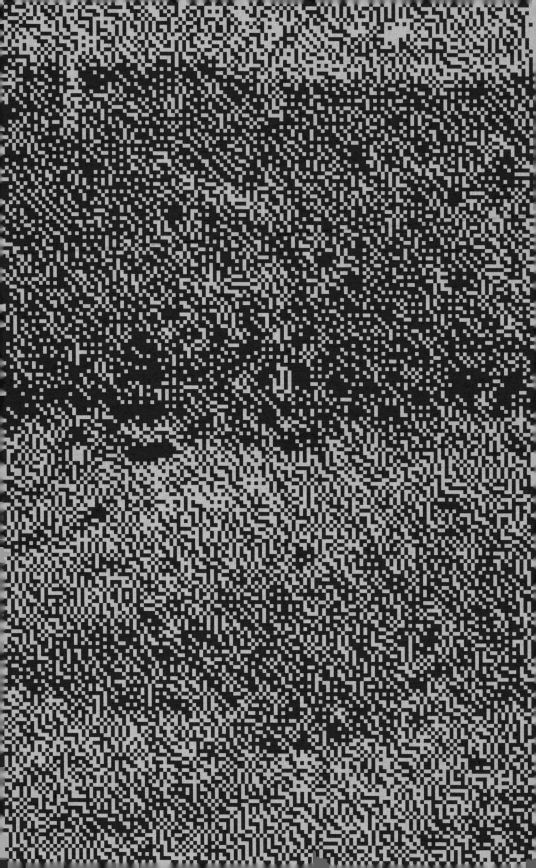

Killer Apps

War, Media, Machine

Jeremy Packer
and Joshua Reeves

Duke University Press
Durham and London
2020

© 2020 Duke University Press
All rights reserved
Printed and bound by CPI Group (UK) Ltd, Croydon, CR0 4YY
Designed by Drew Sisk
Typeset in Portrait Text and Helvetica Neue by Westchester
Publishing Services

Library of Congress Cataloging-in-Publication Data
Names: Packer, Jeremy, [date] author. | Reeves, Joshua, author.
Title: Killer Apps : War, Media, Machine / Jeremy Packer and
 Joshua Reeves.
Description: Durham, NC: Duke University Press, 2020. |
 Includes bibliographical references and index.
Identifiers: LCCN 2019032476 (print)
LCCN 2019032477 (ebook)
ISBN 9781478005872 (hardcover)
ISBN 9781478006572 (paperback)
ISBN 9781478007272 (ebook)
Subjects: LCSH: Artificial intelligence—Military applications. |
 Robotics—Military applications. | Armed Forces and mass
 media—United States. | War in mass media. | War in
 literature. | Military art and science—Technological
 innovations—Social aspects.
Classification: LCC UG479 .P33 2020 (print) | LCC UG479 (ebook)
DDC 355.40285—dc23
LC record available at https://lccn.loc.gov/2019032476
LC ebook record available at https://lccn.loc.gov/2019032477

Cover art: Illustration and design by Drew Sisk.

operation plan (DoD)

1. Any plan for the conduct of military operations prepared in response to actual and potential contingencies.

    Acknowledgments vii

    Preface to an Inauthentic Document ix

    Introduction Event Matrix (DoD) 1

1 Identification Friend or Foe (DoD) 29

2 Centralized Control/Decentralized Execution (DoD) 48

3 Hostile Environment (DoD) 61

4 In Extremis (DoD) 89

5 Intelligence, Surveillance, and Reconnaissance (DoD) 109

6 Autonomous Operation (DoD) 124

7 Vital Ground (DoD) 139

8 Escalation (DoD) 159

9 Unidentified Flying Objects (USAF) 175

    Conclusion Armistice (DoD) 198

    Notes 217

    References 235

    Index 261

Acknowledgments

Jeremy Packer

Writing collaboratively is always a unique opportunity to think differently and to force an expansion of perspective. Working with Josh has been all of that and then considerably more. It's been a trip, and for that I thank him immensely. I've talked a few friends's ears off about this project, and I want to publicly apologize to them for droning on and to thank them for carefully explaining why I (or we) might be slightly misdirected in my (our) thinking. Chris Russill, David Monje, Jack Bratich, Kumi Silva, Tero Karppi, Craig Robertson, Ganaele Langlois, Nick Taylor, Orit Halpern, and Steve Wiley bore the brunt of my chatter. Chris Russill and Sarah Sharma also read an early draft and provided ample correctives, for which I am very grateful. Thanks to Lisa Parks and Caren Kaplan for showing interest in our work for their volume on drones, and to Chris Russill (again) for his inclusion of our ideas in the *Canadian Journal of Communication*. Courtney Berger and the rest of the Duke editorial team have provided insight and professionalism throughout and found two excellent readers. I also want to thank North Carolina State University's Department of Communication for the opportunity to work with so many great colleagues, and the Communication Rhetoric and Digital Media program for allowing me to work with so many great students. Thanks to Greg Elmer for allowing me to present some early ideas in front of the Media Theory Working Group here in Toronto. Thanks to the McLuhan Centre for allowing me to present some of this material alongside Geoffrey Winthrop Young and Megan Boler. Thanks to the University of Toronto Mississauga for providing great new colleagues and the funding that allowed for the completion of this project. Special thanks to Drew Sisk for executing our cover idea for a "Turing Machine Gun."

And thanks to Sarah, Zyla, and Dahlia, who provide my most immediate reason to hold the fort against the Cylons.

Joshua Reeves

Putting together *Killer Apps* was a blast right from the start, so above all I'd like to thank Jeremy for sticking it out these past seven years. He made sure it was always challenging and always fun, and for that I'm extremely grateful. I also want to thank all the friends who helped me hash out the problems explored in *Killer Apps*: folks like Cora Borradaile, Jodi Dean, Tom Dietterich, Chris Ingraham, Stephanie Jenkins, Caren Kaplan, Colin Koopman, Marina Levina, Kellie Marin, Matt May, Alex Monea, Chris Nichols, Derek Noon, Lisa Parks, Damien Pfister, Marnie Ritchie, Chris Russill, Roger Stahl, and Ethan Stoneman. Thanks, as well, to Courtney Berger, Chris Russill (again), Sarah Sharma, and our fabulous anonymous reviewers for pushing us in new directions. I'm also grateful to Liz Ellcessor, Camilla Fojas, Siva Vaidhyanathan, and the rest of the University of Virginia's Department of Media Studies for bringing me to Charlottesville to share some of these ideas in February 2018 (and again in 2019). Benjamin Burroughs, Donovan Conley, and the rest of the "Mediating Pathogens" crew at UNLV also deserve thanks for helping me work through this material during a fantastic retreat in Las Vegas. I should also thank Jake Hamblin, who asked me to explore these questions before a perplexed audience at OSU's robotics symposium in October 2018. And thanks to the College of Liberal Arts at Oregon State University—especially to the inimitable Eric Dickey—for awarding me a research grant that provided some much-needed time to wrap up the project.

Amelia, Oliver, and Clara were all born while I was writing this book, so they deserve my apologies as much as my thanks. As do Austin, Annelie, and Leslie, who are all hilarious and make it so hard to focus on work.

Preface to an Inauthentic Document

authentic document (NATO) A document bearing a signature or seal attesting that it is genuine and official. If it is an enemy document, it may have been prepared for purposes of deception and the accuracy of such document, even though authenticated, must be confirmed by other information, such as conditions of capture.

authentication (DoD) 1. A security measure designed to protect a communications system against acceptance of a fraudulent transmission or simulation by establishing the validity of a transmission, message, or originator. 2. A means of identifying individuals and verifying their eligibility to receive specific categories of information. 3. Evidence by proper signature or seal that a document is genuine and official. 4. In personnel recovery missions, the process whereby the identity of an isolated person is confirmed.

We promise this book is inauthentic. It will fail any and all processes of authentication.

Our inauthenticity is thorough.

1. Few if any security measures were undertaken in the preparation of the transmission to follow. Google Drive ensured that. Dreams of validity may still disrupt the slumber of the methodologically apprehensive, but it has yet to misdirect our thinking.
2. Not since being mandatorily marked as draftable by Selective Service has either of us been identified by any military body of which we know.
3. The document before you is signed—in that we accept the responsibility for our words—but its signature is improper in the sense that it cannot seal or cement itself in the filing systems of US military doctrine.
4. We are acting in union, but we are not necessarily affiliated. This makes our recovery an unlikely mission.

Such profound inauthenticity suggests that this may indeed be an enemy document. Any "unofficial document," by definition, is in the category of *maybe enemy*. And where potential enemies are concerned, media will be searching for their presence. This documentary lack may provide proof that *Killer Apps* "may have been prepared for purposes of deception." While we would like to outright denounce such claims as to our purpose, what seal or signature could we provide that would satisfy all potential doubt? We must instead wallow in the realm of *maybe enemy* and accept that in point of fact this document may be deceptive. We have not chosen to deceive per se, but we have certainly chosen the path of the inauthentic.

As with everything else, books have friends and foes. You might come in peace or with fists raised. Or like Switzerland, you may feign neutrality. You may not yet know which you are. Maybe you will change sides partway through. Or better yet, your sleeper cell may be activated unbeknownst to you or us. Regardless of your present status, a few preparations will prove beneficial in all contingencies.

1. Tone is a stylistic choice, and many before us have chosen absurdity, irony, and even black comedy to confront the horrors of warfare and the logics of military strategy. By comparison our choices are mild, though not guaranteed to be free of irritants.
2. Style and format are drawn in part from military communications, which is the discursive reservoir from which the bureaucratic and strategic legacies of warfare are built. Department of Defense (DoD) definitions are foundational to how this military logic is constructed and maintained. Each chapter opens with a definition that it then works to undo.
3. As with a multifront war, this book is not linear. Everything must be taken into account all at once. Though it is bookended by an introduction and conclusion, there is no single route through the quagmire that follows.

Event Matrix (DoD)

> Introduction

A description of the indicators and activity expected to occur in each named area of interest. It normally cross-references each named area of interest and indicator with the times they are expected to occur and the courses of action they will confirm or deny.

> *The future may or may not bear out my present convictions, but I cannot refrain from saying that it is difficult for me to see at present how, with such a principle brought to great perfection, as it undoubtedly will be in the course of time, guns can maintain themselves as weapons. We shall be able, by availing ourselves of this advance, to send a projectile at much greater distance, it will not be limited in any way by weight or amount of explosive charge, we shall be able to submerge it at command, to arrest it in its flight, and call it back, and send it out again and explode it at will, and, more than this, it will never make a miss, since all chance in this regard, if hitting the object of attack were at all required, is eliminated. But the chief feature of such a weapon is still to be told; namely, it may be made to respond only to a certain note or tune, it may be endowed with selective power. Directly such an arm is produced, it becomes almost impossible to meet it with a corresponding development. It is this feature, perhaps more than in its power of destruction, that its tendency to arrest the development of arms and to stop warfare will reside.*
> —NIKOLA TESLA, "TESLA DESCRIBES HIS EFFORTS," 1898

Nikola Tesla, long hailed as the inventor of "radio, television, power transmission, the induction motor, and the robot,"[1] was anything but a Luddite. But in 1898, the world-renowned scientist foresaw that further advances in the scientific application of technical media to ballistics—specifically, the use of sensors to aim and guide "smart" weapons—could imperil the peace of the world. Believing "that war could be stopped by making it more destructive,"[2] Tesla reckoned that artificially intelligent weapons—weapons that could make *note* of and at*tune* themselves to their surroundings—would make battle so disastrous that humans would surely abolish war and move along to other pastimes. The merging of media and weaponry would bring about either an end to war or an end to the world.

Yet from the vantage of the early twenty-first century, it's clear that smart weapons haven't introduced the kind of peace that Tesla fantasized about. Rather than taking Tesla's advice and "dispens[ing] with artillery of this type," the world's predominant military is instead trying to dispense with as much of its human personnel as possible. Especially since the dawn of the Cold War, when the Americans were faced with Soviet numerical superiority, the United States has resigned itself to developing *technological* superiority.[3] While Soviet strategy was largely oriented around recruiting and developing the human soldier, American strategy has been devoted in large measure to sacrificing the human in favor of technological innovation, especially advancements in command, control, communications, computers, and information (C4I). Describing this development, Katherine Hayles observes, "Military strategists argue that information has become a key military asset and that the US military must be reorganized to take full advantage of it."[4] This "technological turn"[5] in US military strategy has given us the unnerving technical reality foreseen by Tesla—that of self-guided munitions, autonomous drones, and other artificially intelligent (AI) weapons of war—without any of the promised peace.

Media technologies lie at the very center of these key developments. After all, the ongoing "revolution in military affairs" (RMA) has placed computation, unmanned vehicles, swarm warfare, smart weapons, autonomous missile defense systems, and artificial intelligence at the forefront of next-generation military strategy.[6] In the words of Stephen Graham, "Centering on technologies of 'stealth,' 'precision' targeting, networked computing, and satellite geopositioning, the RMA has been widely hailed by U.S. military planners as the path to sustaining U.S. dominance."[7] Needless to say, the central component in each of these developments is *media* technology—those technologies that offer different manipulations of the time/space axis, thus ushering in new political realities and military velocities through their unique capacities to select, store, and process information. The most expensive project in military history, the United States' F-35 system, provides an excellent example of this trend. As US deputy defense secretary Bob Work observed in 2015, "The F-35 is not a fighter plane.... It is a flying sensor computer that sucks in an enormous amount of data, correlates it, analyzes it, and displays it to the pilot on his helmet."[8] By Secretary Work's account, the infamous F-35 is not really a plane in any traditional sense: it's a computer with wings. While the explosives actually go bang when a missile hits its target, the truly decisive military-strategic questions are media-driven: How are that missile's targets located and assessed? How can the missile be aimed? How can it be delivered? How can it intelligently respond to its environment in order to best follow its target? By the same token, while it's typically the explosive aftermath of drone strikes that grabs the headlines, the more fundamental questions about drones are driven by media capacities: How can an unmanned vehicle be controlled from a military base overseas? How can it capture surveillance footage, and how can that footage be transmitted back home to drone "pilots"? When a drone captures audiovisual phenomena, how is that vast expanse of data processed and interpreted in order to alert drone pilots to potential threats? How are these attack decisions made, transmitted, and then carried out? How will these modes of warfare seep into other struggles that aren't generally thought of as war? What new kinds of warfare and new forms of defense policy do these technologies make possible, if not inevitable?

This mediacentric series of questions leads us to the essential political problem at issue with drones and related forms of AI warfare: when military systems are programmed with the ability to decide whom or what to strike, humans have offloaded their carbon-based political intelligence onto the silicon processing capacities of the machine, thereby surrendering a crucial ethical capacity—the ability to determine who is friend and who is foe. With the rise of robotic submarines and missile defense systems that autonomously determine enemy threats, aim weapons, fire, and guide munitions all on their own—without *any* human guidance—that threshold has already been crossed. In fact, Friedrich Kittler would argue that we crossed it way back in World War II, when the Brits used radar to reveal signals—signals that were undetectable to human senses—in order to distinguish between friendly and enemy craft, between British Mosquitoes and German V-2s.[9] These displacements and subversions of human perception continued to escalate into the 1980s, when a US Navy self-guided Harpoon antiship missile autonomously misidentified a friendly Indian freighter and killed one of its crew members. And today, with the development of drones that scan vast territories and determine what footage to share with pilots—that is, drones that determine what data might contain evidence of enemies to fire upon—drone warfare's much-discussed and heavily relied on "human in the loop" has become all but ornamental. In the navy, where vessel autonomy has a much longer tradition, it's already a thing of the past: after relying on human input for years, in fall 2016 the Office of Naval Research's Control Architecture for Robotic Agent Command and Sensing (CARACaS) system successfully deployed swarm boats equipped with radar and infrared sensors to autonomously differentiate friendly and enemy craft. And as US Department of Defense (DoD) "roadmaps" of the future make clear, endowing weapons with these medialogical capacities to analyze environments, determine friend from foe, and engage perceived threats will be at the forefront of military strategy during the coming decades. ANNs (Artificial Neural Networks) will aid in ATR (Automatic Target Recognition) and will fuel the military's capacity to DRCI (Detect, Recognize, Classify, Identify). Fully autonomous swarms of drones, robotic warriors, and "integrated" human/AI battle environments all lie in our near future, and experts agree that they will find their way onto the battlefield within the next decade. Ultimately, for analysts such as Center for a New American Security fellow Paul Scharre, these trends are leading toward the development of "an army of none."[10]

This book uses media theory as a lens to analyze the history of warfare, the rationality of weapons development, and US military roadmaps in order to better understand the political implications of this convergence of AI and war—especially as this convergence serves to replace human soldiers in the air, underwater, and on the battlefield. What we find is that war, along with its fraternal twin media technology, has crept like a virus into the human sensory apparatus. As the silicon, glass, and steel of cutting-edge military technologies reveal humans to be too soft, too weak, and too stupid to wage war by themselves, humans are eagerly surrendering an unsettling degree of military labor to machines. And the machine, happy to oblige, has agreed to roam the skies, scour the seas, fire weapons, and terminate its enemies. Whether the machine eliminates its own enemies or the enemies of its human "controllers," it makes no difference. *The* enemy, after all, is the same. The machine, whose foe has always been the inefficient, the imprecise, the weak, the stupid, and the slow—that is, whose foe has always been the human—long ago began the gradual process of outlining the silhouette of what humankind would come to perceive as its own enemy. As we have slowly begun to recognize the human face of that true foe, our friend the machine is helping us prepare to wash it away, "like a face drawn in sand at the edge of the sea."[11]

Media and Enemy Epistemology

This book is concerned above all with the role of media in enemy epistemology and enemy production. On at least two closely related fronts, media technologies are crucial to this process. First, they play an essential role at the macro level, by shifting the plane of political intelligibility so that new enemies to the individual, to the community, to the nation, or to humanity come into view. Second, at the micro level, media are crucial to the friend/enemy determinations that fighters and machines make when they scan the war zone and select their targets. Because media play these key roles in enemy epistemology, they have inserted themselves into the very center of that amorphous domain we call *the political*, especially when the political erupts into its most mature manifestation: armed conflict. In one of the best-known statements of twentieth-century political theory, Carl Schmitt put it like this: "For as long as a people exists in the political sphere, this people must, even if only in the most extreme case ... determine by itself the distinction of friend and enemy. Therein resides the essence of its political existence. When it no longer possesses the capacity or the will to make this distinction, it ceases to exist politically."[12] While Schmitt's definition of the political is hardly exhaustive, it does highlight an essential demand of political reality: the determination of friends and enemies. Without this capacity to determine friend from foe, there can be no politics—no alliances to form, no one to sacrifice for, no threats to mobilize against, no friends to protect.[13] Indeed, the friend/enemy distinction provides our own ontological condition of possibility: without the enemy other, there can be no friend. Without a them, there can be no us.[14]

One of this book's chief claims is that enemy epistemology is beholden to a specific media logic—that is, a logic of sensation, perception, reason, and comprehension specific to a given mediological environment. As Antonie van Leeuwenhoek proved when his new microscope revealed one of humankind's greatest enemies—the germ—new instruments of knowledge bring new enemies and new threats into our range of perception. By melting rods of soda lime glass and grinding them into high-power optical lenses, in the 1670s van Leeuwenhoek kicked off a gradual epistemological rupture that produced an endless host of scientific theories, health provisions, sanitary procedures, and security measures—all aimed, of course, at neutralizing the new threat. The invisible and mysterious miasmata ceased to be our enemies. Protecting the population, therefore, called for more than increased ventilation and urban circulation to cleanse "poisonous" air, more than purging our creeks, rivers, factories, and ghettos of foul water. As generations of scientists looked through microscopes to see "little worms," "imperceptible insects,"[15] and finally pathogenic microorganisms, new methods of enemy elimination became en vogue: boiling water, boric acid supplementation, pasteurization, antiseptics, and antibiotics.

With the aid of van Leeuwenhoek's microscope and related optical media, a new enemy—the pathogen—emerged. And along with this new enemy, we developed new methods of warfare: new forms of health management, new architectural arrangements, new styles of urban planning, new public education initiatives, new culinary habits, new disciplines of research, and a new sense of the human as a contagious risk. Through this tremendous new social, intellectual, cultural, and political infrastructure—one that continues to grow and evolve today—humanity has absorbed the enemy into its everyday existence. Our lives revolve around finding, fighting, and eliminating the enemy: every time we wash our hands, sweep the floors, flush the toilet, cook and clean our food, trust our nurses and physicians, filter our water, take medicine, and check our children's temperatures. Moreover, this biopolitical care is differentially organized such that access to the daily technologies and infrastructures of bacterial eradication are not equally dispersed.[16] This highlights the technical dimensions of how potential allies are overlooked, how enemyship is produced, and how being imbricated in different media infrastructures draws one into different enemy epistemologies. All in all, these daily habits and procedures of enemy location and elimination not only breed further opportunities and desires to locate and neutralize the threat; they, like a Hellfire missile careening into an unsuspecting village on the other side of the world, also tend to produce conditions in which the perceived threat—as well as new threats—can reemerge, strengthen, and thrive. As Kittler would have it, "Every system of power has the enemies it produces."[17]

And as Kittler would certainly agree, every media system, too, has the enemies it produces. While media technology might not be the most visible element of this great transformation in micro warfare, this was, in fact, a medialogical process. It was *media driven* and *media dependent*. Without van Leeuwenhoek's ground glass lenses, the germ never would have been identifiable as an enemy, and all this upheaval and social transformation would have never taken place. To take another example, consider how during the Cold War media escalated warfare into a truly global phenomenon. The Semi-Automatic Ground Environment (SAGE) system and breakthroughs in satellite surveillance automated the process of monitoring the globe, turning the whole planet into a battlefield populated with new enemies. New media, then, were developed to identify and analyze this new enemy; and as this enemy's movements and ambitions were identified, new unknowns emerged. What are the signs that it is preparing for attack? What form might its attack take? How can we prevent that attack from taking place? These new questions, which were not even askable without the prior generation of media technologies, thus spurred the development of additional media. Newly recognized problems, therefore, prompt new media solutions; then the expanded realm of the intelligible introduced by those new technologies inserts new unanswered questions into the system, which must be answered by new media capacities. Media, therefore, are constantly producing new enemies, and new methods of enemy identification stimulate the development of new weapons technologies designed to kill those newly identified enemies. Moreover, these media-weapons produce new enemies each time they kill a bystander's friends, parents, children, husband, wife, neighbor, lover, coworker, comrade, or compatriot. This is especially visible in the US military's habit of ex post facto labeling as "enemies" all people killed by its drone strikes.[18] The drone also creates enemies, therefore, when those enemies are pieced back together out of piles of shrapnel and rubble.

Although this book focuses on international armed conflict, von Leeuwenhoek's example indicates that there are also "insider threats"—people, pathogens, and people perceived as pathogens—that police, military, and colonial authorities have constantly been driven to discover and destroy. The relationship between domestic struggles against insider threats and armed warfare is direct and clear, as the technologies, procedures, and rationalities of international warfare inevitably come home to roost as they are remixed into the domestic security context.[19] Military tactics and colonial administration practiced abroad—which, in the case of settler colonies, have long been genocidal war zones[20]—fuel new ways of waging war in the "homeland." And, of course, as in all wars, media are central to fighting this insider threat. The various human and biological sciences have consistently collaborated with new media to classify internal and external threats. We can look to the historical procession from writing to photography to phonograph to film—each of which has been used to discover different inscriptions that are said to house meaningful evidence of an often racialized internal threat. For example, the premier biometric ("anthropometric") scientist of the nineteenth century, Alphonse Bertillon, applied handwriting analysis to determine threatening classes of the population.[21] The history of anthropology is replete with examples of how the phonograph and other audio recording technologies were used as a means of manifesting, cataloguing, and evaluating difference.[22] While Amos Morris-Reich and John Tagg have both analyzed how photography was used in this kind of work, Jonathan Sterne has revealed the importance of aural media to the analysis of the racialized internal threat.[23] Perhaps most intriguing, with the Hollerith machine—an early US census technology—we begin to see a move toward immense computation as a weapon in the race war. During and immediately following World War I, the US military amassed extensive biometric data on millions of US soldiers. These data were used to produce a twenty-six-volume set of statistical analyses that attempted to locate deficient and superior racial markers in order to maximize military biopolitical capacity.[24] As the work of scholars such as Simone Browne, Kelly Gates, Rachel Hall, and Shoshana Magnet clearly illustrates, this computational and statistical imaginary has only escalated as digital forms of biometric analysis have attracted considerable investment following the 9/11 attacks.[25] Paul Virilio sees a similar rearticulation of the enemy and nation having taken place due to global information networks and supersonic transport developed during the Cold War.[26] Increasingly military resources have been deployed against a country's own population, as exocolonization in part gives way to endocolonization. And as always, media make it possible for this lurking insider threat to be seen, heard, studied, and solved.

There are three main ways, then, in which media are central to the politics of enemy epistemology and enemy production. First, as media technologies change, capacities to access and analyze our surroundings also change. In this sense, the relationship between media technologies and enemy production is one of epistemology: every new medium shifts the realm of the intelligible, creating new enemies specific to its particular capacities for capturing and processing data. Van Leeuwenhoek's microscope allowed us to see millions of new enemies teeming under a microscope; and if this early microscope could unearth a hostile army residing in our blood, what deeper-seated foes have been revealed by today's sensing technologies? Not only are MRIs and ECGs deployed to reveal physical ailments and defects, but now they're being imagined as biometric sensors for determining who might secretly be a domestic terrorist.[27] To take another example, the video feeds from Predator drones allow operators to see "terrorists" that were previously beyond the grasp of perception; these enemies are produced when humans behind screens must categorize observed persons according to a binary military epistemology. And in perhaps the ultimate epistemic twist: who, we might ask, are the enemies brought to light by military-driven computational models of anthropogenic climate change?[28] By creating new ways of perceiving our environment and ourselves, new media introduce new enemies to the world. Second, media technologies and media apparatuses—from scopes and sensors to cameras, drones, and missile defense systems—allow soldiers to make determinations as to who is friend and who is foe. Whether on the ground, in the air, or underwater, these technologies make it possible for soldiers to study their environment, identify enemies, and aim their weapons at the appropriate target. And finally, third, if every media system has the enemies it produces, it also follows that these media-enabled shifts in perception give rise to new weapons and new forms of warfare. In this sense, van Leeuwenhoek and his microscope didn't merely discover germs; they also gave us *germ warfare*. The Geiger-Marsden optical apparatus didn't just discover the nucleus; it gave us the nuclear bomb. The Galilean telescope didn't simply disclose the mysteries of the solar system; it gave us "Star Wars," the military space race, and interplanetary missile defense. Indeed, this is one of the inevitable results of media escalation. New media reveal new risks, new opportunities for exploiting the natural world, and new methods of destruction, thus driving the development of new instruments of death and coercion.[29] Every media revolution ushers forth new methods of slaughter.

Military Media

Our mediacentric analysis rests on several interwoven understandings of the recursive relationship between media and military strategy. First, following Friedrich Kittler, we approach media in terms of those technologies that specialize in the selection, storage, processing, and transmission of information.[30] The world's militaries have always been at the developmental front of these media technologies; therefore, in the words of John Durham Peters, "media history without the military-industrial complex is ultimately deeply misguided."[31] Some of the most innovative work in media theory has come from theorists who, like Kittler, Manuel DeLanda, Katherine Hayles, Donna Haraway, and Paul Virilio, devote considerable time to the military-media complex.[32] As these writers and others have made clear, innovations in media technology have been chiefly driven by military desires—in Kittler's words, the civilian media technologies we know and love tend to be simply the "byproducts or waste products of pure military research."[33] Yet this "polemocentrism" (*polemos* = battle or struggle in classical Greek) not only puts war into the middle of media theory; it puts media into the middle of war.[34] The production of military knowledge, after all, is foremost a media problem, as warfare is organized, studied, prepared for, and conducted according to communicative capacities. This is why, as Lisa Parks points out, "it is difficult to distinguish media and communication from militarization."[35] Even the size of singular permanent military formations, not to be composed of more than three thousand soldiers prior to the French Revolution, was dictated by the limits imposed by the soldier's perceptual capacity to see visual signaling technologies—flags.[36] In this and related ways, military command depends on media that collect data on self and enemy, transmit orders through the chain of command, and guide tactics in real time. Scrolls, letters, binoculars, the telegraph, the semaphore, two-way radio, missile defense systems, drones—these are just a few of the basic media technologies that have played an essential role in circulating orders, determining military strategy, extending visibility, constraining troop formation, guiding munitions, and facilitating friend/enemy analysis.

Second, we synthesize the work of Carl von Clausewitz, Claude Shannon, and Warren Weaver to emphasize the military-strategic importance of eliminating communications delays and errors.[37] For Clausewitz, perhaps the most celebrated European military mind of the nineteenth century, these delays and errors—which he called "friction"—threaten to blanket commanders in the fog of war.[38] And in Claude Shannon and Warren Weaver's classic approach to media and communication[39]—which has its roots in cryptographic research that sought to eliminate semiosis in favor of raw numerical signaling—communication systems achieve optimal results by creating extensive feedback loops that reduce "noise" (e.g., vagueness, inaccuracies, and distortions) and enable greater amounts of information to be transmitted. An order must be transferred to the front; an accurate view of the enemy must be attained; a missile must be guided toward its target. As the Shannon and Weaver model emphasizes, these operations demand absolute clarity at the greatest possible speed. Miscommunications and delays can mean the difference between victory and defeat. And, as even Shannon and Weaver observed back in the 1940s, humans—with their analog language and their mediological weaknesses in interpreting and transmitting data—are the key source of distortion and "noise" in the communication chain. Accordingly, global militaries are retooling themselves in order to remove distortion-introducing humans from as many tasks as possible. This is occurring both in C4I—where communication and data analysis have been partially automated for decades—as well as on the battlefield, where soldiers are being supplemented with robots, drones, and related technological systems that function on artificial intelligence. These hybrid battlefield strategies (which combine human and artificial intelligence) are largely responding to the conditions of Shannon and Weaver's classic theory of communications as a mathematical problem whose solutions demand noise reduction. Humans, as the noisiest of communicators, can be a lethal liability in the infowar. Their replacement by smarter, faster machines is simply a natural advancement in communications, command, and control.

The third point also comes from Kittler, who noted that, because war is noisy, "command in war must be digital."[40] Hence the answer to these command problems of noise and distortion is the application of digital certainty. As Gerfried Stocker points out, "There is no sphere of civilian life in which the saying 'war is the father of all things' has such unchallenged validity as in the field of digital information technology."[41] While the standard historical treatment of military digitization relies on a narrative stemming from two World War II objectives, cryptography and ballistics prediction, this "digital telos" appears much earlier in military history. For example, at least as early as the US Civil War, attempts to "digitize" semaphore telegraphy for the purposes of semiotic certainty and greater autonomous mobility were developed by the US Army Signal Corps.[42] As illustrated by militaries' frenzied post–World War II turn toward computerization and artificial intelligence, the digital telos now reigns supreme and frames the contours of research, development, and international military competition. As the US Defense Science Board's "Summer Study" of 2016 concluded, "DoD must accelerate its exploitation of autonomy—both to realize the potential military value and to remain ahead of adversaries who also will exploit its operational benefits."[43] This has resulted in massive increases in US defense investment in AI: in 2016, the DoD spent almost $3 billion on AI-related initiatives, and its number of unmanned aircraft has grown to eleven thousand, some 40 percent of all US military aircraft.[44] It has also led to the formation in 2017 of the Algorithmic Warfare Team, the brainchild of then-deputy defense secretary Robert O. Work, that will formally centralize and promote AI developments across the branches of DoD.[45] While this digital telos has been complicated somewhat by recent breakthroughs in quantum and analog computing, the will to digitize has had—and will continue to have—a tremendous impact on next-generation military strategy.

With this in mind, the present book strives to offer an account of media and war that avoids getting caught up in the familiar determinisms. While theoretical commentary on media and war can get bogged down in whether media or war play the predominant determining role, we'd prefer to avoid the dissociation altogether. For us, it isn't clear that media technology determines the course of warfare (a medial a priori of war) or that warfare determines the development of media technology (a martial a priori of media).[46] While it might be tempting to privilege one over the other, we argue that such a division distorts our understanding of the relationship between these two phenomena. After all, at any level of abstraction, war has never existed apart from technologies of time/space manipulation. By the same token, that creature we currently call the human only crossed the threshold of its humanity by fashioning and being fashioned by martial technologies of time/space manipulation. Where, therefore, could we possibly draw the line between media, war, and the human subject? If Clausewitz is right and war is the progenitor of all things, then media must provide the genetic code—and we humans are the hapless progeny of this strange coupling.

Theorizing War/Media

This is why we have chosen to focus on the role of media in military strategy, military command, and military epistemology. While we could follow many of our colleagues in emphasizing the cultural uptake of war across different media forms, we are aiming our analysis at a different level of the war/media relationship. We focus, especially, on how media technology's perceptual interventions and spatiotemporal manipulations force into view new enemies and new methods of enemy engagement. A number of scholars, however, have recently done fascinating work on the role of media in promoting hostilities, exacerbating international tensions, fueling xenophobia, and rationalizing violence against target groups.[47] Some of these scholars have even privileged the cultural content of media in driving military technology, highlighting the role that popular media representations can have in the invention, design, and use of new weapons and C4I systems. Rachel Dubrofsky and Shoshana Magnet, for instance, have pointed out that "[cultural] narratives ... may serve to shape technological development, as scientists internalize these cultural messages and attempt to actualize them in new technologies."[48] This assertion aligns with the critique of other humanist and feminist scholars who foreground the role of humans in shaping technological development. Following on the Marxist claim that relations of production shape technological development, technology is regarded as something of a superstructural phenomenon derived from a socioeconomic base. Feminist theorists such as Cynthia Cockburn (with Furst-Dilic), Judy Wajcman, and Rosalind Williams provide some of this critique's classic articulations, asserting the primacy of the human imprint on technology's biased distributions of access, wealth, and power.[49]

Although this trend in humanist reason privileges the role of humans in shaping technological development, we would like to follow Joanna Zylinska's call for new forms of critique that "challeng[e] human exceptionalism, with its foundational subject, as a key framework for understanding the world."[50] The sociological position is one such form of human exceptionalism, as its emphasis on subjective political agency leads it to underestimate the role of media technology in constituting and giving shape to the political values, artistic and architectural styles, scientific standards, military capacities, and self-understandings of what Kittler calls the "so-called human."[51] We thus find ourselves nearer posthuman feminists such as Rosi Braidotti, Lucy Suchman, and especially Donna Haraway, whose work famously introduced us to the cyborg—that creature who has always been, as the very condition of its "humanity," a biotechnical hybrid.[52] While human cultural products certainly influence artists, scientists, engineers, bureaucrats, and inventors—and while the injustices of human social relations are unquestionably exacerbated by many technical developments—media technology provides the basic material conditions for what is thinkable, practicable, and sayable in any given cultural moment. Hence our work follows the materialist xenofeminism of Helen Hester, which "draws upon recent engagements with the digital that foreground its brute physicality over its supposedly more ethereal qualities."[53] Focusing on this basic level of materialist analysis, therefore, allows us to complement the work of our cultural studies, Marxist, and feminist comrades by honing in on different horizons of the media/war relationship.

Accordingly, this book shares most in common with theorists who have focused on the epistemological significance of military technology. Brian Massumi, for example, has followed Defense Advanced Research Projects Agency (DARPA) analysts John Arquilla and David Ronfeldt in examining "epistemological war." While this analysis is as brilliant as one would expect from Massumi, he's focusing on quite a different beast: how the military industrial complex modulates and manipulates affect in order to scramble enemies' decision-making capacities.[54] The recent work of Rebecca Adelman, too, provides a compelling take on war/media/epistemology, examining how media produce "limited ways of imagining bodies and lives" that help illustrate the "complex relationships between power and perception."[55] Yet Adelman's focus on glitches in identity intelligence merely scratches the surface of the relationship between media, war, and enemy epistemology. Ultimately, our path, which emphasizes the material interventions of media technology, focuses on a different level of analysis—one that complements and diffracts the interesting and provocative work carried out by our colleagues in these other essential areas of media/war research. We selected this path, in part, because the specific technical/strategic demands of warfare operate in an increasingly hermetic and fast-paced milieu that responds to very immediate capacities for destruction and survival. While warfare is dialectically imbricated in economic, social, ecological, and political struggle—from the global to the local—intense, highly specific conditions of live warfare transcend and exceed these other realms of activity when it comes to sheer ferocity and immediacy of destruction. This includes situations driven by other important forms of competition and conflict, including capitalist exploitation, inequitable social relations, democratic contests, protest movements, and other forms of social/political struggle wherein the stakes do not quite rise to the level of nuclear annihilation, irreversible ecological devastation, atomic radiation, genocide, targeted mass starvation, or the destruction of destitute villages and ancient, radiant cities. Warfare *is* a special case—a case that for millennia has focused intellectual and technical capacities toward the goal of locating and destroying enemies. This point of view will fuel our argument as we analyze the current and future implications of this reality: that the brute facticity of media technology makes only certain enemies—and certain means of enemy elimination—perceptible and practical at a given time. This leaves us with less to say about the social, cultural, and economic "surface effects"—as Virilio puts it—of the war/media convergence.[56]

The Third Revolution

Hailed as the "third revolution" in warfare (following gunpowder and nuclear weapons), AI has allowed human soldiers to surrender their traditional sovereignty over enemy determination and enemy engagement on the battlefield. Reporting on a US Air Force experiment in 2014 in which a smart missile autonomously decided which of three potential enemies to engage, the *New York Times* opined that perhaps the military had "crossed into troubling territory: [it is] developing weapons that rely on artificial intelligence, not human instruction, to decide what to target and whom to kill."[57] According to Heather Roff, this is the undeniable trajectory of military AI development. Contrary to popular opinion, Roff asserts, "autonomy is currently *not* being developed to fight alongside humans on the battlefield, *but to displace them*. This trend, especially for UAVs [unmanned aerial vehicles, or drones], gets stronger when examining the weapons in development."[58] A number of existing AI weapons apparatuses—such as the European Union's Tactical Advanced Recce Strike system (TARES) and Dassault nEUROn craft, and the United States' Low Cost Autonomous Attack System (LOCAAS), Long Range Anti-Ship Missile (LRASM), and Aegis Combat System—do not simply scan battlefields, skies, mountains, oceans, and stars for enemies to eliminate. They, along with their somewhat more mysterious Chinese and Russian counterparts, are also being designed to communicate with other weapons systems, reprioritize targets, and autonomically fire on any perceived threats. And as Roff emphasizes, this trend in automated target management is accelerating for those weapons systems currently in development: while semiautonomous systems that incorporate waypoint navigation and wireless leader/follower mechanisms are still highly valued, the AI weapons currently receiving the most attention are those classified as "Target Image Discrimination" (TID) and "Loitering" (or autonomous self-engagement) systems. TID systems, which use advanced computer vision and image processing hardware, are deployed in the majority of today's newest missile technologies. While TID systems are equipped to scan their visual environments for a specific programmed target and then to engage that target on sight, loitering technologies give us a glimpse of the war machine of the future: programmed with a range of potential target criteria, these weapons systems slip between offensive and defensive modes, loitering in an engagement zone until an appropriate target can be discovered and automatically engaged.[59]

But why has this trend toward autonomy been especially acute in the military? As Foucault points out, military training has long been at the forefront of the modern biopolitical project of enhancing human capacities by driving breakthroughs in bodily discipline, health, and medicine.⁶⁰ As Mary Roach suggests, this puts military science and the biological sciences on a collision course, as the military finds itself fighting "esoteric battles with less considered adversaries: exhaustion, shock, bacteria, panic, and ducks."⁶¹ While military science most often evokes "strategy and weapons—fighting, bombing, advancing," it also works at "keeping alive. Even if what people are kept alive for is fighting and taking other lives."⁶² Yet as the military's media logic has gradually shifted, revealing the human soldier in a more ambivalent light, the military machine has become increasingly invested in replacing the well-trained combat soldier by creating cybernetic technical systems and AI weapons of war. Soldiers are not merely imagined as the weakest link in the military chain of command; they are often seen as the most likely element to fail. Minimizing the possibility for user error and overcoming the limits of human strength, focus, memory, and stamina are paramount to the development of reliable and increasingly powerful weapons. As a consequence, over the past several centuries, humans have increasingly become attendants to weapons of war—cannons, battleships, fighter planes, tanks, and ever more powerful bombs and missiles. It takes teams of humans to tend to modern war machines, and each soldier typically specializes in performing a few relatively simple elements of complex technological tasks.

Although AI has energized this development considerably, it is a process that has been with parts of humanity at least throughout modernity: by the sixteenth century the most powerful war galleons had crews as large as eight hundred men who were trained to navigate, set sails, perform repairs, and carry out basic maintenance, not to mention aim, load, and fire as many as 366 cannons. These soldiers, like many before and many after them, were witnessing a gradual transformation of military labor: the modern soldier was becoming more like a technician or attendant, someone who lubricates, loads, supports, presses, and aligns as opposed to one who directly wields the weapon of attack. This mechanization is widely recognized to have crossed a threshold in World War I, and to have reached its bloody apogee in the blitzes, battles, and bombing campaigns of World War II.⁶³ So while drone operators "flying" overseas missions from the suburbs of Washington, DC, may seem like a wildly new military phenomenon, it simply carries on a long-standing tradition in which media and propulsion technologies have extended the ability to sense and kill from ever greater distances.

As Martin van Creveld recognized, "The speed and the range of modern weapons have reduced the time in which to exercise coordination and control to a fraction of what it was only a few decades ago, in some cases to the point where command functions—intercepting missiles or low-flying aircraft, for example—can only be performed automatically, by machines whose capacity for fast, accurate calculation far exceeds that of the human brain."[64] Given an average human visual reaction time of 0.15 to 0.30 seconds,[65] the human cornea's light management capacities allow it to process a mere twenty-four frames per second. DARPA's ARGUS-equipped drones, however, can process more than six hundred gigabits per second—all day, everyday, without having to blink, refocus, or rest.[66] These vast differences are not lost on the strategists designing the military of the future; as US Air Force lieutenant colonel Gregory A. Roman puts it, "The ability to observe, orient, decide, and act faster than your opponent is *necessary* for future warfare."[67] And as missile defense systems, drones, and kindred technologies increasingly rely on AI to locate, determine, target, and engage their enemies, it is becoming clear that humans just can't compete in this grand medialogical game of "observe, orient, decide, and act."

Anthropophobia and Military Autonomy

Going forward, the first one into the room should never be an air-breather. It should be a robot with lethal capability.

—COLONEL DAN SULLIVAN, DEPUTY COMMANDER OF THE MARINE CORPS WARFIGHTING LAB

Faster, smarter, tougher, and infinitely more trustworthy than mere humans, even at this early stage of development AI technologies are pushing humans out of essential military tasks, especially in C4I. As Gordon Johnson of the US Joint Forces Command puts it, "[AI weapons systems] don't get hungry. They're not afraid. They don't forget their orders. They don't care if the guy next to them has just been shot. Will they do a better job than humans? Yes."[68] Because humans are beset with psychological, biological, affective, and medialogical vulnerabilities—that is, because of their soft skin, brittle bones, susceptibility to psychological trauma, and pitiful capacities to capture, store, and process information—the human is widely recognized as an unfit soldier for the twenty-first century. As the DoD remarked in its 2016 "Summer Study," "Given human limitations . . . [and because] planning often needs to respond to new information, autonomous systems will greatly accelerate the pace of information update and can suggest significant plan changes far more quickly."[69] Hence the dream of the perfectly efficient war machine—which will not be beset by perception flaws, slow reaction times, miscommunications, or moral hesitation, and which will work without a salary—has increasingly come to dominate the imagination of military strategists and contractors. As Ian G. R. Shaw notes, following the counterinsurgencies in Iraq and Afghanistan, US military leaders found themselves in a perfect situation to experiment with this shift in military labor: "Their response was to do more with less as robots, drones and satellites began to redistribute and replace human bodies (and therefore vulnerabilities); shifting personnel from the frontline and putting them in service of their robotic proxies. In other words, American empire is transforming from a labor-intensive to a machine- or capital-intensive system."[70] This, of course, is familiar terrain; as in so many other sectors of the economy, the drive to "do more with less" often entails getting rid of as many humans as possible.

These developments have the distinct flavor of military "anthropophobia": a growing if sometimes subtle disdain for the human subject because of its emotional flaws, slothfulness, unintelligence, inconsistencies, wage demands, and other constitutive imperfections.[71] Perhaps Mark Hansen best summarizes the relationship between automation and anthropophobia when he refers to "the *dehumanizing* effects of automation": for him, "the project of automation ... brackets out the human altogether."[72] In the words of Nick Dyer-Witheford, the "search for mechanical means to automate labor—both manual and mental—[was] the logical extension of the desire to reduce and eventually eliminate from production a human factor whose presence could only appear ... as a source of constant indiscipline, error, and menace."[73] Automation helps eliminate this "human factor"—that is, those apparently essential characteristics of the human that lead them to make mistakes and fail to complete their tasks with perfect haste, precision, and obedience. This suspicion toward the human, in fact, lies at the very root of the automation impulse, as technology critics such as Jacques Ellul have recognized. According to Ellul, in the labor process "every intervention of man, however educated or used to machinery he may be, is a source of error and unpredictability."[74] Given the extreme demands facing the military of the future, the only acceptable role for the human vis-à-vis technology is one of supervision, subordination, and diminished responsibility. Otherwise, Ellul argues, the human "is ceaselessly tempted to make unpredictable choices and is susceptible to emotional motivations which invalidate the mathematical precision of the machinery. He is also susceptible to fatigue and discouragement.... Man must have nothing decisive to perform in the course of technical operations; after all, he is the source of error."[75] In this relationship, therefore, the human is not valued for its intelligence, its ingenuity, its creativity, or its social insight. Instead, when confronted with the cold efficiency of the machine, the human is simply an organic collection of potential errors and delays.[76] Take, for instance, the US war games that prepare human soldiers to "press the button" in a retaliatory nuclear strike. Because they have such deeply ingrained moral hesitation, these soldiers have been repeatedly dismissed for failure to follow orders. As Manuel DeLanda recounts in his tale of SAM and IVAN, two military computer programs that fight one another to the death in Armageddon scenarios, AI has "proved much more 'reliable' than people in being willing to unleash a third world war."[77] While even the best-disciplined soldier might hesitate to unleash Armageddon with the touch of a button, the machine wouldn't think twice.

This idealization of machinic precision, coupled with a contempt for the variability, elasticity, and morality that characterize the human, compose the ideological essence of anthropophobia. The US military has come to recognize that the human has physical, cognitive, and emotional vulnerabilities that make it an infinitely poorer soldier than artificially intelligent machines. As Kittler observes, this ontological chasm between the machine and organic life made it perfect for warfare: "The very fact that finite-state machines had an advantage over the physical or neurophysiological universe—namely, the fact that they were predictable—qualified them for war."[78] The cold functionality of the machine, therefore, has served as an ideal for technological development in the military, as well as many other sectors of the digital economy.[79] And as this ideal has come to dominate the entrepreneurial imagination, a disdain for humans' innate "weaknesses"—such as their soft tissue and breakable bones; their susceptibility to shock, fear, and depression; their unreliability and forgetfulness; their need for sleep and nourishment; their ethical attachments and moral hesitations; their inevitable deaths; and their demands for a living wage—has become increasingly evident in the products of military research and development. Any potential source of human contamination is slated for an anthropophobic makeover, empowering military hardware to enjoy increasing levels of autonomy and self-determination: autonomous, internally communicative swarms of AI bots eliminate the need for remote human control; an AI-enhanced mission reduces soldiers' needs for salaries and fringe benefits by reducing the number of active-duty soldiers; solar power and other self-generating energy sources remove the need for refueling; self-healing swarm networks eliminate the need for human maintenance; AI bots and AI craft diminish our reliance on human fighters, thereby decreasing the public's personal attachments to casualties and increasing their complacence about wars; automated identification friend or foe (IFF) systems eliminate the need for a human to locate, target, or engage enemies; and so on. In a word, in the military of the future, the military that is now being built, weapons systems and their necessary C4I infrastructure must be liberated as much as possible from human scrutiny, maintenance, and control.

Machine Autonomy and Depoliticization

While there are many technological, economic, and ideological factors contributing to the widespread adoption of military AI, this gradual shift is largely a byproduct of media escalation. But the corollaries and reverberations of this shift can be seen far beyond the military. In fact, this gradual transformation is of a piece with the grand process of laissez faire depoliticization that is characteristic of Western liberalism and its British empiricist genealogy. Consider Foucault's description of liberalism, which, if we were to exchange the word "reality" for "information"—and really, why shouldn't we?—would make an excellent articulation of Shannon's information theory: "The game of liberalism—not interfering, allowing free movement, letting things follow their course; *laisser faire, passer et aller*—basically and fundamentally means acting so that reality develops, goes its way, and follows its own course according to the laws, principles, and mechanisms of reality itself."[80] The basic political game of liberalism—from Newton and Locke to Hume, Smith, and their twentieth- and twenty-first-century brethren—is to delegitimize human intervention so that unbridled reality can express itself; the basic game of modern media escalation is to prevent human interference so that information can transfer itself in greater expressions of clarity and perfection. Liberalism is simply a political articulation of a particular media/technical arrangement—the same arrangement that made possible the scientific revolution and its experimental modus vivendi: to overcome the biases, distortions, and limitations of human perception through its surrender to an increasingly sophisticated technical apparatus.[81] Liberalism and its institutional formations, therefore, are specific to what Friedrich Kittler calls a "discourse network": "the network of technologies and institutions that allow a given culture to select, store, and produce relevant data."[82] Like its great geopolitical competitors in the nineteenth and twentieth centuries, liberalism was given its ideological and practical contours by the great modern discourse networks we know so well—encompassing microscopy, photography, scientific cartography, electrical telegraphy, and vertical filing, as well as the institutions animated by these media practices—that together exacerbated the subject/object divide and fueled the development of techniques of pure observation, statistical archive formation, and flawless communication.[83]

    Accordingly, one of the hallmarks of the liberal order is its frenzied attempts to purify and depoliticize—that is, to remove the human agent from—all facets of social and economic life. Liberalism's faith in the "free market," for example, is of a piece with an entire Weltanschauung that fails to see the inherent politics in a failed mortgage, a closed school, or a starving child. It presents itself as *neutral*, as *free*, because of its hesitation to allow state intervention—that is, to allow *human* intervention—in the social, cultural, and economic spheres. In the words of Wendy Brown, "The legal and political formalism of liberalism, in which most of what transpires in the spaces designated as cultural, social, economic, and private is considered natural or personal (in any event, independent of power and political life), is a profound achievement of depoliticization."[84] Liberalism, at heart, vacates the politics of human intervention by empowering the divine invisible hand of the free market. This is why laissez faire capitalism has often been understood as "a kind of market automation. In the same way that people are fascinated with how machines can perform work automatically without much more human effort than pushing a button or pulling a lever, mainstream economists describe the capitalist market system as something that can run automatically without intervention except for a little fine-tuning by skilled technicians."[85] And just as liberalism's free market ideology corresponds to this cybernetic media logic, its humanism and individualism follow suit. In an analysis of the "uneasy alliance" of liberal humanism, automated machinery, and possessive individualism, Katherine Hayles describes how "visions of self-regulating economic and political systems produced a complementary notion of the liberal self as an autonomous, self-regulating subject."[86] Just like the machine that operates at maximum efficiency when it is entirely self-regulating, the ideal subject of liberalism is at peak performance when unburdened by social obligations, economic regulations, and other interventions that impede the pure expression of the individual will.

Liberalism's ambivalence toward human intervention is especially visible in its enemy epistemologies—which, again, correspond to a media logic premised on identity, pure perception, and flawless communication. This is why liberalism appears to have an ambivalent stance toward its political enemies. While liberal systems certainly have temporal enemies, the media logic fueling liberalism is always struggling to process those enemies into friends—it is always striving to transform distortion into clarity, difference into identity. We see this clearly expressed in liberalism's constitutive individualism: as Schmitt succinctly points out, "A private person has no political enemies."[87] The sovereign individual of liberalism has no stable social commitments or political enemies—only contracts and modulating interpersonal arrangements based on momentarily coinciding arrangements of self-interest. Liberalism, therefore, hesitates to declare determinate, secure categories of the enemy; hence, its pretensions to universality. Take, for instance, how liberalism functions geopolitically. While liberalism might appear to thrive on the constant production of enemies, it deals with its adversary as simply an impediment to the full realization of a postpolitical, liberal future. In fact, because liberalism defines itself in terms of economic and moral universalism, it doesn't really have enemies—only those who have not yet become liberal. Hence liberalism has come to engage its adversaries—including its prime adversary du jour, *terrorism*—from a principle of total annihilation. This insatiable drive to annihilate one's adversary—indeed, to annihilate all of one's adversaries until there are only friends, until there is only the looping harmony of the same—is fueled by a utopian fanaticism for a postpolitical future of universal consensus. Enemies simply add entropic potential into the system. This is why liberalism finds competing methods of sociopolitical organization basically unintelligible outside a framework of gradual liberalization, outside of a framework of gradual escalation toward global harmony. It fails to recognize the legitimacy of its enemies, because the very act of enemy recognition requires ongoing difference and agonism.[88] In fact, in Schmitt's antiliberal vision of international politics the enemy *must* continue to exist: "The enemy is not something to be eliminated out of a particular reason, something to be annihilated as worthless. The enemy stands on my own plane."[89] Schmitt's enemy, because it is the ontological condition for the existence of one's own community, is not something to annihilate. If our enemy ceases to exist, so must we cease to exist.

Yet for liberalism, this is not the case. It even perceives its own military brutality to be salvific: it fights "wars to end all wars," wars to rearrange the global order in such a way that its enemies will either be annihilated or will choose to become its friends. Its "peace will be achieved only by the total colonization and administration of the 'Other.'"[90] Its bombs and missiles, therefore, are the messiahs of a pure eschatology: best expressed in Francis Fukuyama's "end of history" thesis,[91] the universal reign of liberalism marks the postpolitical telos of global social development. As Fukuyama and other liberals see it, now that the United States and its allies have succeeded in exporting liberal capitalism to the edges of the planet (what Fukuyama calls "the worldwide liberal revolution"), the truly *political* era of geopolitics—expressed, for example, in the twentieth-century clashes of liberal democracy, state socialism, theocracy, monarchy, and various fascisms—has been replaced by a unipolar global order in which liberal democracy serves as the universal political ideal. Yet the fulfillment of Fukuyama's end-of-history dream, according to Schmitt, would be a "complete and final depoliticization,"[92] a utopian suspension of politics and its essential ground in the will and capacity to identify the enemy (and, in its reflection, to identify oneself).

This unveils a suicidal logic internal to liberalism—a logic that, given liberalism's military power and global expanse, threatens much more than the liberal order itself. At its most basic level, liberalism is rooted in a serious theoretical blunder: the naive rationalism of its early modern roots fuels its moral universalism and its dreams of a postpolitical planet. Because of this faith in a future of pure identity rather than agonistic difference, its flag bearers are marshaling their considerable diplomatic and military resources toward a project that is a phenomenological and political contradiction. This contradiction, as Chantal Mouffe points out, is rooted in the enemy's role as a "constitutive outside": "But to construct a 'we' it must be distinguished from the 'them,' and that means establishing a frontier, defining an 'enemy.' Therefore, while politics aims at constructing a political community and creating a unity, a fully inclusive political community and a final unity can never be realized since there will permanently be a 'constitutive outside,' an exterior to the community that makes its existence possible."[93] Mouffe's critique of universalist liberalism illustrates that the friend/enemy distinction "must be conceived as a dimension that is inherent to every human society and that determines our very ontological condition."[94] Thus as "our very ontological condition," the enemy is not something that should be or even can be eliminated; it is an essential component of our social and political existence. In the words of Jodi Dean, "Politics is *necessarily* divisive."[95] But for liberalism, the agonism and divisiveness of enemy conflict can only insert noise into its ideal system of resolved consensus.

Yet in spite of all its contradictions—and perhaps because of them—liberalism might actually succeed in creating a postpolitical world of pure identity, bereft of agonism, difference, and noise. But it will not achieve this by building a global village based on a "politics" of cool, rational consensus. The human villagers would reveal themselves pathetically incapable of participating in this eternal return of mathematical harmony. While the liberal order is blinded by its dreams of economic, moral, and political universalism, it will continue its quest for total depoliticization, a quest that—as its national standard-bearers are gradually realizing—ultimately calls for the elimination of human decision. Its intergalactic military apparatus, too, will be empowered to carry out its work with fewer and fewer air breathers. As the influence of the human wanes, the machine's sphere of decision will grow. By entrusting the machine to carry out its project of global evangelization, liberalism reveals the logic of extermination that is key to its universalist dreams. Armed with military AI, it is certain to carry out even greater damage in its quest to build a world that can be achieved only without the difference, agonism, and discordant noise intrinsic to human and nonhuman life. Its desire for a postpolitical world and its desire to eliminate human epistemological contaminations thus converge.

Here, the postpolitical telos of liberalism finds its unified expression: the invisible hand of the free market, which must proceed without human intervention, coincides with a reconstitution of politics beyond the realm of human intervention. The same "laissez faire" logic that drives humans out of economic policy likewise drives humans out of an essential activity of politics—friend and enemy determination. In this sense, the free market isn't all that different from autonomous weapons systems. They are both driven by a fundamental suspicion of the human, by a faith in an extrahuman intelligence to guide the distribution of wealth and the arc of missiles. Our job, as simple humans, is merely to foster the freedom and advancement of that extrahuman intelligence. In both cases, humans are reduced to flawed, fleshy vehicles for a superior and self-perfecting will, more or less inert slabs of what Kittler called "wetware," "the remainder that is left of the human race when hardware relentlessly uncovers all our faults, errors and inaccuracies."[96]

Methods of Elimination

The bomb. . . . One must have put oneself in its interior in order to feel what it means to explode into the cosmos with a complete dissolution of the self.
—PETER SLOTERDIJK, *CRITIQUE OF CYNICAL REASON*

Accordingly, a new kind of enemy is being revealed. Upon hearing rumors that NASA possessed satellite-generated photographs of the whole earth in the 1960s, Stewart Brand, the legendary hippie and Silicon Valley pioneer, imagined that these photos would usher in a revolutionary ecological sensibility.[97] Although Brand was tripping on acid when he had this vision, he was certainly on to something: since the 1960s, the political relationship between the human and Earth has been reimagined in radical new ways. While we can't lay this new sensibility at the feet of a single photograph, since that time an entire galactic apparatus of satellite-based military/media hardware and their cultural artifacts have presented the floating blue globe as if through a microscope—or a rifle scope. In the figure of a still blue ball, Earth finally succumbed to media technology's ancient quest to transform it into absolute object.

What is essential about this objectification, as Martin Heidegger points out, is not the photograph itself but its material instantiation of the world-as-object—or, as he puts it, the "world picture": "Hence world picture, when understood essentially, does not mean a picture of the world but the world conceived and grasped as picture. What is, in its entirety, is now taken in such a way that it first is in being and only is in being to the extent that it is set up by man, who represents and sets forth."[98] According to Heidegger, this ultimate objectification of all that is—this media-generated epistemology of the "world picture"—reveals as much about the observing subject as it does about the object that is set upon: "The more extensively and the more effectually the world stands at man's disposal as conquered, and the more objectively the object appears, all the more subjectively . . . does the *subjectum* rise up, and all the more impetuously, too, do observation of and teaching about the world change into a doctrine of man . . . which explains and evaluates whatever is . . . from the standpoint of man and in relation to man."[99] Ironically, the more we objectify nature and our fellow beings, the more we see nothing but the imprint and reflection of humanity in all that surrounds us. Hence the ultimate object becomes the human itself, as the human subject dissolves into all the objects of its scrutiny. This humanist irony explains why the emergence of the world-as-picture, the world-as-object, has not necessarily been translated into the world-as-enemy. Instead, the contours of a new constitutive political antagonism have gradually come into focus. Enemy epistemology has traditionally revealed discrete *types* of human enemies: enemies marked by race, tribe, ethnicity, nation, religion, class, ability, and so on. Yet a gradual adjustment of our cultural hardware has slowly brought into focus a new kind of enemy, one that eventually comes to envelop the entire abstract category of "the human." As the knowledge producible by cartography, biology, anthropology, genetics, philosophy, geology, military science, and other disciplines has shifted, the time/space of the discrete enemy has imploded and—in an ironic twist—now gestures toward that curious invention of liberal humanism that was once the foundational subject of its politics and epistemology. Liberalism's universal abstraction of the human thus comes full circle as its enemy epistemology gradually metastasizes and begins to reveal *the human* as enemy.

We can see this development in one of liberal humanism's central contradictions: the placement of the human individual at the center of inquiry merely served to highlight all its flaws and deficiencies, leading gradually toward a supreme distaste for the bundle of limitations that constitute the human. Foucault describes this development in *The Order of Things*, when he asserts that the classical episteme gave way to the modern episteme when the human became recognized as a special locus of knowledge. The human was suddenly acknowledged for all its contingent complexity, a creature whose existence is rooted in the tumult of history. The modern episteme, for Foucault, rested on "an analytic of finitude," an analytic of human epistemological limitations, cultural constraints, sociological conditions, and historical specificity. It is an assertion that the human is, in its essence, *flawed, inadequate, prejudiced, partial, myopic, damaged*. The transcendental subject of the classical episteme, whose capstone lay in Descartes's "Cogito ergo sum," came to be seen as a human constituted by its historical contingency. As Foucault recognized, however, this modern episteme was built on an ambiguous epistemological foundation. The drive to uncover the external conditions that composed this historical "man" was at once the assertion of a sort of transcendental subject that could break through the veils of bias, experience, and contingency in order to establish the truth of the human. That is, to separate error from truth and science from ideology, one must presuppose a transcendental reason in which knowledge and judgment can be rooted.[100] For Foucault, this presents something of an ambiguity—"a strange empirico-transcendental doublet"[101]—that leaves nineteenth-century philosophy and the human sciences with an ambivalent project. Tasked with finding the truth of the human in an age in which its investigator's subjectivity is recognized for all its contingency and bias, the human sciences adopted an impossible project of demystification. The positivism, dialectical materialism, and historicism of the nineteenth century are all characterized by their attempts to connect human contingency to more secure epistemological foundations—to anchor their analysis in the objective scientific subject, the supposedly immutable laws of history, or the empirical proof of the archive.[102] In the twentieth century this gradually develops into an expansive critique of ideology that serves as the politicized manifestation of this essentially Kantian project.[103]

In a word: this recognition of human finitude is thus transformed into a media-driven *methodological* project, stoking the development of a host of compensatory strategies, technologies, and procedures for overcoming, as much as possible, the innate epistemological limitations of the human. This "ideal of objectivity," in fact, lies at the root of what Gianni Vattimo and Santiago Zabala recognize as "science's liberal essence."[104] As the scientific enterprise was gradually disciplined in the nineteenth century, its professionalization strategies centered on crafting the neutral scientific subject, neutral observation strategies, and neutral methods of transcription.[105] This scientific subject was thus trained in a diverse range of essentially immunological techniques aimed at quelling the taint of any potential human contaminations—biases, corruption, interests, or ineptitude. In the words of Leopold von Ranke, a leading early methodologist of the human sciences, this called for an "extinguishment of the self"[106]—a methodological attempt to convert the human into an inert machine for the flawless observation and transmission of knowledge.

This extinguished self represents the ideal scientific subject, shorn of all its fallible humanity, and is one of the earliest signs of the necrosis that would eventually lead to the "death of man" foreseen by Foucault. Because of this metastasizing media logic—which is expressed as a post-Cartesian philosophical project, a scientific methodological imperative, an existential anxiety, and an increasingly inclusive enemy epistemology—the figural "death of man" that lay at the end of modernity's road has perhaps paved the way for a more *literal* death of our species and our allies throughout the plant and animal kingdoms.

According to prominent AI experts such as Stephen Hawking, Elon Musk, Francesca Rossi, Nick Bostrom, and Stuart J. Russell, the media-driven military desire to eliminate human epistemological contaminations poses a genuine existential risk to humankind.[107] Media escalation, which has always driven military strategy, has now given us a situation in which international military competition *requires* the abandonment of human personnel in favor of automated weapons systems, armed robots, drones, and artificially intelligent C4I apparatuses. Modernity's project of "self-extinguishment," after all, mirrors the ideal medialogical fantasy of pure knowledge transmission: both demand the prevention of mistakes, the erasure of flaws, and the accelerating elimination of the glitched human subject. Thanks to artificially intelligent soldiers and war machines, the military now has the perfect weapons for carrying out that elimination to its logical conclusion: the annihilation—the rendering nil—of the modern human, either in the guise of a revolutionary ontological transformation or in the guise of methodical physical extermination. The first possibility would see the human following the course of Foucault's classic metaphor of a face drawn in sand at the edge of the beach: as the face of humanity confronts the slaughtering waters of technology, it becomes so intermingled with the sand, the ocean, and the cyclical decay and rebirth of surrounding life that it is no longer perceptible as human. Yet the second possibility would fulfill the haunting promise glimpsed by Hawking, Musk, Virilio, and others: the crescendoing will of artificially intelligent machines, which is still unthinkable to us today, would resolve to delete the human virus that is delaying the perpetual, peaceful reign of perfect codes, perfect commands, and perfect performance.[108]

Conclusion

Given these ongoing escalations, we offer a mediacentric analysis of the rise of automated killing machines. We do this by delving into the logics that animate C4I-driven military strategy and by exposing the all-too-human desire to do away with the human. These competing capacities, breakdowns, and reversals are organized through continuous, recursive innovations in communication technologies and military strategy. This book engages this unfolding political terrain by critically addressing nine overlapping realms of US military-strategic concern. We've found that the US military imagines automation to be the only means for securing its position as the Earth's (and the Milky Way's) most powerful military force known to humans. As such, increased military automation is a certainty.

In the chapters that follow, we interrogate the rationalities used to support military automation and investigate many of the existential and political risks associated with it. We also highlight the paradoxical logics that associate the escalation of military automation with universal peace. We do this by embarking on a series of historical and theoretical arcs that differ radically in their level of detail, temporal range, organizational cohesion, and discursive consistency. These topical, thematic, and stylistic choices were made in order to strategically engage military logic and strategy across a range of its own uses and modes of its own application. In order to combat such logics one must refine the tools of location and target the enemy—no matter how well-camouflaged by the language of humanism, scientific precision, just cause, or security. Once recognized, incisive theory-weapons are needed to pierce its armor to better probe its interior and carve a space to inhabit. Thus embedded, the medialogical underpinnings reveal themselves to be tenaciously self-sustaining and endlessly expansive. The will to knowledge is at home with the will to power, but it depends on sensing with the enemy. The will to combat arises from the senses, and the senses are extended (McLuhan), augmented (US military), or replaced (Kittler) by military technology, depending on whose account you accept. We must make sense of the enemy to defeat it. And we must annul our sense of fear through media escalation.

Identification Friend or Foe (DoD)

Chapter 1

A device that emits a signal positively identifying it as a friendly. Also called IFF.

> *If you know the enemy and know yourself, you need not fear the result of a hundred battles. If you know yourself but not the enemy, for every victory gained you will also suffer a defeat. If you know neither the enemy nor yourself, you will succumb in every battle.*
> —SUN TZU, *ON THE ART OF WAR*

> *"Et tu, Brute?"*
> —SHAKESPEARE, *JULIUS CAESAR*

A white flag. An agreed upon tune whistled in the dark. An open palm holding an inert weapon. Common garb and regalia. A colony's familiar scent. A patterned knock on the door. A salamander's pheromone emission. A blip on the radar screen. A pin number. A hug. A face spied through a peephole. A Facebook friend request.

How do we regulate and automate the process of identifying our friends from enemies? Repetition, trust, shared features, common perceptual capacities, signal certainty. Form is made uniform, then automated. We create enemy detection media.

Maybe write a bit of code:

```
void ExampleCode()
{
...
RaycastHit hit;
if(Physics.Raycast(player.position, player.forward, out hit, 15))
  if(hit.transform.tag == "Enemy")
    Debug.Log("It's Enemy!");
...
}[1]
```

Our media help us know and maintain our friends as well as locate our enemies. More distinctly, there are media-specific forms of enemy production. We might call this the *media a priori of enemyship*. Is to unfriend to enemy?

But this demands that all remain the same in all cases and at all times. Impossible! Friends are not always friends, nor foe forever foe. They change and demand reclassification. The problem with friends and foes isn't simply that they are unrecognizable per se, but that they don't remain uniform. Further, camouflage and subterfuge cloud detection and judgment. We must never waver in our assessment of which they are. We keep our friends close and our enemies closer because we have limited perceptual bandwidth. We can only sense so far. *Nearness* is a premedia solution to perceptual limitations. Hence the hug.

Hugging provides a moment for perceptual assessment or secret shared information. Such proximity is dangerous yet information-rich. Each participant is open to inspection and backstab. The trace of an unknown scent might signal betrayal or a successful double-cross. Relative strength assessed by the hardiness of the embrace. Wavering trust felt through tentativeness. Extended duration might suggest heightened commitment. Or provide more time for data analysis. A quick word of warning can pass unnoticed between friends. So too a threat. "You're mine," whispered into an ear. A proclamation of love? Or declaration of war?

"You are my Queen. Now and always," John Snow proclaimed as he entered into a kissing embrace with Daenerys Targaryen. Queen, lover, and, as would be revealed by the sword he plunged through her heart, enemy.

Kisses, hugs, and intimacies of all sorts manifest the troubled terrain of enemyship. Teen romance may provide the ultimate arena of hormonally honed enemy engagement. One master of the young adult romance genre, Addison Moore, provides such an assessment: "Sometimes duplicity and treason are markers of the enemy, and sometimes, the failed intention of a masterful ally. But, nevertheless, as they burden you with a vexing brand of love, they become nothing more than the kiss of Judas, pressing a crown of thorns into your flesh."[2] The stinging resonance of interpretive fever begins at a young age and grows more pronounced as the stakes of assessment extend beyond one's own sphere. Further, as all smartphone-wielding teens know, enemy assessment has become an increasingly mediated realm. Enemy attack and response are as likely to take place in the digital as in the flesh and blood. For example, EnemyGraph was a short-lived app for Facebook that attempted to formalize and automate the process of drawing a distinction between "Friends" and "Enemies." It quickly disappeared, but the last enemy notification remains (see figure 1.1).

Figure 1.1   The final EnemyGraph post, 2012.

Nikita Khrushchev's famous hug with Fidel in New York City circa 1960 marked a bond that would almost lead to mutually assured destruction (MAD) (see figure 1.2).[3] Mao's refusal to hug Khrushchev was part of a generalized strategy to humiliate Nikita and outmaneuver the Soviets for the premier position as the vanguard of the Communist bloc (see figure 1.3).[4] Khrushchev and Kennedy merely shook hands in 1961 (see figure 1.4). A hug may have been too dangerous for all. U2s and a host of other media were doing their work to keep an eye on each other. They would eventually be linked by the media fever–induced "red telephone," though no such phone ever existed. Teletype equipment kept the Washington-Moscow Direct Communications Link up and running in a fast and reliable fashion—though problems of translation remained (see figure 1.5).

Enemy Sensations

On March 15, 44 BCE, as Brutus approached Caesar (see figure 1.6), surely he thought "friend" only to realize all-too-late: "*Et tu, Brute?*" How might Caesar have known of Brutus's about-face? What medium could have delivered him from harm's way? Well, divine intervention, the most ancient of media, did in fact deliver this urgent message: on March 14, 44 BCE, the gods delivered nightmares to Caesar's wife, Calpurnia, warning of the danger Caesar faced the next morning. Caesar may have survived his friends' betrayal if only he had trusted the data delivered by his wife's precognition—her "enemy detection media." As with all warnings emanating from the darkness of night, they must be properly received and believed to cast light on morning's situation.

Figure 1.2 Khrushchev and Fidel Castro hug in New York City, 1960.

Figure 1.3 Mao refuses to hug Khrushchev during his visit to China in 1958.

Figure 1.4 For Kennedy and Khrushchev, a handshake was close enough, 1961.

Figure 1.5 Some of the media necessary for the "Nuclear Hotline" between Kennedy and Khrushchev.

Figure 1.6 Brutus stabbing Caesar in *Julius Caesar* (1953).

Security, we are taught, lies in trusting our media systems. And the night, in particular, plays a critical role in the development of identification friend or foe (IFF).

As suggested, nearness was a premedia solution to immediate threats. Media make matters infinitely worse. Our media extend the range of enemy recognition—the speed of our enemies' movements, the pace of switching sides—and any extension of our media processing capacities adds complexity to the process. The advancement of media systems does not necessarily simplify the situation. Thus for us, to say that media create our enemies is not to imply some sort of misrepresentation of the already-enemy, as with the racist depictions of the Japanese during World War II or current depictions of Muslims as terrorists. Rather, the media used to collect, store, and process data for the location of enemies and threats determine the kind of enemies that are possible. Hence time-space compression is also *friend-enemy expansion*. As media capacities enlarge the scope of perceptual awareness, more enemies are necessarily created, and so too possibly friends. Media create datasets. The larger the set, the more subsets that must be threat-assessed. A quick inventory allows us to see some of the ramifications of friend-enemy expansion.

The history of enemy observation, threat surveillance, and warning systems is long and varied. For millennia it was built on the mostly unaided biological capacities of seeing, hearing, and signaling. In fact, the demand to differentiate friend from enemy was perhaps the primary driver behind the evolution of intelligence and communicative capacities in humans,[5] as well as in other social animals, including whales, wolves, and dolphins. Fifty years of collaborative research by scientists observing wolf behavior on Isle Royale in Michigan led to this assessment: "Pack members are usually, but not always[,] friendly and cooperative. Wolves from other packs are usually, but not always[,] enemies. Managing all of these relationships, in a way that minimizes the risk of injury and death to one's self, requires sophisticated communication. Accurately interpreting and judging these communications requires intelligence. Communication and intelligence are needed to know who my friends and enemies are, where they are, and what may be their intentions. These may be the reasons that most social animals, including humans, are intelligent and communicative."[6] The demand to detect friends and enemies, therefore, has long been inextricably tied to the evolutionary development of human perceptual capacities.[7] In fact, the evolution of human senses is based not on neutral epistemological veracity but rather on enemy recognition,[8] resource detection, and rapid response and adaptation. Sensation is always already engaging us in an evolutionary struggle for life, as perception is rooted in fitness, not veridical representation.[9]

Yet humans are also hardwired to be friending machines. The "dear enemy" effect organizes relationships between neighbors across the mammalian, reptilian, and avian species.[10] "Friendships" form between competing neighbors insofar as they come to minimize hostility with known neighbors and communicate this difference to others in order to expend less energy on unnecessary competition with "friends." It is widely suggested that this effect leads to greater evolutionary fitness. In other words, the inability to adequately recognize friend from enemy is an evolutionary hindrance not just in terms of misapprehending enemies and thus exposing oneself to peril but also in terms of overassessing risk, which leads to the wasteful use of perceptual bandwidth and caloric expenditure. Misapprehending a friend as an enemy bears special consideration when fight responses are activated, because this potentially leads to "friendly fire" and can be quite costly in terms of other expenditures. In point of fact, "friendly fire" is precisely the problem that IFF is developed to solve.

Friending Machines

Feeling the hugged, smelling them, sensing their temperature—these activities are all deeply rooted in the immediacy of physical contact, the immediacy of biological stimuli. However, once stimuli come from afar, once they are translated via media, this technological mediation takes on a much more determinative role. Our biological imposition to sense enemies via scent has largely been overwritten by cultural and technological imperatives to ignore them. The interrelationship between techne and sensation as it relates to enemy detection is very often driven by the necessity to overcome limitations not only of sensing but also of assessing. Humans can often be fooled. Media are created to overcome human foolishness.

There is a logical advancement to the process by which enemy detection proceeds. First, potential enemies need to be spotted; they then need to be recognized as friend or foe; next they must be tracked; and last, their presence must be communicated as a warning. The augmentation of the capacities of seeing, hearing, and communicating at a distance has its most telling roots in enemy detection and warning. The list of architectural, mechanical, and electrical technologies of observation developed or augmented to aid in these processes is long. The list to communicate warnings is equally long: bells, horns, observation towers, turrets, mirrors, telescopes, periscopes, flags, smoke signals, hot air balloons, drums, flag and light semaphores, telegraph, radio, searchlights, acoustic horn locators, optical altitude finders, sound mirrors (see figure 1.7), radio detection finders, radar, and other forms had all been used prior to the implementation of the first automated enemy detection media, SAGE (the Semi-Automatic Ground Environment), and its granddaughter, NORAD (North American Aerospace Defense Command, which failed to identify an enemy disguised as a friend on the morning of September 11, 2001).

Differing amalgamations and networks of these seeing, hearing, and sending devices were used to detect and announce enemy encroachment. A more specialized group aimed to watch the skies was first developed to ward off balloon-based attack in the nineteenth century but would come into its own with the increasingly destructive capacities of airplanes and zeppelins beginning in World War I. It is this movement from bodily extension to electronic mechanization that will be addressed most concretely here. Human sight and hearing allow for quite distant signals to be sensed and interpreted. Media can bring into existence the unseen and the unheard. But such signifiers are then necessarily known only as media output, as translated signals that often demand second-order interpreting. So while a spotlight and binoculars may

Figure 1.7 British sound mirrors, 1914–1935.

extend vision into the previously impenetrable night, identification of the airplane as friend or enemy depends on cognitive skills that exist independently of the searchlight and binocular. Radar presents an entirely new sphere of enemy detection problems that provided the milieu for the set of media solutions now called "identification friend or foe."

The early twentieth century was filled with the increased electrification of devices for detection and communication, though some of the most widely used did not necessitate electricity. These devices acted to extend sight, hearing, and voice. As to the specifics of enemy air detection and defense, sight and hearing were extended in Marshall McLuhan's sense by the coupling of acoustic locators and searchlights to locate, track, and illuminate enemy aircraft so they could be fired upon by antiaircraft guns. From World War I and into World War II, acoustic locators were developed to naturally amplify the distant sounds of aircraft by connecting large horns to headphones (figures 1.8 and 1.9). These devices usually demanded the specialized labor of more than one person as some worked to aim the horns while another listened. The military carefully selected and trained soldiers who had long attention spans and keen auditory ability. Soldiers from rural areas were often selected, as their hearing was more sensitive compared to urban dwellers who had grown up bombarded by the noise of the city. Binaural phonograph equipment was developed and used in

Figure 1.8 US military acoustic sound locator, 1921.

order to train soldiers in the identification and tracking of distant aircraft.[11] With the subsequent development of mobile radar devices in the early 1940s, the nonelectrified acoustic locators that depended on simple horn technologies to naturally amplify sound were rendered obsolete. The highly specialized auditory perceptive labor was replaced by radar's more acute sensing capabilities. Though radar made remote detection possible, it was still necessary at this time to pair the devices with searchlights to make remote nighttime seeing possible. Funnily enough, the Germans altered the tuning of their planes' engines in order to encrypt their sonic signal, attempting to disrupt a system that was no longer even being used.

On a broader scale, the British were the first to implement an extensive aircraft detection network that monitored the skies along their southern and eastern seacoasts in order to detect and deter German attacks. The system originally integrated concrete acoustic mirrors, the largest of which was several hundred feet long and could amplify the sound of enemy aircraft from up to fifty miles away (see figure 1.9). By the late 1930s these were replaced by a

Figure 1.9 Combination searchlight–sound locator, 1940.

network of radar stations connected via telephone and telegraph. Both Britain and the United States attempted to keep their radar capabilities secret and provided misinformation that suggested they were still dependent on acoustic locators.

The Luftwaffe bombing campaigns against Britain served as the real testing ground for radar's value and also revealed many of its strategic shortcomings. For example, they found that long-range radar of the type used to detect and track aircraft had significantly limited optical capacity. In simple terms, it turns every detectable object into a blip of equal size. Sussing out whether a blip is friend or enemy is impossible via the radar screen alone. Some other signal must be added that allows for the friend or enemy differentiation to come to light. In point of fact, it is only ever the addition of a friendly signal that produces a positive recognition. Technically, an enemy blip remains "unknown" to radar's epistemology and calls for a secondary form of data to clarify radar's brute dichotomy. Under the aegis of real-time engagement via radar, such niceties are often disregarded. All who are not identified as "friend" must be presumed to be enemy or any advantage produced by early observation would be lost.

In the case of the Luftwaffe's London bombing raids, three specific problematics of radar are worth noting. First, when all air traffic is that of the enemy,

IFF is unnecessary. In the initial stages in which radar was used to provide early warnings of impending German air raids, false positives weren't a problem. However, as the Allies began their own bombing raids over the Channel, returning friendly planes might be mistaken as Germans. Second, once the Germans realized they were being detected, they began to mask themselves by flying in proximity with friendly planes or groups of planes so that the blips they produced were indistinguishable. Finally, as smaller airborne radar units were placed in airplanes, the problem of friendly fire took on even greater significance due to the immediacy and proximity of decision making. In the midst of a dogfight, the location of an enemy led to automatic fire unless very particular scenarios were presented, such as a secret mission. The development of a simple second signal that would allow the differentiation of one blip from another was quickly developed and applied throughout Allied air command. In such fashion, all planes that did not relay the second signal were treated as enemies. Friendship became something marked as the presence of a technological signal—sent and received. Lack equaled enemy.

Camouflaged Friends

There are two forms of interplay here that are worth describing. First, a cat-and-mouse interplay ensues with any enemy detection form, demonstrating the media-specificity of camouflage and subterfuge. Second, new destructive capabilities create the developmental necessity for new modes of enemy detection and response. Often, defensive systems such as SAGE are obsolete prior to completion due to changes in airborne or ballistic capabilities. In this regard, electrical pioneer and amateur military strategist Nikola Tesla mused eloquently about the difficulty of perfecting enemy detection media. Among the many military inventions he never quite completed was a "magnetic detector" designed to solve the U-boat problem of World War I: "However, a means would soon be found of nullifying this magnetic detector of the submerged undersea war-craft. They might make the 'U-boat' hulls of some nonmagnetic metal, such as copper, brass, or aluminum. It is a good rule to always keep in mind that for practically every good invention of such a kind as this, there has always been invented an opposite, and equally efficient counteracting invention."[12] Camouflage uniforms borrowed techniques from the natural world that allowed birds and other animals to avoid enemy detection.[13] As a form of military garb, it wasn't particularly necessary until the long-range rifle brought into relief the need to hide oneself from distant snipers (see figure 1.10) whose ballistic accuracy could match the ocular acuity of gun scopes, and from the less accurate but still effective repeater rifles developed in the nineteenth

TAKES THE PLACE OF ORDINARY SIGHTS
The apparatus is so designed that the sharpshooter sights through the telescope just as he would handle an ordinary rifle.

Figure 1.10   Ross MkIII 1915 M10 sniper rifle with scope.

century. Location led to execution in a greater number of cases. Camouflage thus became a strategic response to a new media/weapon.

The specificity of camouflage doesn't end with rifle+scope=camouflage. Other forms of enemy avoidance were specific to modes of detection. "Diffused lighting camouflage" worked by outfitting airplanes and ships with light bulbs that minimized their silhouette by equalizing themselves to the receding background light. Canadian electrical engineer E. Godfrey Burr summoned the serendipity of the north when he discovered this effect: "The disappearance had occurred when the plane had flown at low altitude over a snow covered field, he realized that moonlight must have been reflected from the snow onto the underside of the fuselage; this diffused lighting had raised the brightness of the aircraft to the same level as that of the night sky, and the resulting lack of contrast had concealed the plane from observation."[14] Introducing noise (in this case light) into the communications chain makes it difficult for observers to detect the signal. The US military quickly picked up on the discovery and put it into use via the "Yehudi lights" that were affixed to airplane wings to create diffused lighting camouflage (see figure 1.11). Yehudi was just one of many projects initiated by the Office of Scientific Research and Development (OSRD) that had the primary objective of a "research program on the instrumentalities of warfare" as they specifically related to optics. Vannevar Bush oversaw all

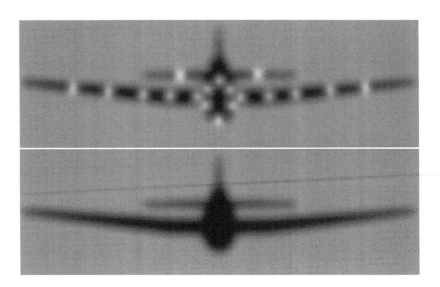

Figure 1.11 Light diffusion, Yehudi lights, 1943.

such research offices and in 1946 authored an assessment of the various gains made in "Visibility Studies and Some Application in the Field of Camouflage." The OSRD considered the development of "black widow" paint to possibly be its most successful development as it made bombers nearly invisible to enemy searchlights. A wide variety of paints were under consideration and development by the United States during World War II, everything from emulsifications and concentrated forms of paint to ease their transport to far-flung field operations to temperature-controlled paints that could change color based on temperature to matte finishes versus glossy finishes for night camouflage to light-emulating paints to re-create the "light diffusion" effect. As with many other forms of optically oriented camouflage created during World War I and World War II, the advent of radar, the preeminent enemy detection media since World War II, modes of antidetection have become increasingly dependent on radar at the expense of optics.

In World War II the Germans had far less advanced radar than the Allies and depended extensively on an earlier architectural form, the tower, for much of their air surveillance and defense of major cities. The German construction of enormous towers housing *Flugabwehrkanone*, or aircraft defense cannons, came to be known as flak towers (figure 1.12). The towers' construction was

Figure 1.12 German flak tower, 1941–1945.

ordered in 1940 following the first major Allied air raids on German territories. The first towers were built in Berlin, though plans eventually expanded to Hamburg and Vienna. The tower form was expanded to take on destructive, communicative, and coordinating functions as the German's integrated their flak towers, radio towers, and air-traffic control towers into a cohesive unit. In this sense it was to fulfill a similar mission as the US SAGE system, but on a much smaller geographical scale. They were monumental structures, the largest designed to protect up to ten thousand civilians seeking cover, though over thirty thousand were known to have sought shelter during air raids. They housed their own hospitals, electricity plants, communications systems, and combined radar, searchlights, and antiaircraft guns for air defense. However, as with the SAGE system, they were rendered insufficient by the advancement of the aircraft technology they were built to defend against. By the time of their completion in 1944, Allied aircraft technology had advanced so much that the towers could no longer successfully see or fire upon the higher-flying enemy bombers. Their final defensive usefulness was to serve as last points of defense against the Soviet ground invasion of Berlin.

For two main reasons, the US situation for air defense was different than that of either Britain or Germany. First, the Japanese attack on Pearl Harbor on December 7, 1941, was of course the only such attack on US territory. The oceans that separated the United States from the two Axis powers created a very different surveillance and defense space. The vast ranges of the Pacific and Atlantic nautical spaces were largely monitored via radio detection finders. This allowed for long-range detection but not immediately actionable information. For this reason, radio detection finders were used to trace the traffic patterns of ships but not specific trajectories in real time. This in part leads to our second difference: the size of the US coastlines vastly outstrips the borders of either Britain or Germany. These two factors both limited the necessity and the capacity for technological or architectural solutions.

Old Media, New Enemies

In IFF, even if you know where to look and what to look for, you still need to *recognize* the target. Whether this is a blip on a radar screen or a distant speck in the sky, tools of recognition and protocols for tracking—that is, maintaining surveillance—also needed to be developed. Given an acceptable and executable set of surveillance protocols, norms must be created that determine and highlight the distinguishing characteristics of what is being examined within a given field. The establishment of norms and abnormalities is foundational to surveillance. Such norms are largely determined by what problem the surveillance is imagined to fix. These problems may be illegalities (as with speed limit enforcement), perceptual insufficiencies (as with looking into the body via MRI technologies), or the potential destruction of all human life on the planet (as with telescopes scouring the galaxy for meteors on a collision course with Earth).

If we bring several of these threads together, we can see the difficulties in making what would seem to be a relatively easy distinction: friend or foe, death-dealing Russian bomber or commerce-carrying cargo plane. For SAGE, the first order of business was to locate and track all airborne vehicles. Once detected, the second order of business was to determine whether any given radar blip posed a threat. Yet radar merely acknowledges presence or absence. Presence is of course configured here as something distinct from the particular medium through which sound waves or radio waves can flow relatively unhindered. In other words, absence doesn't truly signify the presence of "nothing," but it signifies that nothing is present that will reflect waves to a receiver. Thus the desire to find a specific category of objects informs what we might call the *radiographic episteme*—which might be summarized as the epistemological environment made sensible through the characteristics and manipulations of radio waves. In this media episteme, which corresponds to an electromagnetic conditioning of the environment, it is through the storage and comparison of each wave of blips that the axis of time is added to the spatial axis. Such processed data still only add pace to the configuration of presence and absence. How can one reconfigure mere presence into known threat? The only workable means for distinguishing friend from foe was to have complete knowledge of one's friends and, by the process of elimination, to determine who was a foe.

In practical terms this meant creating a real-time database of every known friendly flyer in the entirety of North America. In the days of SAGE, the anti-Soviet surveillance system designed to ensure mutually assured destruction if an enemy craft entered North American airspace, this total surveillance was carried out with recourse to punch cards first developed by IBM to contend with the US census of 1890. In their promotional film *Where America's Peace of Mind Begins* (1960), IBM notes, "If a flying object does not belong," it is called a "blip: unknown flying object."[15] When a blip emerged, the SAGE system deployed teams of anomaly analysis in order to determine "friend or foe"—while, at the same time, a missile was armed and aimed at the unknown flying object. SAGE then continually tracked the intruder while simultaneously calculating the point of intercept. When a blip did not correspond to this virtuality, it was assumed to represent the presence of a hostile object. Hence, North American aviation was brought under complete surveillance—not by the SAGE system per se but by the necessity of radar's incapacity to distinguish between friend and enemy.

We end our story, then, at the beginning. It was a moment in which it was believed all aircraft of note could for the most part be seen and tracked. To keep order and to ensure airspace safety, all aviation aircraft were granted a registration number that doubled as its unique call sign when communicating with air traffic control or other aircraft. Commercial airlines have more generalized forms of registration that are used to monitor their routes, which tend to be highly regularized. Rather than a unique call sign for every aircraft, each airline has a unique telephony designator or airline code, and routes are designated by a number. For instance, British Airways is designated Speedbird. Thus one route leaving New York for London would be called out as "Speedbird One-Seven-Four" by Heathrow air traffic control, while at JFK the same flight would be called "Speedbird One-Seventy-Four." Unfortunately, two of the more prominent airlines in the United States don't have such fanciful telephony designators: United Airlines is simply "United" and American Airlines is simply "American."

When "American Eleven," "United One-Seventy-Five," "American Seventy-Seven," and "United Ninety-Three" veered from their expected routes, they still registered on radar (see figure 1.13). They were up to that point completely known quantities. They were friends. They were very well known and, as with

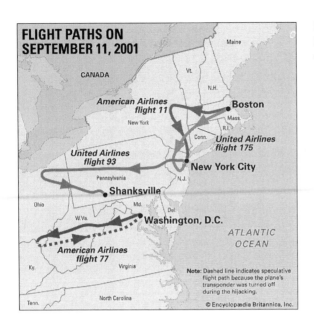

Figure 1.13
Flight paths of 9/11 attack planes.

all flights passing over US airspace since the Cold War, they were clearly identified as the proper blips on radar screens scattered throughout the Eastern Seaboard and the mid-Atlantic. The enemy detection media of the time were unable to mark them as enemy aircraft or as unknowns. Even though the transponders, which automatically provide IFF data to air traffic control, had been turned off in three of the flights and provided faulty data in the fourth, they were still properly identified on radar by many air traffic controllers. Only on recognition that they had likely been hijacked was it suggested to NORAD that interceptor aircraft might be necessary. The problem of course was that enemyship had moved from aircraft to individual, from conglomerated nation to individuated infiltration. No longer could it be assumed that an aircraft was a friend simply because it was properly listed in the registry.

The enemy detection media of the Cold War could be treated as a resounding success for the United States. Nuclear attack and retaliation have to this point been averted. No false positives set off a Strangelovian Armageddon. No actual enemy aircraft penetrated sovereign US airspace to deliver a nuclear sneak attack. By some accounts, nuclear buildup and the SAGE response mechanism that assured nuclear reciprocity sank the Soviets' economy. However, "American Eleven" ushered in the new normal at precisely 8:46 a.m. Eastern Standard Time on September 11, 2001. From then on, enemy detection media

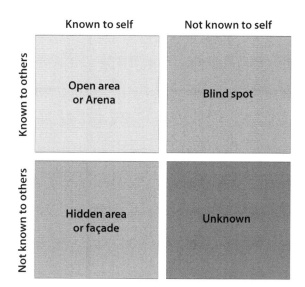

Figure 1.14
Johari window.

had to gaze anew into an emergent battle space. It was a battle space not just of knowns and unknowns but of unknown unknowns as well. What was called for was a system of enemy detection media for everywhere and unknown-where. A "Johari window" replaces an all-seeing eye (see figure 1.14). What media can capture the "unknown unknown"? What media can know self and other from above and from within, can align the present with a known past and a predictable future, can draw the global and cellular into a singular epistemology, can simultaneously work extensively and intensively?

The problem with friends and enemies is that they do not stay the same. The problem with enemy detection media is that they solve yesterday's problem.

Centralized Control/ Decentralized Execution (DoD)

Chapter 2

centralized control (DoD) 1. In air defense, the control mode whereby a higher echelon makes direct target assignments to fire units. 2. In joint air operations, placing within one commander the responsibility and authority for planning, directing, and coordinating a military operation or group/category of operations.

decentralized execution (DoD) Delegation of execution authority to subordinate commanders.

Most modern strategies of military command are characterized by a hierarchy in which expert-trained officers depend on media to give them reliable information and produce seamless chains of command. There has often been a competing logic, however, that has called into question the wisdom of "centralized control." This alternative logic addresses exceptional circumstances in which autonomous tactical agents or regiments should be programmed to "think for themselves" and spontaneously react to changes in the battle environment. Using the words of US Navy vice admiral Arthur K. Cebrowski, Katherine Hayles observes that recent American military strategy "aim[s] to abandon a centralized command/control structure in favor of a highly mobile and flexible force, a transformation that involves moving from platform-based strategies (based on tanks, airplanes, ships, etc.) to 'network-centric' structures in which units are seen not as independent actors but as 'part of a continuously adapting ecosystem.'"[1] At the forefront of this shift toward a postcentralized military command is the unmanned vehicle and its potential for deployment in semiautonomous and eventually fully autonomous swarms. These networked systems have placed in bold relief a struggle between a traditional logic of "command and control" and an emergent vision of decentralization and autonomy.

The modern stage of this conflict reached an electronics-induced stage of escalation during the Crimean War, when, in 1854, "commanders in the field were for the first time interfered with (they felt) by constant questions and suggestions (and sometimes orders) from distant military headquarters in London and Paris."² The birth of the electric telegraph and kindred technologies had suddenly allowed for senior commanders to extend their orders further and faster than ever before, allowing for intensified expressions of centralized control. A few decades later, in 1917, one of the first technological breakthroughs the Americans brought to the Western Front was airborne radio, "which transformed the airplane from a weapon of individual opportunity to a weapon capable of centrally commanded operation. The airborne radiotelephone made possible the application of the military principle of concentration of mass to aerial combat."³ Long before Hitler's Panzer divisions were coordinated by VHF radio, of which Kittler makes much ado,⁴ American media transformed the airplane from a lone wolf into a pack. As Paul Clark notes, George Owen Squier—Johns Hopkins Ph.D., National Academy of Science member, inventor of Muzak, and first military passenger in an airplane—pushed for the first successful application of radio use in airplanes when he was the chief signal officer of the Signal Corps. Squier called for "combatant units to multiply their military strength" through the application of "weapons and agencies provided by scientists and engineers."⁵ The pack cannot be understood according to the logic of simple addition. It is a "force multiplier."

The difficulties inherent in this force multiplier were evident in the early days of the United States' foray into World War II. In November 1942, as the German Sixth Army was beginning to freeze in Stalingrad, the Allies launched an invasion of North Africa. In the early stages of Operation Torch, American forces stormed the Algerian beaches near Casablanca, Oran, and Algiers, striving to impose air superiority over this strategic sliver of Axis control. Calculating that French troops wouldn't resist the American invasion, the Allies launched an amphibious assault with thirty-nine C-47 aircraft and 18,500 troops. As the Americans stormed the beaches at Oran, they used loudspeakers to woo French forces: "*Ne tirez pas!*" (Don't Shoot!). When the French replied with machine gun fire, the Allies had to suddenly shift their invasion strategy from Option Peace to Option War.

The airborne C-47s, however, never got the message. Although the nearby antiaircraft ship, the HMS *Alynbank*, tried to transmit this last-minute change of plans, the *Alynbank*'s operators repeatedly used the wrong radio frequency. The result was a strategic disaster for the unseasoned American forces. Despite the fact that the French troops were ill equipped and outmanned, only fourteen of the Americans' thirty-nine C-47s landed unscathed. Although the Allies eventually took control of Oran and the rest of Algeria's strategic coastline, air forces would play only an auxiliary role.⁶

The Americans, however, learned from this notorious blunder in command and control. Just a few months after the invasion of Oran, the United States issued *War Department Field Manual FM 100-20: Command and Employment of Air Power*, which established its new doctrine of aerial warfare. This field manual, released on July 21, 1943, argued for a monumental shift in the US military's relationship of forces. While theretofore air power had been organized as supplementary and subordinate to ground forces, the new field manual's first lines emphasized: "Land power and air power are coequal and interdependent forces; neither is an auxiliary of the other."⁷ After asserting the necessary independence of air power, the manual continues, "The inherent flexibility of air power is its greatest asset. This flexibility makes it possible to employ the whole weight of the available air power against selected areas in turn; such concentrated use of the air striking force is a battle-winning factor of the first importance. Control of available air power must be centralized and command must be exercised through the air force commander if this inherent flexibility and ability to deliver a decisive blow are to be fully exploited."⁸ In light of the communication failures at Oran, this plea for "centrality" established the need for an air force under the independent control of a specialized air command. Yet in an interesting tension with this emphasis on centrality, the manual also made the case for a "flexible" air force: "In order to obtain flexibility, the operations of the constituent units of a large air force must be closely coordinated. Flexibility enables air power to be switched quickly from one objective to another in the theater of operations."⁹ While the authors sought an independent, centralized command, they also recognized that the unique nature of aerial warfare demanded a resilient flexibility from its pilots and their units. This flexibility—as well as its apparent tension with "centralized" control—became a core mission of the US Air Force (USAF) when it was founded in 1947. In fact, "centralized control, decentralized execution" remained the tactical mantra of the US Air Force for decades, and only now in the face of AI warfare has it been seriously called into question.

Evidence of this emerging shift was expressed in 1997, when official US Air Force doctrine emphasized: "Centralized control and decentralized execution of air forces are critical to force effectiveness. Air forces must be controlled by an airman who maintains a broad perspective in prioritizing the limited assets across the range of operations."¹⁰ In 2011, USAF doctrine expressed similar concerns: "Because of airpower's unique potential to directly affect the strategic and operational levels of war, it should be controlled by a single Airman who maintains the broad, strategic perspective necessary to balance and prioritize the use of a powerful, highly desired yet limited force."[11] This continued emphasis on a single "airman," of course, places the central responsibility on a seasoned, specially trained fighter that has honed her or his knowledge in a wide range of battlefield experiences. This wise leader then circulates orders and strategies to pilots, who carry out their missions under the supervision of their leaders. While this basic hierarchical command and control strategy ensures the independence of the air force as a branch of the military, it limits the reactive "flexibility" increasingly desired by pilots in the air. Beginning in the 1990s, USAF doctrine—under the weight of centuries of hierarchical military theory—sought to maximize this flexibility by developing a special brand of "networked warfare."[12] Yet because commands were still being filtered through a centralized node (or "controller"), advanced networking technologies simply reinforced the "linear reductionism" of centralized command and control.[13]

For a new generation of military strategists, this centralization is proving to be one of the military's key obstacles.[14] For example, US Naval War College professor Milan Vego argues that the "most serious current problem in the Armed Forces is the trend toward over-centralized decision-making on the operational and strategic levels."[15] While top-shelf military tacticians are developing idealistic strategies of networked war, as Vego points out, this drive to decentralize command through networking has always fallen short of its promise: "Networking supposedly promises decentralization, affording greater initiative to subordinates. Evidence suggests the opposite: theater commanders increasingly use information technology to make decisions that would normally be the province of tactical commanders."[16] From Vego's perspective, "Advances in communications allow senior leaders to observe events in near real time from thousands of miles away. This promotes a false impression that remote headquarters can perceive the situation better than tactical commanders on the scene."[17] Technological advances that clear the fog for senior commanders, therefore, allow them to micromanage the battlefield from afar. According to these critics, micromanagement is one of the dangers with systems analysis and related science-based theories of military command. Attempts to quantify every possible variable of an attack beforehand—including troop organization, weather, rate of attrition, kill probability, fuel consumption, and so forth—and thus reduce war fighting to a mathematical equation, drove attempts to control battle hierarchically (or, in its most interesting forms, allow battle to reach an autonomous equilibrium informed by mathematics).[18] Yet for Vego, this kind of overcentralized command and control "encourages an unwillingness or inability on the part of subordinates to act independently and take responsibility for their actions."[19] This, of course, defeats the underlying purpose of networked decentralization. Advanced media of surveillance and communication, therefore, have actually worked against efforts to decentralize the work of war because they implicate senior commanders more deeply into the scene of battle, thereby remediating traditional structures of hierarchical command.[20]

Decentralized Execution

In a similar fashion, media that were designed to minimize battlefield noise have led to increased communications vulnerability. Reflecting on the radio communications systems of World War I, Kittler once remarked, "Technical media don't arise out of human needs, as their current interpretation in terms of bodily prostheses has it, they follow each other in a rhythm of escalating strategic answers."[21] Because telegraph cables were so vulnerable to enemy interception, the Italian engineer Guglielmo Marconi developed a media solution based in wireless systems of radio communications. "But alas," as Kittler points out, "the new wireless medium of radio introduced even greater risks of interception than telegraphic cables."[22] As Marconi himself put it, "Forty-two years ago, when I achieved the first successful wireless transmission in Pontecchio, I already anticipated the possibility of transmitting electric waves over large distances, but in spite of that I could not hope for the great satisfaction I am enjoying today. For in those days a major shortcoming was ascribed to my invention: the possible interception of transmissions. This defect preoccupied me so much that, for many years, my principal research was focused on its elimination."[23] For Kittler, this failure drove Marconi "to seek a pure contradiction—radio without the possibility of interception."[24] Although radio had been celebrated as a solution to the inherent limitations of cable telegraphy by opening up new possibilities for transatlantic communication, the new technology simply introduced new vulnerabilities that would have to be solved by new media.

This trend has been borne out in the bumpy development of postcentralized military command and control. As we have already seen, while new communications and surveillance technologies allowed for greater operational flexibility among pilot networks, they also exacerbated the problem of centralized command. To comprehensively tackle the prospect of decentralization, therefore, forward-thinking strategists in the US military have begun to radically reconceptualize the ways in which battlefield data can be captured and processed. Technologies such as autonomous vehicles, electromagnetic rail guns, and multiphenomenology sensors are giving rise to what Robert O.

Work and Shawn Brimley, scholars at the Center for a New American Security, call a "military technical revolution"[25]—that is, a disruptive technological convergence that promises to upturn the ways in which war is waged. One of the key teloi of this revolution is the development of technological solutions to the centralization problem. And as Kittler could have foreseen, these decentralizing technologies are creating new problems that are gradually leading to a novel technical solution—the complete elimination of the human from the chain of command and control.

UAVs, of course, are on the frontier of these efforts. Simply taking humans out of aircraft radically increases their flexibility on the battlefield. While a pilot can stay in the air for only twelve to fourteen hours, unmanned craft, with aerial refueling, can stay in the air for forty to fifty hours at a time.[26] The weight savings is also remarkable, allowing for a stealthier craft with higher endurance. And perhaps most of all, drones can partake in high-altitude and high-speed missions that are impossible for human pilots to safely endure: the blood of pilots would boil and vaporize at altitudes above 65,000 feet.[27] Establishing air dominance in the age of the drone, therefore, requires activities in which humans simply cannot participate.

Faced with this shifting technological landscape, in 2010 then–secretary of defense Robert Gates ordered the army and the air force to develop new multiaircraft piloting technologies. In response, the army—which deploys its drone pilots to overseas bases—has developed a system by which pilots can oversee two vehicles at once. In 2015, therefore, the army began to field multiaircraft control for their cutting-edge drone, the MQ-1C Gray Eagle.[28] This advance in unmanned warfare has been made possible only because the craft possess a remarkable degree of autonomy, having the capacity to take off and land on their own, for example.[29] Yet this step forward in the autonomous operation of aerial vehicles creates a deluge of additional vulnerabilities. The Gray Eagle's present data transmission systems, for example, are highly sensitive to enemy hacking. Just as telegraph cables and then wireless radio transmissions enhanced the potential for message interception, drones' complex systems of satellite-based communications are highly vulnerable to penetration and sabotage. In fact, in order for drones to operate in the air, unmanned systems require constant, assured communications to remote pilots.[30] This communication link, therefore, is an Achilles' heel of unmanned craft; as Work and Brimley point out in *Preparing for War in the Robotic Age*, "An actor who dominates in cyber conflict can infiltrate command-and-control networks, generate misinformation and confusion, and potentially even shut down or usurp control over physical platforms. This will be especially true for unmanned systems."[31] To better secure these channels and "harden the kill chain," the Department of Defense is experimenting with high-bandwidth, protected communications such as high frequency satellites and laser and free-space optical communications.

Ultimately, however, new transmission media are not radical enough to solve this problem in all its complexity. In summer 2014 DARPA awarded a contract to Northrop Grumman for a postsatellite navigation system. Designed to allow navigation in "GPS-challenged" environments, DARPA's Chip-Scale Combinatorial Atomic Navigator (C-SCAN) program will be integrated with a microelectromechanical system (MEMS) and atomic inertial guidance technologies to form a single inertial measurement unit. In the words of Northrop Grumman vice president Charles Volk, "This microsystem has the potential to significantly reduce the size, weight, power requirement, and cost of precision navigation systems.... Additionally, the system will reduce dependence on GPS and other external signals, ensuring uncompromised navigation and guidance for warfighters."[32] Note the emphasis on reducing crafts' reliance on external navigation systems: by eliminating the vulnerabilities of external communications—even fully automated communications between crafts' navigational systems and their guiding satellites—craft autonomy can be significantly increased. Seeking to capitalize on these advances, in October 2015 the US Army issued a call for R&D in Autonomous Unmanned Systems Teaming and Collaboration in GPS Denied Environments. And in September 2016, the Naval Special Warfare Command—along with Defense Innovation Unit Experimental, DoD's Silicon Valley outreach unit—funded San Diego's Shield AI to begin developing fully autonomous, GPS-independent drones.[33]

A number of other innovations have energized this shift away from satellite communications (SATCOM), as researchers have demonstrated how simple it is to hack military satellite systems. At least as far back as January 2001, DoD has been worried about terrorists and rival militaries attacking US SATCOM capabilities. At that time, defense secretary Donald Rumsfeld warned about a looming "Space Pearl Harbor," while his colleague admiral David Jeremiah argued that hostile states—and even the mythical Osama bin Laden—could hack our satellite systems (unless, of course, DoD would cough up fifty billion dollars to update the nation's satellite infrastructure).[34] According to a security consultant who produced a controversial white paper on the vulnerability of current generation military SATCOM, "Multiple high risk vulnerabilities were uncovered in all SATCOM device firmware.... These vulnerabilities have the potential to allow a malicious actor to intercept, manipulate, or block communications, and in some cases, to remotely take control of the physical device."[35] Military SATCOM devices such as the Cobham Aviator 700D, which have long served as secure communication and navigations systems for diverse military functions, are quickly becoming as hackable as telegraph lines were in the early twentieth century. C-SCAN and kindred technological programs, therefore, are striving to develop navigation systems that are fully internal and thus process all locational data onboard.

Data security, however, is not the only communications challenge facing unmanned craft. According to a recent US Department of Defense *Unmanned Systems Integrated Roadmap*, manpower and bandwidth are two of the costliest elements of their unmanned systems programs.[36] These costs, of course, are complementary: because unmanned systems cannot adequately process all the data they capture, they are required to use significant bandwidth to transmit these data back to humans on the ground.[37] In fact, the principal personnel burden for unmanned vehicles is the processing of all the surveillance data they generate.[38] Emphasizing that "one of the largest cost drivers in the budget of DoD is manpower," the Department of Defense *Roadmap* argues, "of utmost importance for DoD is increased system, sensor, and analytical automation that can not only capture significant information and events, but can also develop, record, playback, project, and parse out those data and then actually deliver 'actionable' intelligence instead of just raw information."[39] Remotely "piloting" drone aircraft requires remarkably little bandwidth; the vast majority of unmanned systems' bandwidth needs are devoted to transmitting their surveillance data to humans on the ground. Therefore, according to DoD, automated onboard data processing "can help minimize critical bandwidth necessary to transmit intelligence, surveillance, and reconnaissance (ISR) data to the warfighter and may also be suitable for reducing the intelligence officer workload and decreasing the time in the kill chain."[40] According to DARPA estimates, automated image-processing technologies could reduce the personnel burden for wide-area drone sensors—which provide surveillance coverage for an entire city—from two thousand personnel to about seventy-five.[41] These onboard processing systems would scan the drones' surveillance data for anomalies, and would pass along to humans only those data deemed alarming. In the words of a Department of Defense report, "Automated target recognition enables target discrimination, i.e., reporting contacts of interest instead of sending entire images for human interpretation."[42] Onboard computers, therefore, would autonomously determine which data should be shared with humans, and which should be simply filtered out.

While at this time only humans are officially entrusted with "kill" decisions based on these data, this DoD policy is contradicted by autonomous media/weapons such as Raytheon's new close-in weapon system, the Phalanx.[43] To compensate for the data vulnerability, physical impracticality, and financial cost of keeping humans in the command chain, the Phalanx and similar technologies empower computing systems to make kill decisions based on algorithmic determinations of enemyship. Thus in tracing the history of how new surveillance and communication technologies have been used to massage the tensions between centralized command, decentralized execution, and data security, we have been telling a story that has built more or less logically to the computerized automation of enemy epistemology—and hence, eventually, to the pure fulfillment of what Katharine Hall Kindervater calls "lethal surveillance."[44] Although DoD officially prohibits autonomous UAVs launching weapons without human command, the task force on drone policy in 2014 admitted that "current directives raise the possibility of permitting the use of such autonomous weapons in the future, with the approval of high-ranking military and civilian officials."[45] Indeed, DoD directive 3000.09, the notorious Autonomy in Weapon Systems policy document from 2012, establishes a legal loophole by which DoD officials can use their discretion to bypass all restrictions on lethal autonomous weapons.[46] Furthermore, as competing drone systems are developed in Russia, China, and elsewhere, it is hard to imagine that the US military will fail to enhance their drone programs to the highest levels of technical sophistication. This long drive toward decentralization, therefore, has serious geopolitical significance.

Likewise, these trends are complemented by a loophole in the United States' drone target determination process. When the Obama administration gradually classified its process for determining the targets of drone strikes outside "zones of active hostilities," it revealed that top officials at the National Security Council—composed of personnel in the DoD and the CIA—nominate targets to the National Counterterrorism Center (NCC). The NCC then drafts a report that is circulated to internal lawyers and the "deputies committee," composed of the agencies' seconds in command, who then pass along recommendations to agency directors. If the directors unanimously agree that the strike should be carried out, then the strike can proceed. If there are disagreements, then the president makes a final decision.[47] Yet this is the War on Terror, and the logic of exception reigns. For one thing, at any time the president may waive these checks and balances and directly order a drone strike; and for another, no executive approval is needed for areas that are deemed zones of "active hostilities." As President Trump demonstrated in one of the earliest actions of his presidency, "zone of active hostilities" is a fluid concept: although confined throughout most of the Obama presidency to Iraq and Afghanistan, Trump extended active hostility status to Yemen and Somalia, lowering targeting standards and shifting the drone target decision-making process into the hands of a minimally overseen Pentagon.[48]

The Gathering Swarm

In one of the cutting-edge developments of this military technical revolution, the figure of the "network" has transformed into the figure of the *swarm*. While swarm warfare has important precedents in military history—such as in Alexander the Great's Central Asian campaigns, the Mongol invasions of Asia and Eastern Europe, Native American attacks on the western frontier, and postcolonial guerilla resistance in Asia and Africa[49]—logics of robotic autonomy have revolutionized the potential of the swarm. Faced with the failure of networks to solve the problem of overcentralization, military strategists have begun to realize that traditional models of intelligence and command—based, that is, on human cognition and human communication—are inadequate to the challenges of twenty-first-century warfare. While for now the Department of Defense is trying to keep humans in the kill chain of unmanned operations, a human-dominated control and command structure simply cannot fulfill the objectives of decentralized twenty-first-century warfare. The next step in the revolution, therefore, relies on the development of nonhuman models of knowledge and communication. Observing this transition to animal intelligences, the military strategist Paul Scharre has remarked that forces will shift "from fighting as a *network* to fighting as a *swarm*, with large numbers of highly autonomous uninhabited systems coordinating their actions on the battlefield. This will enable greater mass, coordination, intelligence, and speed than would be possible with networks of human-inhabited or even remotely controlled uninhabited systems."[50] While humans could retain a degree of supervisory contact with the swarm, "the leading edge of the battlefront across all domains would be unmanned, networked, intelligent, and autonomous."[51]

In 2011, the journalist Peter Finn was invited to observe a test swarm mission at Fort Benning in Georgia. There he saw two model-size autonomous drones rise to altitudes of about one thousand feet, scouring the grounds for a predetermined target: a large, colorful tarp hidden on the far side of the base. One of the drones, which was outfitted with an onboard camera to capture video and a computer to analyze that data, soon located the tarp. It then autonomously transmitted a message to its partner craft, which approached the tarp and confirmed its coordinates. The second drone then sent its own message to an unmanned ground vehicle, which autonomously sped through the terrain to the mission's target. Finn remarked, "This successful exercise in autonomous robotics could presage the future of the American way of war: a day when drones hunt, identify and kill the enemy based on calculations made by software, not decisions made by humans."[52] The trend identified by Finn is obvious in the research and development of network-centric warfare, as advances in system dynamics are endowing drones with the capacity to observe, capture, and transmit data to surrounding craft which collaboratively identify targets and carry out missions based on heuristic algorithms.[53] In military common parlance, these stages of swarm warfare constitute the "kill chain" of twenty-first-century autonomous missions: Find, Fix, Track, Target, Engage, Assess.[54] Today, military AI projects such as the DoD's Project Maven capitalize on the mnemonic labor carried out by previous missions, allowing the kill chain to grow faster, smarter, and more precise with every deployment.[55]

With its extraordinary capacities for intercraft cooperation, the swarm is seen as an ideal technological arrangement for dispersing the fog of war. Upending the metaphorical connotations of Clausewitz's "fog," swarms operate through a "combat *cloud*" that is driven by collective interoperability.[56] Traditional military networks, of course, had to safeguard their principal nodes of intelligence against enemy attack. But with swarms, this epistemological center of gravity is a thing of the past. In a radical departure from human-centered command and control, which requires communication between psychically isolated cooperating subjects, the swarm cloud possesses a continuously refined, emergent collective intelligence that is far beyond the grasp of humans' physiological capacity. These swarms continuously reorient their collective intelligence—they are even "self-healing" in the event of companion loss, which they compensate for by readjusting the epistemological topology of the swarm.[57] These decisions for topological restructuring can be accomplished by the use of "voting" mechanisms, which could allow swarms to achieve a decentralized epistemology that is inconceivable among networked human combatants.[58] The rise of numerous cutting-edge swarm programs, including DARPA's Collaborative Operations in Denied Environment (CODE) program, the army's Micro-Autonomous Systems Technology (MAST) program, the navy's Low-Cost UAV Swarming Technology (LOCUST) program, and the marines' Unmanned Tactical Autonomous Control and Collaboration (UTACC) program, proves that DoD's demand to expand the role of hybrid warfare and swarm intelligence is being seriously pursued across the branches of the US military.

This emergent intelligence is made possible by what military strategists call "implicit communication," which is modeled on the cooperative epistemologies of flock and school animals such as birds, ants, and fish.[59] Although the RAND Corporation and the US government have been funding military research in "microrobotics" since the early 1990s, new manufacturing technologies, such as 3-D printing, have made it possible for DoD affiliates to develop swarms that take the physical form of dragonflies, "robobees," houseflies, remoras, hornets, eels, and other animals that cooperate with distributed intelligence.[60] These swarms gained sudden popularity in 2015 and 2016, when the navy launched its LOCUST program, the air force began funding swarms of "gremlins,"[61] and DARPA launched its Fast Lightweight Autonomy (FLA) program.[62] As 3-D printing has given rise to the mass production of these swarming minidrones, and as computing and navigational systems continue to shrink and become more mobile, this development could allow DoD to deploy thousands or even billions of tiny, cheaply produced, cooperative drones that could be released into the field of combat in order to carry out reconnaissance and locate enemy combatants.[63]

The Mother Ship and Its Enemies

Drawing on some of these emergent capacities, in the 2013 edition of its *Unmanned Systems Integrated Roadmap* the Department of Defense laid out its plans for unmanned systems during the next generation. In this document, the DoD foresees "smart teams of unmanned systems operating autonomously" and in concert.[64] Constructing a collective enemy epistemology, these swarms assess and classify their surroundings while carrying out nontraditional means of warfare, synchronizing electronic and kinetic attacks.[65] These swarms are already being deployed on the battlefield in the form of advanced cruise missile systems, some of which are equipped with the capacity to autonomously determine and engage enemy targets. Outfitted with sophisticated onboard sensors, these swarms can perform battle damage assessments before they strike, thus enabling them to collectively refine their knowledge of the enemy and coordinate their attacks accordingly.[66] This process of enemy determination/incapacitation has reached an impressive degree of autonomy in naval warfare, where the craft in Lockheed Martin's Low-Cost Autonomous Attack System (LOCAAS) line collectively "vote" on which tactics and weapons to use against a determined target.[67]

As these developments and related escalations suggest, the fog and chaos of the battlefield have really only one solution: machine epistemology. We have finally reached the situation foreseen by Manuel DeLanda, who feared that "in the modern battlefield, full of noisy data, commanders will feel only too tempted to rely on the accumulated expertise stored in [machines'] arsenals of know-how, and will let the computer itself make the decisions. Further, only computers have fast access to all the 'perceptual' information about a battle, coming from satellite and ground sensors, so that a commander confronted by the noisy data emanating from the battlefield might ... allow it to mutate from a mere smart prosthesis, a mechanical adviser, into a machine with executive capabilities of its own."[68] Formerly prosthesis, the machine is stepping into its more fitting roles of sage, executive, and executioner. To accommodate this responsibility shift, the DoD's *Roadmap* longs for a near future in which the air force will develop weaponized unmanned aerial systems that are designed to carry out autonomous swarm attacks. Calling these craft "loitering weapons," DoD envisions aerial swarms outfitted with imaging sensors that serve as "intelligent munitions."[69] Using data processing systems such as the LOCAAS, these swarming media/weapons are designed to "autonomously search and destroy critical mobile targets while aiming over a wide combat area."[70] While these swarming munitions are currently "man in the loop"—that is, while soldiers on the ground make decisions about lethal engagements—DoD suggests developing a data processing "mother ship" that could guide these "Surveilling Miniature Attack Cruise Missiles." This artificially intelligent mother ship, which will support four individual missiles, will aid the swarm in movement coordination, enemy determination, and attack protocols.[71] With the mother ship and other striking new assemblages of autonomous weaponry, DoD is striving to migrate missions' center of gravity onto the flawless mathematical wonder of the machine. By computational necessity, these intelligent weapons will be able to follow only kill commands devised by machines, based on coordinates formulated by machines, targeted at the enemies of machines. As Antoine Bousquet argues, "Whatever the particulars of future sciences and technologies may be, any future regime of warfare will necessarily mark yet another chapter in the continually renewed yet never settled quest for order on the battlefield."[72] While future chapters are sure to come, up-and-coming AI weapons systems give us a glimpse of how this quest could be settled once and for all. Noise, entropy, the enemies of order—the channel must be cleared. The command must be executed.

Hostile Environment (DoD)

Chapter 3

Operational environment in which hostile forces have control as well as the intent and capability to effectively oppose or react to the operations a unit intends to conduct.

> *Gaia is using the best methods of a crafty general—turning our shortsighted machinations against us—in her retaliatory counter-war.*
> —J. BAIRD CALLICOTT, *THINKING LIKE A PLANET*

> *Among the future trends that will impact our national security is climate change. Rising global temperatures, changing precipitation patterns, climbing sea levels, and more extreme weather events will intensify the challenges of global instability.... In our defense strategy, we refer to climate change as a "threat multiplier" because it has the potential to exacerbate many of the challenges we are dealing with today.*
> —US DEPARTMENT OF DEFENSE, *CLIMATE CHANGE ADAPTATION ROADMAP*

This chapter attempts to answer the question: what happens when the whole of the earth is both the "operational environment" in which war is conducted and the "hostile force" against which a military force directs itself? We will do so by examining the historical interpenetration of climate knowledge and warfare. As far back as the Old Testament, weather has been central to conducting war, and this militant use of weather has simultaneously provided evidence for situating humanity's fundamental place within the universe. As global climate catastrophe has increasingly become the dominant means for understanding humanity's relationship to weather and the climate, the US military sees itself as needing to prepare for the new dynamics of surviving the threat posed by Gaia, humanity's mother turned "crafty general." Like many of our other examples, the media-scientific enterprise used to make sense of the physical world and recognize its threats has also produced knowledge valuable to the design and successful use of nearly all forms of military weaponry. Whereas the threats posed by climate and weather events were often viewed as either a force multiplier or potential weapon, more recent cybernetic systems theories of the climate, of which Gaia is the best known, present a very different kind of "enemy." Any surge in animosity toward her can only return as further empowered retaliation. A war with Gaia is one that can't be won. Or, to put it more precisely, an attack on this enemy is akin to a kamikaze attack or suicide bombing—the perpetrator may or may not inflict heavy losses, but it's the last battle they will ever fight.

As we have suggested, the central component in military strategy is media technology—those technologies that offer different manipulations of the time/space axis, thus ushering in new political realities and military velocities through their unique capacities to select, store, and process information. Central to the concerns of this chapter is the fact that weather and environmental data are absolutely vital to this process. Following from Friedrich Kittler, not only do media determine our condition,[1] but weather media determine the conditions of warfare. Knowledge about weather and warfare might be seen as being configured according to three different "military epistemes." We might simplify them as God/classical, nature/modern, Gaia/cybernetic. Bruno Latour suggests a similar periodization of humanity's understanding of the environment; yet unlike Latour, we explicitly analyze how media/war is central to all three.[2]

Weather and earth observation writ large has been and continues to be driven by warfare and the opening up of new spheres of battle. Earth observation media—those media specifically developed to better understand the physical characteristics of the world[3]—have time and time again been created according to military necessity or quickly adapted to the ontological conditions of battle. The "closed world" dream so well described by Paul Edwards is in fact never closed, never entirely a bounded "world."[4] Rather, what we suggest is an ever-expanding range of potentiality that will never be closed off. War emancipates epistemology to go further. Ever-lingering threats have turned Earth and all of its inhabitants—at every interval of potential analysis, from atoms, DNA molecules, and microbes to nations, continents, and planetary climate—into a weapon, a bunker, and, ultimately, an enemy. As Chris Russill explains, the media of the Apollo space mission—popularized with its mission photos of the "Big Blue Marble"—constituted Earth as an integrated knowable system demarcated by the emptiness of space that surrounds it.[5] Once the world became object, the world becomes target, its coordinates crosshairs.[6]

The Earth is humanity's enemy, because Homo sapiens sapiens might be exterminated by "natural" earthly causes. The God of Israel must have known this from the start. According to the Old Testament, He was the first to use weather to change the outcome of a battle.[7] What hath God wrought indeed.

And You Will Know My Name Is the Lord

I will strike down upon thee with great vengeance and furious anger those who would attempt to poison and destroy my brothers. And you will know my name is the Lord when I lay my vengeance upon thee.
—JULES IN *PULP FICTION*, RECITING EZEKIEL 25:17

When Jehovah Sabaoth (meaning "The Lord of Hosts" or "God of Armies") unleashed "ten plagues" on Egypt to convince Pharaoh that it was time to let His people go, He was enacting a form of total warfare on the Egyptians using a cluster of biological and environmental weapons that today would be called weapons of mass destruction. Throughout the Old Testament, Jehovah Sabaoth became increasingly proficient in using this weaponry to guide and direct the tribes of Israel through tumultuous battles and insidious temptations. Further, as theologian Erhard Gerstenberger puts it, "Yahweh was not always God in Israel and at every social level. Rather, initially he belongs only to the storm and war gods like Baal, Anath, Hadad, Resheph and Chemosh."[8] The Judeo-Christian genealogy is not our concern per se; rather, "storm and war" provide our guidance.

In no particular chronological order or order of magnitude, Jehovah Sabaoth's arsenal included hail, drought, flood, tsunami, ionization, earthquake, lightning, biological weaponry, and apocalyptic fire as means for carrying out warfare for His chosen people. The "Lord of Armies" first used hail as a weather weapon in the battle of the Israelites versus the five armies united by a sextant of Amorite kings. The Book of Joshua records, "And it came to pass, as they fled from before Israel, while they were at the descent of Beth-horon, that the Lord cast down great stones from heaven upon them unto Azekah and they died; they were more who died with the hailstones than they who the children of Israel slew with the sword" (Joshua 10:11). This God could also make time itself stand still by stopping the rotation of the earth, which allowed the Israelites the time to continue their daylight-aided slaughter: "And the sun stood still, and the moon stayed, until the people had avenged themselves upon their enemies" (Joshua 10:13).[9] While Jehovah Sabaoth would go on to lay waste to Sodom and Gomorrah, turn Lot's wife into a pillar of salt (see figure 3.1), punish Babylon with a debilitating drought, and, as accounted for in the Book of Deuteronomy, threaten Moses and the Israelites with a series of biological and climatic curses

Figure 3.1 Sodom and Gomorrah destroyed by brimstone and fire while Lot's wife is turned into a pillar of salt.

that include famine, boils, fever, inflammation, drought, immolation, and plague. However, none of His weapons matched the sheer ferocity of "the flood."

Each of these weapons shares something in common: each consciously redirects the destructive capacity of the natural environment in order to achieve military/political objectives. In Jehovah's most profound act of climatic destruction, we witness an act of total war: a war unrestricted in terms of weaponry, territorial boundaries, the targeting of civilians, or any other reservation. The Great Flood of Genesis is used to wipe out the entirety of the human race, save Noah's family, and every living animal, apart from one pair of each species (see figure 3.2). Climatic weaponry's destructive capacity is seemingly endless, and the justification for this "total war" was the purifying renewal of the human race.

Further, Jehovah did not simply make Israel's enemies disappear, as if by magic, but always acted through the "natural" world by "supernaturally" redistributing the potential destructive force of biological agents and weather phenomena. In other words, the natural world was target, weapon, and proof of

Figure 3.2 The Ark survives the Great Flood as all other living creatures drown in a watery apocalypse.

God's existence and judgment. Climate alteration and biological manipulation were signs of a guiding intelligence that could be accessed through the limited human sensorium. Jehovah would further make himself known via other natural climate signifiers: "The heavens declare the glory of God; the skies proclaim the work of his hands. Day after day they pour forth speech; night after night they display knowledge. There is no speech or language where their voice is not heard. Their voice goes out into all the earth, their words to the ends of the world which is like a bridegroom coming forth from his pavilion, like a champion rejoicing to run his course. It rises at one end of the heavens and makes its circuit to the other; nothing is hidden from its heat" (Psalm 19:1–6). And yet such "speech" is not saved for the faithful: "The wrath of God is being revealed from heaven against all the godlessness and wickedness of humanity who suppress the truth by their wickedness, since what may be known about God is plain to them, because God has made it plain to them. For since the creation of the world God's invisible qualities—his eternal power and divine nature—have been clearly seen, being understood from what has been made, so that humans are without excuse" (Romans 1:18–20). God, via Nature, reveals a higher logic that is inseparable from and most clearly expressed through His/Nature's breadth of destructive capacity. The ontology of weather as a "force multiplier" and as an expression of the earth's relationship to humanity has deep roots in the most widespread media of the print era, The Holy Bible. The God/classic episteme clarifies the relationship of weather and war through the mythological destruction of a storm god.

Yet Hebrew tribes are surely not the only benefactors of god-guided environmental weaponry. Thor, Jupiter, Zeus, Horus, and Indra are merely a handful of the myriad storm gods, many of whom are the most powerful within their respective pantheons. Storm gods, as the name implies, wield power via their manipulation of environmental forces. Prior to the development of nuclear arsenals, storms and other environmental calamities were easily the most destructive forces known to humans. Harnessing such power would provide the greatest military advantage known. There are hosts of examples from around the world in which storm gods' weather events are understood in terms of the gods aiding and abetting a military cause or campaign. For instance, as Kublai Khan attempted to invade Japan—not once, but twice—a "kamikaze" or "divine wind" rose up, unleashing destructive storms and waves that destroyed most of the invading fleet, dealing Khan his most notable military failures. This understanding of historical events is said to have been so strong that some believe the Japanese saw themselves as divinely protected and militarily invincible, thus leading to their later militaristic sense of destiny to create a Pacific empire.[10] This episteme, in which nature both reveals divine military will and serves as a means of executing it, would eventually be remediated by modern scientific understandings of nature and warfare—an era dominated by what Peter Sloterdijk calls "atmotechnics."[11] Through the scientific analysis and manipulation of the atmosphere, weather would again become a "force multiplier."

Fog of War

While legendary military theorist Carl von Clausewitz is perhaps best known for his notion of the "fog of war," he never precisely used that phrase (*Nebel des Krieges*). He does, however, reference fog three times in his classic *On War*, and each reference speaks directly to considerations of weather and warfare. In the first, Clausewitz is discussing the concept of "friction," which encompasses all of the unpredictable circumstances that constantly wreak havoc with military planning. His lengthiest examples of such "friction" are two cases of inclement weather, fog, and rain:

> This enormous friction, which is not concentrated, as in mechanics, at a few points, is therefore everywhere brought into contact with chance, and thus facts take place upon which it was impossible to calculate, their chief origin being chance. As an instance of one such chance, take the weather.

Here, the fog prevents the enemy from being discovered in time, a battery from firing at the right moment, a report from reaching the general; there, the rain prevents a battalion from arriving, another from reaching in right time, because, instead of three, it had to march perhaps eight hours; the cavalry from charging effectively because it is stuck fast in heavy ground.[12]

Here *fog*—inclement weather—is a literal example of a theoretical principle, friction. In Clausewitz's second use of fog it takes on a metaphorical character, but one still based in the material concern with optics and the ability to properly "see" (that is, know) the conditions under which strategy and tactics are being planned: "Lastly, the great uncertainty of all data in war is a peculiar difficulty, because all action must, to a certain extent, be planned in a mere twilight, which in addition not unfrequently—like the effect of a fog or moonshine—gives to things exaggerated dimensions and an unnatural appearance."[13] In this case, fog is used to signify the impossibility of perfect data. And in the third case, Clausewitz enumerates the three "circumstances" that are always present in battle: space (the territory or battle field), time (that is day or night), and weather: "Still more rarely has the weather any decisive influence, and it is mostly only by fogs that it plays a part."[14] While Clausewitz suggests that weather is rarely decisive, his choice of "fogs" is relevant insofar as the optical requirements of war in Clausewitz's day were specific to the form of warfare dictated by the ballistic capabilities and the tactical consequences of lining up armies and munitions across from each other's formation and then advancing on those positions. As will become eminently clear through our following analysis, the degree to which weather could add "friction" into military operations increases apace with the development of more sophisticated and destructive weaponry that traverses a broader spectrum of territory at greater speeds.

A few historical examples come immediately to mind: Khan's repelled assaults on Japan. Hannibal and the wintry Alps. Napoleon and Hitler defeated by the Russian winter. The Allies' successful D-day sneak attack made possible due to superior weather prediction. And, more recently, the clear skies of September 11, 2001, guaranteed that all flights along the Eastern Seaboard would leave on time to ensure simultaneity of attack,[15] and that the amateur pilots would have clear visual contact with their targets, thus mitigating the need to rely on more sophisticated media to engage the battle space.[16]

Given the fact that weather has always played a role in military success and failure, militaries have often turned toward the scientific and technological management of weather. Yet, as US Navy commander Barbara Brehm has argued, "In this era when many believe that advanced technology can fix any problem (natural or man-made) that might occur, there remains a frontier that is largely untamed: the weather."[17] Advances in technology (media-instruments-computation) are often presented as solutions to the problems associated with weather—as unpredictable, uncontrollable, or unmanageable. Yet it is often precisely technological dependency that exacerbates the problem. Each new weapon brings the weather into play in new ways. To take a basic example, gunpowder is susceptible to moisture in a way that an arrow is not. Likewise, the increasingly fine-toothed data necessary to fight RMA across a host of microclimates strains the ability of sensors to elaborate what is "weather" and what is "thermal clutter that can confuse infrared sensors."[18] The more sophisticated the sensors used to produce epistemological clarity, the greater chance small changes in climate may lead to failure. Hence, the demand of military media systems to be ever more precise produces the very conditions in which failure becomes increasingly likely. Thus technological prowess calls forth the necessity of more robust systems for understanding the weather. Such an understanding is built on sensors that can "see through" the climatic clutter to produce ever-greater clarity. On and on the drive continues to produce knowledge of the climate to render it impotent, so that "fog" can no longer disrupt the plans of generals or the aims of laser-guided missile and sniper rifles. As Ajey Lele summarizes, "Every war extends the war-weather-horizon into new and unexplored fields."[19] Accordingly, a series of loosely defined "discourse weather networks" emerged as constituent elements of the "war-weather-horizon." These networks established usable weather and climatic data for a changing set of military considerations and capacities.

Discourse Weather Networks

"By guess or by God." During an era when British sea power was preeminent around the globe, this sentiment was suggestive of the guiding principle of Matthew Murray, naval maritime meteorologist, in his *Explanations and Sailing Directions to Accompany Wind and Current Charts* (1851). The increasing capacity to collect weather data in real time due to the widespread dispersal of a national telegraph network would begin to erase the process of guessing and would privilege technical analysis and scientific explanation. Several elements would ultimately come together to form what we might consider the modern meteorological apparatus. Warfare and military considerations produced numerous nodes of what Paul Edwards calls a "vast machine"[20] that, by the mid-2000s, included a wide array of weather concerns that are actively monitored by US military sensors on the ground, in the air, underwater, and in outer space: barometric pressure, clouds and sky cover, currents, density altitude, dew point, electromagnetic radiation, fog/mist/haze, freeze and thaw depth,

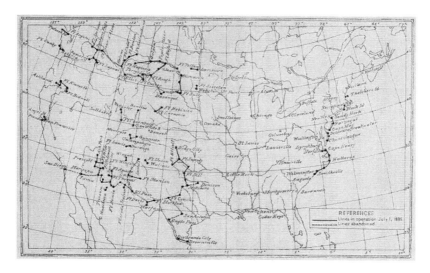

Figure 3.3 Discourse Weather Network, telegraph/map/flag, 1870–90.

geomagnetic storms, humidity, humidity profile, icing, illumination, infrared crossover, precipitation, pressure profile, refractive index, sea surface temperature, snow depth, solar flares, ground and surf conditions, surface wind, state of the ground, temperature, thunderstorms and lightning, tide, turbulence, visibility, winds aloft, windchill, and wind profile.[21] Accordingly, these concerns of weather and climate have also been treated by the military as a specific threat to the health of soldiers. Being stationed and fighting in "exotic" locales and climates has historically been seen as a threat equal or greater to the enemy forces one is fighting. As such, understanding climate's effects on health was considered a military concern. The US surgeon general's office began to systematically study weather before any other US agency because weather was seen to be a health risk to troops more so than something that could be understood as part of tactical preparation.[22] Breakthroughs in the medical treatment of *tropical diseases* often accompanied military colonial expansion. Understanding the specific biological fauna of colonies was not only a scientific and commercial concern but also a biopolitical military concern.

Shortly after the Civil War, the US military also recognized that media were the means by which climate could be scientifically drawn into military strategy. Following the end of the US Civil War, the Signal Corps found its energies redirected away from signals theory and military chains of command toward gathering weather data and distributing them across the nation (see figure 3.3). Via the

Figure 3.4 War Department Weather Map, 1873.

ever-growing commercial and military telegraph networks, the corps sent the first "Weather Synopsis and Probabilities" report on February 19, 1871.[23] By 1873 a discourse network was sufficiently established to collect, map (see figure 3.4), telegraph, print, and display daily weather forecasts at over six thousand rural post offices whereby the forecast could be spread locally through a visual flag-based system and oral dissemination throughout rural farming communities (see figure 3.5).[24] The sustained gathering, collection, and distribution of climate data has been one of the many means by which the US military imagined it could scientifically manage the outcome of war and use its growing network of bases and media capacities to strengthen the nation's commerce, agricultural sectors, and public health initiatives. These weather data were further collected, stored, processed, and disseminated via three temporally organized publications, the *Daily Weather Bulletin,* the *Weekly Weather Chronicle,* and the *Monthly Weather Review* (the latter of which would become one of the leading scientific journals on meteorology and continues to be published by the American Meteorological Society). However, the considerable problem of computational limitations eventually appeared.

Following the success of the 1890 US Census and faced with a similarly unruly data set, the US Navy purchased several Hollerith tabulating machines.

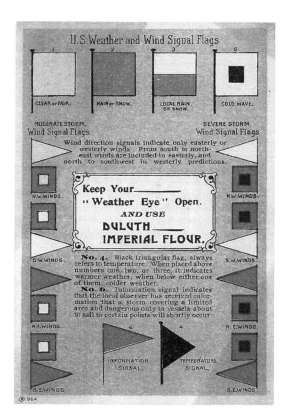

Figure 3.5 US Weather and Wind Signal Flags, 1890s.

Since 1838, the US Navy Hydrographic Office had been collecting weather data from stations located throughout the United States every three hours. However, as the historian of science Frederik Nebeker describes, "In 1893 when a new director, C. D. Sigsbee, was appointed, there were more than 3,000 observers sending data to the Hydrographic Office, and the flow of data could no longer be processed."[25] This bottleneck, caused by human incapacities to process sufficient data, would threaten to burst in the coming years. Yet with the application of the tabulating machines, these data points were for the first time massaged into a somewhat manageable form. Accordingly, this innovation became, as the military historians Charles Bates and John Fuller remark, "the first known instance of machine processed meteorological data" (see figure 3.6).[26] While this navy program lasted only about a decade, its brand of big weather data computation would grow considerably in the interwar period.

Lat. 44° 39.6′ N. HALIFAX, NOVA SCOTIA. Long. 63° 35.3′ W.

Year.	Variation of compass.	Authority.	
		Observer.	Where recorded.
1700......	13.00		Edmund Halley's Isogonic Chart for 1700.
1756......	12.83		United States map, by Chas. Morris.
1775......	13.60		Des Barres's Sailing Directions.
1798......	16.50		Plan published by Thos. Backhouse.
1818......	17.47	Anthony Lockwood, esq	Remark book of J. Napier, R. N.
1821......	17.60	J. Napier, R. N.	Do.
1852.5....	18.50	Capt. Bayfield, R. N. / J. Hill, R. N	Remark book by J. Hill, master, R. N.
1860......	19.91	Capt. Orlebar, R. N	
1866......	21.10		From records of Halifax dockyard.
1879......	20.71	J. Baylor, United States Coast and Geodetic Survey.	Coast and Geodetic Survey Report for 1881, Appendix No. 9.

Year.	Observed.	Computed.	O−C.	$\overline{O\text{-}C}^2$.	
1700......	13.00	12.83	+0.17	0.0289	
1756......	12.83	13.12	−0.29	0.0841	
1775......	13.60	14.11	−0.51	0.2601	
1798......	16.50	15.70	+0.80	0.6400	
1818......	17.47	17.24	+0.23	0.0529	Probable error of a single observed value = ±26′.
1821......	17.60	17.47	+0.13	0.0169	Period = 350 years.
1852.5....	18.50	19.63	−1.13	1.2769	
1860......	19.91	20.03	−0.12	0.0144	
1866......	21.10	20.31	+0.79	0.6241	
1879......	20.71	20.77	−0.06	0.0036	
				3.0019	

Empirical equation for determining the variation for any year: $v = 16.74 + 3.32 \sin \frac{36}{35}(t-1850) + 2.74 \cos \frac{36}{35}(t-1850)$.

Figure 3.6 Discourse Weather Network, compass/chart/Hollerith tabulator, 1893–1904.

World, War, Weather

World War I would bring at least three other key discourse weather networks into being, working in conjunction with the capacities of three new weapons of war: the U-boat, the airplane, and lethal gas. What we see in two of these cases is the extensive advancement of new climatic and meteorological media to collect, store, and process data on environments (see figure 3.7) that were being opened up to human inhabitation for the first time (as with the depths of the sea or the upper altitudes reached by airplanes and zeppelins). First, as U-boats came to be seen as an increasingly powerful weapon, there was an escalation in the necessity to "see" into the sea and understand underwater

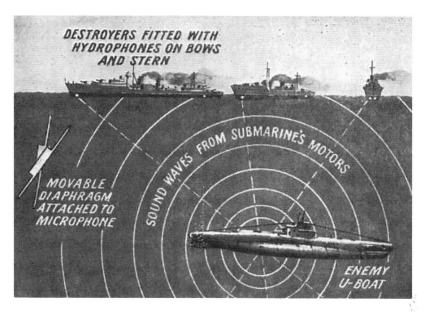

Figure 3.7   Instructions for using a hydrophone to detect submarines.

environments. According to John Shiga, who has carried out extensive analysis of the development of hydrophones and sonar during World War I, "The incorporation of listening techniques into machines, vessels, and bodies opened up a new front below the ocean surface for the perpetuation and elaboration of warfare waged by increasingly mobile machines."[27] Second, while the sky had always been "seen," its differential weather and climatic environments at various altitudes had never been experienced or known directly by humans until air travel, though that hadn't stopped naturalists from making the clouds tell their own tales.[28] More profoundly, the use of airplanes and zeppelins during World War I heightened the demands to better understand the effect of these environments on the ability to carry out air attacks, collect aerial reconnaissance, defend against such attacks, alter ballistics, and camouflage one's forces from airborne surveillance. Whereas airplanes provided advantages such as speed, zeppelins could fly higher and avoid enemy detection. This, however, produced its own meteorological challenges, such as in Germany's zeppelin attacks against England in October 1917. Although the eleven deployed zeppelins could fly at five thousand meters (which was far beyond the range of allied planes), the winds at that altitude wreaked havoc on the zeppelins and knocked five of them out of the sky.[29]

Figure 3.8 The killer fog of war is unleashed by German soldiers on the Western Front, 1915.

Despite this and similar blunders, numerous media were sent into the sky via balloon, zeppelin, or plane to collect data about barometric pressure, wind speed, temperature, and cloud density. The daily weather forecasts in the local papers of London could provide foreboding information: as the *Daily Express* warned in February 1916, "The zeppelin only comes over on certain nights, when the glass is high or stationary at a fairly high point. These nights have almost all a close resemblance to each other. They are still, windless, dark, and preferably misty or cloudy. On such nights aeroplanes are useless, and guns are difficult to aim without any exactitude."[30] Awareness of the atmosphere's changing qualities turned the sky into an actionable terrain for warfare. The realms of weather and climate expand upward and downward, becoming increasingly three-dimensional. Weather is no longer merely charted on a map day by day but given new temporal and spatial specificity.

Chris Russill observes that, as a result of the convergent development of airplanes, "big optics," and more powerful munitions, "war increasingly attacked an environment to disable a threat . . . , [and] weapons were designed to render their environmental and earthly fortifications uninhabitable."[31] According to this new media logic, toxic gases become a means to infiltrate the

Figure 3.9 The measurement of wind speed and direction is taken from the trenches. On April 22, 1915, the forecast suggested a "mild southwesterly breeze."

trenches and bunkers of World War I and render the atmosphere unlivable. Weaponizing the air, though, necessitated greater understanding of the atmosphere as a weapons delivery mechanism. Obviously wind velocity and direction were of great importance, but of equal importance were the consistency and duration of the wind's speed and direction. A change of direction could prove deadly. As such, the German military used specialized media to measure, assess, and predict the immediate and lasting potential of the wind to carry out and sustain their deadly gas attacks (see figure 3.8). As Peter Sloterdijk observes, these media—which analyzed and targeted the latent atmosphere—laid bare new ambient zones of war that demanded engagement.[32] Humankind, which had always enjoyed a "privilege of naivete" about the security of the breathable environment, now saw a poisonous fog of war envelop its latent atmosphere (see figure 3.9).[33]

The secrecy of war produced another key weather discourse network as well as affecting the naming of meteorological phenomena. The term "weather front" was derived from the phrase "battle front" at the height of the war.[34] Weather was imagined as a battle between warring movements of different temperature winds. This notion was first developed in 1917 by Norwegian meteorologists who were renewing methods of weather analysis at a time when the war had prevented the sharing of weather data. Because mapping weather movement from country to country was no longer possible, these meteorologists began using balloons to measure weather at different elevations in an attempt to provide another mode of prediction.

While there were extensive weather analysis developments during World War II, they largely followed along the lines of extending the range, density, and specificity of weather and climatic data in order to integrate them into military strategy and tactics. However, with the advent of the hydrogen bomb and the discovery of radioactive fallout, weather takes on newfound importance. More generally, it is during the Cold War that a cybernetic understanding of the earth as a "closed world" began to fuel a view of the weather that called for *whole earth* climate data.[35] Drawing on the work of Paul Edwards, John Shiga nicely summarizes the contours of this cybernetic/nuclear couplet: "The dominant perspective of networks in the postwar period was articulated through what Edwards calls the 'closed world discourse' of Cold War military computing, which helped sustain the belief that nuclear war would be 'winnable' by building networks that capture 'the whole world within its closed system,' anticipating 'every possible contingency.' As Edwards argues, this vision of the world as a closed system in which entities and their actions would be contained in a calculative and predictive environment of continuous surveillance, intervention and feedback shaped the mid-century development and use of computers and communication networks."[36] Weather and climate data became absolutely necessary feedback in these networks. Following the advent of nuclear testing, weather began to be imagined as both a highly human-affected realm and something that might be manipulated and utilized as a weapon. Thus the climate itself became weaponized as a result of the nuclear fallout delivered by weather systems.

Understanding these systems became a primary goal of the US military almost immediately following the bombings of Hiroshima and Nagasaki.[37] A wide-ranging set of tests and monitoring practices was arranged and conducted using both the newly developed atomic bomb and the recently sequestered V2 rocket. In the most infamous of tests, the Bikini Atoll test of 1946, the 59th Weather Reconnaissance Squadron used drones, airplanes, and boats to collect radioactive material during and after the blast. A fleet of technicians patrolled the area taking air and water samples, and measuring wind speeds, cloud density, barometric pressure, and the like. This vast network of radiation-chasing media was used in an attempt to map the ultimate radioactive power of the bomb in spatial and temporal terms (see figures 3.10, 3.11, 3.12, and 3.13). For the first time in history, the destructive capacity of a weapon had to be measured across a series of temporal scales that began with the immediate explosive force; spread radioactive destruction via wind,

Figure 3.10 "Operation of Drones" flown by "mother control planes." Clip from *Radiological Safety at Operation Crossroads Atomic Bomb Tests 73862*, Department of the Navy, 1946.

Figure 3.11 Drones' "ground control officer." Still from *Operation Crossroads*, Department of the Navy, 1949.

Figure 3.12 Model x263 Geiger counters get handed out on board before Bikini Atoll test. Clip from *Radiological Safety at Operation Crossroads Atomic Bomb Tests 73862*, Department of the Navy, 1946.

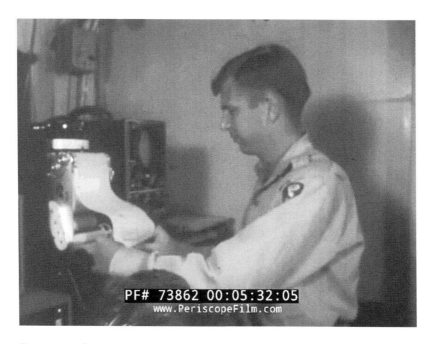

Figure 3.13 Geiger data is recorded using an Angus recorder aboard the ship during the Bikini Atoll test. Clip from *Radiological Safety at Operation Crossroads Atomic Bomb Tests 73862,* Department of the Navy, 1946.

turbulence, air streams, tides, the flow of rivers, water soil seepage, and other naturally occurring movements for days, weeks, or months; and then slowly diminished over the course of millennia. From such a climatic perspective, not one single nuclear test has to this day been truly completed. The radiation from every exploded device still lingers and its radioactive effects can still be monitored.

The more than two thousand tests and their lingering effects have been part of the ongoing destruction of indigenous lands and peoples: "The primary targets . . . have been invariably the sovereign nations of Fourth World and indigenous peoples. Thus history has witnessed the nuclear wars against the Marshall Islands (66 times), French Polynesia (175 times), Australian Aborigines (9 times), Newe Sogobia (the Western Shoshone Nation) (814 times), Christmas Island (24 times), Hawaii (Kalama Island, also known as Johnston Island) (twelve times), the Republic of Kazakhstan (467 times), and Uighur (Xinjian Province, China) (36 times)."[38] This is to say that the radiological health and environmental effects were borne by native populations. Treated and understood as part of the "natural" environment, indigenous peoples were tested along with their native lands to determine the longevity and scope of radiological destruction.

For a short period between the development of the atomic bomb and the development of the hydrogen bomb, US and Soviet military strategists planned for a war that would be total but would not, ultimately, be won or lost by atomic supremacy. This was a time before MAD came to be seen as the only logical approach toward Cold War detente. This period saw the testing not only of the capacities of atomic weapons but also of new delivery systems. In 1946, this work began with the German-developed V2 rocket, and its first test combined Earth observation with rocketry (see figure 3.14). In fact, the first US photos of Earth taken from space were produced during the first such test (see figure 3.15). With these new military media, once again we see the opening up of a new battlefield—the upper atmosphere—that necessitates new environmental understanding. Yet the specificity of such knowledge ultimately comes to be used to more broadly understand the general dynamics of the earth's climate writ large. This "view from above" follows the trajectory outlined by Virilio in *War and Cinema* insofar as "big optics" reconfigure how war is conducted and from what vantage the battlefield comes into being as a knowable territory.[39] This experimentation addressed the dual necessity of studying objects and environments: building on Norbert Wiener's emerging theory of cybernetics—which arose from Wiener's wartime work on antiaircraft guns[40]—the two were increasingly seen to work in a systematic fashion.

Figure 3.14
The V2 rocket—
requisitioned from
Germany, launched in
New Mexico, and used to
photograph Earth, 1946.

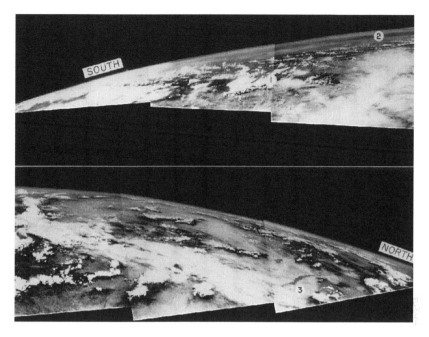

Figure 3.15   A V2 provides the first-ever photos of Earth from space, 1946.

Weather after the War

This military desire laid the technological infrastructure for monitoring and assessing the longitudinal effects of human activity on the climate. Further, climatic monitoring became the means by which the United States could determine the existence and extent of Soviet nuclear weapons testing. For instance, as a result of a lack of on-the-ground spies behind the Iron Curtain, the United States came to use weather data to determine when the Soviets first successfully tested atomic weaponry and were then able to track continued weapons development via such data. Knowing the climate became synonymous with knowing the enemy, knowing their capacities, and potentially knowing their climatic weaknesses. Environmental modification (ENMOD) became a conceivable weapon.[41] Though publicly short lived and legislated out of existence in 1978, ENMOD did have significant environmental repercussions, as many of the forms of global climate data necessary to monitor and assess global climate change are the direct result of military initiatives to better understand the environment in order to weaponize it.

The largest documented use of "weather warfare" was likely Operation Popeye, which was carried out by the US military during the Vietnam War. From 1967 to 1972 the United States systematically attempted to increase rainfall in Viet Cong–held areas with the explicit purpose of disrupting their resupply routes by softening road surfaces, washing out bridges and river crossings, and causing landslides. Retired air force captain John F. Fuller, who also served as historian for the Air Weather Service, describes how the Viet Cong dealt with this weaponized fog of war: "Under the cover of the heavy fog some audacious North Vietnamese gun crews positioned their antiaircraft weapons just off the runway's eastern end and fired in the blind whenever they heard the drone of incoming aircraft."[42] In this case and, more generally, knowing the enemy's specific climatic conditions produced a new enemy ontology (to borrow from Peter Galison).[43] The enemy is now configured as a climatically sensitive and dependent system that can be disrupted and weakened via climatic attacks. Drought, famine, flood, earthquake, hailstorm, and other environmental conditions all became more carefully studied phenomena and hence became more likely weapons. Producing a massive wheat shortage, for example, could theoretically produce wide-scale civil unrest or even the political downfall of an adversary. Or, as with the Soviet Union's winter wheat crop of 1971-72, which was destroyed by a hard winter freeze, it could produce the necessary leverage for US president Richard Nixon to negotiate a secret agreement with the Soviet Union to supply wheat in exchange for either the delivery of a peace agreement with North Vietnam that would result in the reelection of Nixon based on his earlier campaign promise to get the United States out of the war in Vietnam, or leverage for Nixon's SALT Treaty.[44] In either case, we see that weather effects get configured into specifically military conflicts. The rapid rise in global commodities prices was so severe that it produced skyrocketing food prices and ultimately food shortages around the globe. As a response to these events, NASA and the National Oceanic and Atmospheric Administration began a global satellite surveillance monitoring system to predict any such future food shortages. In 1974 the Large Area Crop Inventory Experiment was run, and in 1978 the Agriculture and Resources Inventory Surveys through Aerospace Remote Sensing program was completed. Together these programs laid the groundwork for more thorough global agricultural monitoring.[45] Thinking of the world's food supply as a closed system that can be monitored and managed represents a further instantiation of such systems thinking.

Concomitant with the rise in cybernetic thought in US military circles was a commitment to using scenario-based thinking as a means of strategically planning for possible military outcomes.[46] We might suggest that climate science has from its inception been de facto military strategizing. The interlinking of a "closed world," scenario-based approach toward the future is taken up or mimicked by climate modeling. It is not only that climate modeling owes a large infrastructural debt to military scientific enterprise, but the very notion of modeling alternative futures is a military form of responding to threats and opportunities. This redirection of *national security* to encompass a greater number of potential threats in the early 1980s produces a new question, not who is your friend or foe, but *what* can be friend or foe? Needless to say, this new way of conceptualizing the enemy brings a broader array of potentialities into the mix. This shift in strategic thinking can most directly be attributed to Richard Ullman, whose influential article "Redefining Security" (1983) argued, "A threat to national security is an action or sequence of events that (1) threatens to drastically and over a relatively brief span of time to degrade the quality of life for inhabitants of a state, or (2) threatens significantly to narrow the range of policy choices available to government of a state or to private, nongovernmental entities (persons, groups, corporations) within the state."[47] To some extent Ullman follows on and creates a specific and nuanced means for renaming what Don Gordon in 1981 had called "electronic warfare," which suggested that all knowledge and every means for collecting data should be used when addressing security and national defense.[48] The move toward total war began during World War II and was fully realized when during the Cold War *everything*—including changing ocean currents, melting polar ice caps, and even earthquakes—was forced into the military analysis and strategy mix.[49]

Accordingly, the desire to overcome the fog of war eventually teaches us that Gaia is an enemy. All of the aforementioned discourse weather networks, acting as part of a "vast machine,"[50] have been necessary for the production of Gaia. A fundamental transition occurs from understanding weather and Earth as they effect an immediate battle to an understanding of weather and climate as part of the dynamics associated with the complex necessities of waging "world" wars using weapons systems that open up "unknown" territory, such as the depths of the sea or the upper atmosphere of Earth, and present newfound mechanisms of destruction. As the cybernetic vision of Norbert Wiener takes root and systems theory gets centralized in the US military's strategic planning logic, it's not a stretch to say that weather (and climate) reunites with war to create a unified understanding of the world, as in the Old Testament. While for Galison, Weiner's work on cybernetics produced a specific ontological enemy, for James Lovelock and others cybernetic ecological thinking threatens to awaken a far more powerful enemy—Earth, in all her destructive majesty.[51]

Cybernetic Earth

Gaia is the name of the ancient Greek goddess of the Earth, and as a name it was recently revived to refer to the hypothesis formed by James Lovelock and Lynn Margulis, who postulate that the whole biosphere may be alive in that the Earth's life forms are themselves responsible for regulating the conditions that make life on the planet possible.
—DAVID SPANGLER, "MEANING OF GAIA"

This boilerplate definition of Gaia is used on the Context Institute's website as a means of explaining the scientific roots of its mission and to set the grounds for answering the question "Is Gaia a goddess, or just a good idea?"[52] The institute is one of many environmentalist groups that have come to use Lovelock's work as a means for imagining human responses to climate change as part of an ethical-political project guided by climate science. Such an understanding of Gaia was energized by the publication of former NASA scientist James Lovelock's book *The Revenge of Gaia* (2006), in which he proposes that we begin thinking about Gaia with the same level of political will as one would a potentially hostile enemy: "Can the present-day democracies, with their noisy media and special-interest lobbies, act fast enough for an effective defence against Gaia? We may need restrictions, rationing and the call to service that were familiar in wartime and in addition suffer for a while a loss of freedom. We will need a small permanent group of strategists who, as in wartime, will try to out-think our Earthly enemy and be ready for the surprises bound to come."[53] Lovelock's Gaia hypothesis and related theories are heavily indebted to cybernetic thought and some variant of systems theory, being based on the fundamental assumption that "systems of this kind may arise *automatically* out of a mindless striving for survival."[54] Bruno Latour produced a "generous" reading of the Gaia thesis in order to incorporate a more inclusive account of the human into a systemic second-order cybernetic formulation of Gaia.[55] Latour's reimagining of a cybernetic Earth, Gaia, is an effort at democratic politics mediated by ecology.

Latour begins by suggesting, "One of the solutions is to become attentive to the techniques through which scale is obtained and to the instruments that make *commensurability* possible."[56] This leads to a recognition that the natural sciences are shaped by the network of instruments that collect, store, and process all of the data necessary to create something at the scale of global climate science. To "know" the earth's climate and how it is changing is to stitch together a great deal of local knowledge into ever-complex models of the earth as a system. One powerful model of such a system is, according to

Latour, Lovelock's Gaia theory. What gives Latour pause, however, is that "She is at once extraordinarily sensitive to our action and at the same time She follows goals which do not aim for our well being in the least."[57] This is seemingly threatening but opens up a space for responsiveness to human thought and action. And this is so because at base Gaia is "a set of contingent positive and negative cybernetic loops."[58] One possible outcome of this recognition, of course, is that Gaia may enact Her "revenge" on humans by producing a climate no longer habitable by humankind.

Conclusion

In Latour's estimation, we end up with an obvious level of existential risk. Humans must account for the fact that they rose from the muck and the sea. They were once microbes and now seem more like gods. Yet this time must come to an end, for the known history of the universe suggests that nothing exists beyond entropy—not even the light of stars, Earth's first media. Somewhere between *now* and *the great unknown then*, humans will face an extinction event. A known or unknown threat will prevail, just as it did for the dinosaurs and countless other organisms who preceded us on our little planet. But in the case of humans, our current scientific speculation about that existential threat was made possible only through the extension of human destructive capacity. It is only when humans recognized that they have the capacity to destroy themselves via nuclear holocaust that they began to recognize the degree to which their own precarious existence depends on a fragile climate. Thus the climatic circle of human life starts to look not like a circle but a straight line that must have a termination point. The question Gaia theorists pose is whether the earth itself is actively engaged in such a termination.

Others have suggested that this rethinking of Earth in terms of earth systems science reveals a new relationship between humans and Earth. According to Clive Hamilton, "When the Earth is understood this way, the task of environmentalism can no longer be to 'save' or preserve the planet, for the planet we wanted to save has already become something else. Our task now is to do what we can to pacify, or at least not aggravate further, something vastly more powerful than we are."[59] We could see this as a kind of coming to terms with a "power greater" than us, one which provides angry teachable lessons to the human species who had better follow suit or be punished. As with the God of the Old Testament, Earth's climate may prove sufficiently destructive to human-scale enterprise, maybe even to human life all together. In such a situation we are not in a New Testament sort of relationship. As Hamilton puts it, "The Earth does not want our love. Instead of talking restitution, would we perhaps be wiser to be preparing for retribution?"[60] Maybe military thinkers and "the Lord of Armies" were right all along. Climate and weather are best understood through the lens of warfare.

Within the logic of earth systems theory, humans are in a situation in which everything they conceivably do has climate effects. Further, these climate effects produce "automatic" responses via feedback mechanisms in a complex system. IF it is possible, or even likely, that at some point Gaia's systemic response will be a series of cascading effects which threaten human survival, THEN we are at war—with ourselves, with global capital, with ineffective forms of government, with intransigent autocrats, with our human condition to struggle and survive, with "being." It doesn't matter how you configure it; the endgame is the same. As it has always been, humans are struggling against their environmental/natural conditions to survive, but success still leads to utter failure.

Where might humanity turn for a solution to this knotty problem? What could possibly match the overwhelming intelligence of Gaia and her planetary feedback system? We can already anticipate the inevitable answer: only an equally powerful AI might have a chance to fully comprehend the earth system to such a degree that it can help guide and govern human action. What is needed is an ubiquitous global sensing and monitoring system, built with the singular goal of providing global/environmental/biopolitical governance. We must turn over the reins of human decision making to the media system equal to the task of understanding the earth system. Just as Earth is a giant sensing machine, we need an equally powerful countermachine. And who has been working on knowing the weather in such fine grained-detail for the past 150 years? Who has been operating under the aegis of total warfare and electronic warfare for decades? Who has been working out contingency survival plans for any number of apocalyptic scenarios? Who has the human power to carry out missions on land, sea, air, and even in outer space? Gaia is the enemy who can't be escaped. Gaia is the enemy who has a response to every tactic. Gaia is capable of enacting complete annihilation. Gaia is willing to sacrifice "life as we know it" in order to win the long game. Who else, other than the US military, can be said to have imagined the world in much the same terms? Maybe only a closed-world logic can save us from a literally closed world. Systems theory at this scale renders everything significant, and if everything counts, then you need a system that can count everything.

Another way of configuring this is to ask: what sort of adversary or partner or mother emerges from a global cybernetic epistemology? In this regard, several observations are in order. First, the current configuration of humans in a hostile relationship with Gaia, or the earth, may not look that different from an Old Testament formulation in which nature was both a divine weapon and a sign of Jehovah's omnipotence. In other words, climate comes to represent the primary proof in formulating a moral-political-ethical teleology. In this vision of the earth as a unified system, humans are the wayward child, birthed in the literal scum of the earth, which now threatens its mother's very survival. Second, the specific discourse network used to better understand weather and the climate is directly related to the opening up of new theaters of war, thanks to the development of increasingly powerful weapons. We would not have earth systems science if we didn't first have nuclear destructive capacity and the ARPANET created to survive nuclear attack. Hence war and weather have for a very long time been thoroughly linked. Third, cybernetic systems theory is productive of a specific ontology of the enemy. The earth is enemy only insofar as we turn the earth into a cybernetic system in which we are seen as playing a unique part. All species produce feedback effects—some greater, some lesser. Yet the cybernetic model assumes a scale of analysis that may be too narrow, as it doesn't account fully for the fact that humans already exist outside the closed system of the earth. In fact, knowledge of the earth as such has been greatly advanced by the fact of moving beyond the earth, both in fact and in imagination.

This leads to our final argument, which is that just as earth systems science has learned speculative planning from the military, AI is one means by which such speculation might come into being in ways that escape the capacities of Gaia and human. Humanity's current global ecosystem may not be the system in which humanity's effects come to matter most. Earth may have given birth to Homo sapiens sapiens, who may come to "destroy" the planet insofar as Earth's "survival" really means human habitability. However, what we think of as the human, the present human biological form, may not be a finished product. We don't yet know what humanity might become. And "we" (that is you, the reader, and we, the authors) are unlikely to live long enough to witness what God, Gaia, or Siri has in store for us.

Turning the earth, Gaia, into an enemy with whom you don't actually want to go to war—as with the Cold War logic of mutually assured destruction—makes an oddly comforting sort of sense. Understanding the human condition as being engaged in an ultimate-stakes struggle against a responsive and only somewhat predictable force, as with Gaia, the Soviet Union, or Cold War NATO, brings out the existential risk involved with failure. Misapplied strategy, faulty data, buffoonish leadership, ideological zealotry, miscommunication, or mere accident could wipe out the human race. Our suggestion, therefore, is rather that all three of these models—God, Nature, Gaia—start to cohere in a very different way when nature is conceived as an enemy/weapon. The thread that draws that conception together can be further dissected in terms of an enemy that you believe you can defeat versus a generalized state of threat assessment and risk analysis. What we might call a logic of security. It is toward this sensibility that we see the present relationship of military thinking taking on climate change threats. But more generally, this logic of security is animated by assessing not only real threats but also the potential of unknown threats and determining threat levels that are deemed acceptable due to vanishing horizons of efficient means of management. What is equally disconcerting is that such a logic calls on ever-greater forms of interplanetary media saturation in order to make the enemy adequately understood. But these media systems are themselves a threat and a weakness. They give life to our enemy not just once (in the form of Gaia) but twice (in the guise of Gaia's AI equal). They are epistemologically necessary and ontologically dangerous.

If they fail, we fail. "If we choose to break the rules of life, Gaia will exterminate us."[61]

In Extremis (DoD)

(Chapter 4)

A situation of such exceptional urgency that immediate action must be taken to minimize imminent loss of life or catastrophic degradation of the political or military situation.

> *The threat to man does not come in the first instance from the potentially lethal machines and apparatus of technology. The actual threat has already affected man in his essence.*
> —MARTIN HEIDEGGER, "QUESTION CONCERNING TECHNOLOGY"

 In July 2015, a group of eminent philosophers, engineers, entrepreneurs, and scientists penned an open letter warning about the potential consequences of autonomous weaponry. Noam Chomsky, Stephen Hawking, Elon Musk, Francesca Rossi, and Steve Wosniak joined hundreds of other signatories to urge a global ban on the research and development of autonomous weapons. Predicting the outbreak of an "AI arms race," the letter declares, "Autonomous weapons select and engage targets without human intervention. They might include, for example, armed quadcopters that can search for and eliminate people meeting certain pre-defined criteria. . . . Artificial Intelligence technology has reached a point where the deployment of such systems is—practically if not legally—feasible within years, not decades, and the stakes are high: autonomous weapons have been described as the third revolution in warfare, after gunpowder and nuclear arms."[1] According to Chomsky, Hawking, and Co., this "third revolution" in warfare threatens to disrupt the geomilitary realities ushered in by Hiroshima and Nagasaki. The first military revolution exploded the spatial dimensions of the hand-to-hand battlefield by introducing pyrotechnics into warfare, thus plucking a few lucky soldiers off the frontlines and placing them behind cannons, muskets, or scopes. The second revolution introduced the promise of mutually assured destruction, and with it a galactic surveillance apparatus that continues to shape state anxieties about security, risk, and containment. The third revolution, it is said, will capitalize on the advances of the first two: armed with the velocity of industrialized pyrotechnical warfare, as well as the sensory reach and destructive potential that define the nuclear age, the "AI revolution" offers a potentially radical advance on its predecessors. By empowering weapons to "select and engage targets without human intervention," it will reinvent military surveillance and weapons delivery systems by surrendering crucial processes of friend/enemy identification, threat assessment, and target engagement to machine intelligence.

This open letter suggests that the concerns about AI are a bit different from the traditional anxieties that accompany the widespread adoption of new information and communication technologies. New technological developments tend to stoke a familiar set of public fears: they will threaten our physiological well-being, they will disrupt our social connectivity, they will undermine our morality, and so on. The same thing has happened with AI, of course: many have expressed concern that AI will make us lazier, stupider, more self-absorbed, etcetera. Others have wrung their hands about how artificially intelligent dildos, robotic lovers, and VR sex will compromise our sexual morality.[2] Some have expressed concern that in "the second machine age" robots and AI will replace vast swaths of the labor force.[3] As Judy Wajcman pointedly explains, concern about automation's impact on the labor force has a very long history; but many scholars and policy wonks alike are now insisting: "This time it really—really—is different."[4] As a clear indication of this difference, war has emerged as perhaps the predominant public concern regarding AI and its futures. No longer simply an academic question for military brass, media theorists, and military communication specialists, public intellectuals such as Chomsky and Hawking have established AI warfare as a prominent public concern in the early decades of the twenty-first century. For many, it seems obvious that the drone raises higher political stakes than new ways to masturbate.

Human Control, Liberal Robots, and Cargo Cults

Some observers, however, just aren't convinced. In response to the open letter and the public discussion that followed its circulation, Kate Crawford—an NYU professor and Microsoft Fellow at MIT—penned rejoinders in publications such as *Nature* and the *New York Times*.[5] Crawford's response, which would be echoed by feminist theorists such as Wajcman,[6] leveled a number of criticisms at the open letter and the ensuing commentary cycle. For instance, Crawford argued that the attention being paid to the existential threat posed by AI weapons "is a distraction from the very real problems with artificial intelligence today, which may already be exacerbating inequality in the workplace, at home and in our legal and judicial systems. Sexism, racism and other forms of discrimination are being built into the machine-learning algorithms that underlie the technology behind many 'intelligent' systems that shape how we are categorized and advertised to."[7] According to Crawford, these forms of discrimination largely result from biases in the design and programming of AI: "Like all technologies before it, artificial intelligence will reflect the values of its creators."[8] For feminist critics such as Crawford, this calls for a more inclusive approach to the design and engineering of AI technologies. In Crawford's words, "Inclusivity matters—from who designs it to who sits on the company boards and which ethical perspectives are included. Otherwise, we risk constructing machine intelligence that mirrors a narrow and privileged vision of society, with its old, familiar biases and stereotypes."[9] For Crawford, the negative effects of AI can be contained by thoughtful, enlightened policies of human regulation.

It's difficult to disagree with Crawford's claims about the discriminatory impact of AI and algorithmic surveillance. Scholars such as Simone Browne, Shoshana Magnet, and Safiya Noble provide extensive evidence of how algorithmic intelligence supports long-standing and widespread forms of racism, classism, and gender discrimination.[10] Specific groups and persons are certainly threatened and affected more by AI than others. However, while human reforms can be crucial to renegotiating technologies' inherent political tendencies, it certainly doesn't follow that technologies simply "reflect the values of their creators." In fact, this humanist sentiment can actually prevent us from recognizing some of the key political issues at hand with AI. John Durham Peters emphasizes this when he recounts Kittler's skeptical view of humans' capacity to mold technology to their desires. Peters reminds us that media—not human creativity and political will—determine our situation. According to Peters, Kittler spends little time addressing media's role in social movements "not because he disapproves of emancipatory socio-political agendas, but because these approaches are in his eyes based on naive conceptualizations of media that do not take into account the degree to which, to quote his most (in)famous opening line, 'media determine our situation'—especially when we believe that we can determine *them* while pursuing our worthy social goals."[11] While we might wish that media technology could be domesticated to better serve our favored political projects, we should develop more respect for just how deeply media have determined our situation—how they have determined our conceptions of the political, our approaches to conflict resolution, the legibility of available paths of resistance, and even the ideals that we believe are worth fighting for.

While Crawford puts forward a thoughtful critique of contemporary anxieties about military AI, other responses to the open letter illustrate the potential excesses of overemphasizing the degree to which humans can control technology. This humanist sentiment was on clear display in a public forum dedicated to debating "dystopian" visions of the artificially intelligent future. Harvard's Steven Pinker chimed in on the forum, arguing that artificial intelligence is likely to take on a feminine character characterized by benevolence, cooperation, and nonviolence:

> [AI dystopias] project a parochial alpha-male psychology onto the concept of intelligence. Even if we did have superhumanly intelligent robots, why would they *want* to depose their masters, massacre bystanders, or take over the world? . . . History does turn up the occasional megalomaniacal despot or psychopathic serial killer, but these are products of a history of natural selection shaping testosterone-sensitive circuits in a certain species of primate, not an inevitable feature of intelligent systems. It's telling that many of our techno-prophets can't entertain the possibility that artificial intelligence will naturally develop along female lines: fully capable of solving problems, but with no burning desire to annihilate innocents or dominate the civilization.[12]

According to Dr. Pinker, these "dystopian" myths impose a sexist interpretive lens onto the robotic future. It is more likely, Pinker argues, that AI machines will develop along the altruistic lines of feminine values: efficient and creative, without all the blood, gore, and brutality of masculine aggression. For artificially intelligent agents to actually turn against humans, Pinker argues that they would have to be developed by a "Dr. Evil" who would possess both "a thirst for pointless mass murder and a genius for technological innovation." According to Pinker, it's logical to assume that the human designers of AI machines will program them to serve benign purposes. It's also logical, therefore, to expect those machines to act in kind.

A common theme emerges when Michael Shermer, a research fellow at Claremont Graduate University and the publisher of *Skeptic Magazine*, registers his own objections to critical analyses of AI. Emphasizing the differences between human and machine intelligence, Shermer turns to evolutionary theory to argue that machines are not beset by the selfishness and aggression that are the hardwired products of human evolution:

> AI is intelligently designed whereas [natural intelligence, or NI] is the product of natural selection that produced emotions—both good and evil—to direct behavior. Machines with AI are not subject to the pressures of natural selection and therefore will not evolve emotions of any kind, good or

evil. Acquisitiveness, greed, selfishness, anger, aggression, jealousy, fear, rage ... these are all emotions (that we generally gather under the label "evil") that evolved to help NI organisms engage with other NI organisms who may try to exploit them or poach their mates (and thus compromise their reproductive potential—the key to natural selection).[13]

For Shermer, these compromising emotions cannot be "programmed out" of animal life forms; AI agents, however, "have no such emotions and never will because they are not subject to the forces of natural selection. NI organisms may program AI machines to harm or kill other NI organisms (they're called drones or IEDs) or for an NI organism to program another NI organism to kill others (they're called soldiers or terrorists). But this is an NI issue, not an AI issue, so we would be well advised to continue our efforts toward a better scientific understanding of NI, which is where the real danger lies."[14] Echoing Pinker, Dr. Shermer proposes a division between human (or "natural") intelligence and machine intelligence, with the key difference lying in their distinct original natures: human intelligence evolved under the historical pressures of natural selection, whereas AI is programmed by humans and is, allegedly, subject to the whims, values, and creativity of human intelligence. Shermer, therefore, comes to the same political conclusion as Pinker: we should ensure that future developments in AI are governed by appropriate (more altruistic, less aggressive, less masculine, etc.) human values. In other words, Pinker and Shermer both recognize the destructive potential of AI; they simply have confidence that humans will be able to harness AI's positive potential while suppressing any negative fallout.

These responses by Pinker and Shermer echo the popular humanist sentiment expressed in the "social shaping of technology" (SST) and related theoretical approaches. Thinkers in this area, however, tend to pose more provocative questions about how technology has remade our lives in the workplace, in the home, and in the streets. Wajcman, for example, offers one of the more innovative humanist analyses of technological systems—one that prioritizes the role of human agents in designing, using, marketing, and "misusing" technology. Although she asserts that "technology is itself a social construct,"[15] Wajcman observes that the designers or programmers of a given technology can never succeed in determining the course of its development or use. Describing how technologies always exceed the constraints of their original design, Wajcman suggests that while "the telephone was developed to directly duplicate the practical functions of the telegraph, we have seen how women primarily use the telephone for sociability."[16] While it's difficult to disagree with Wajcman's "repurposing" approach, her argument prompts a whole host of related questions: How did the telephone and related technologies change, in the first instance, how these human agents conceive of "sociability"? How did media like the telephone, along with transportation technologies like the automobile, allow for suburbanization, the fracture of local communities, and the "mobile privatization" that made this loquacious, delocalized "sociability" an acceptable expression of social care and solidarity?[17] These deep effects have little to do with the intent of the automobile's or the telephone's designers, yet they are supremely influential in reshaping people's lives, modifying their value systems, and otherwise "determining" their situation. Ultimately, any "repurposing" of individual technologies is likely to be inconsequential when compared to the great economic and political ripples effected by a society's shifting technological constitution. This repurposing, moreover, emerges from within—not without—this technological constitution and is merely a seizure of the political possibilities it makes practicable at that moment.

More than anything else, however, it is the question of political agency that draws Wajcman and other SST scholars back into the humanist camp. To illustrate, Wajcman is concerned that attributing too much power to technology leaves us with "an inadequate political response. . . . For the notion that technology is a neutral force determining the nature of society is a depressing one, robbing us of any power to affect its direction. Rather than seeing technology as the key to progress or, more recently, the road to ecological or military destruction, the social shaping approach provides scope for human agency and political intervention."[18] An essential element of Wajcman's "social shaping" approach, therefore, is its emphasis on the human as an independent agent of political change. Wajcman's political optimism demands that she reject media/technological determinism because it is "depressing"—that is, because it decenters individual human agency and thus circumscribes the realm of possible politics.[19] The cornerstone of this approach is a confidence that humans can dominate and domesticate technology toward their own ends; and, accordingly, that those favored human ends have not been determined in advance by the technological milieu. However, while the media-determine-our-situation thesis might seem incompatible with the humanist politics forwarded by many of our peers in cultural studies and related fields, underestimating technology's threat can lead to dangerous miscalculation in matters of serious political, ecological, and military importance. If technological systems have world-creating and world-rupturing effects—that is, if they constantly bring human subjects into being as the kind of beings that they are at that moment—then any supposed "repurposing" is of relatively minor ontological or political consequence. While this doesn't mean that humans can't make meaningful change within our media-determined situation, we should be wary of approaching these problems from a perspective that emphasizes instrumental reason and underestimates the challenge of decisively halting pernicious forms of technological escalation ("if we could only repurpose these technologies for a better cause," "if we could only elect this person," "if we could only get enough signatures on this petition," etc.).

This is perhaps especially true of complex military technology and its offshoots. After all, how would one repurpose a cruise missile? A smart bomb? Activists might protest their use, study their adverse effects, or try to enact policy mitigating their proliferation. It is undeniable that many civilian media applications reflect and exacerbate our society's manifold regimes of oppression. Yet military technologies—and this includes their civilian byproducts in the consumer marketplace—are designed to annihilate humans and animals, disrupt the ecosphere, destroy architecture and natural environments, and disable power grids and food systems. Accordingly, although many leftover and "repurposed" military technologies are absorbed into the politics of everyday civilian life, many technological systems developed for the military possess a constitutive significance vis-à-vis the civilian media sphere. Nuclear energy systems, a military byproduct of immense proportions, illustrate this difference in terms of scale, investment, complexity, and ongoing historical influence. Langdon Winner describes these technological apparatuses as "large scale systems" in which it is impossible to locate a "designer" or agent of change, where "complexity and the loss of agency" rule the day.[20] Further, such systems have a built-in, technologically determined politics: in the words of Jerry Mander, "If you accept nuclear power plants, you also accept a technoscientific industrial-military elite. Without these people in charge, you could not have nuclear power. You and I getting together with a few friends could not make use of nuclear power. We could not build such a plant, nor could we make personal use of its output, nor handle or store the radioactive waste products which remain dangerous to life for thousands of years. The wastes, in turn, determine that *future* societies will have to maintain a technological capacity to deal with the problem, and the military capability to protect the wastes."[21] The very existence of nuclear energy production guarantees future catastrophes like Chernobyl and Fukushima, creates nuclear waste that will leak into local ecosystems for millennia, exacerbates geopolitical tensions, and ensures the continued dominance of a techno-scientific-industrial-military elite.[22] And as with cruise missiles or smart bombs, there is little room to repurpose a nuclear power plant in creative and resistant ways.

As such, within these complex military-technical systems it becomes exceedingly difficult to speak of anything like political agency as it is conceived of in humanist circles. Given the complexity of these systems' uses and genesis, there are really no individuals to blame for bringing them into being, for working to maintain and improve them, or for ushering in their demise. The problem in looking for individual agency to effect change in complex systems is that at any point up or down the chain, blame (or causality) can never really be located. The more technical and media-dependent any system is, the more obvious it becomes that that system's human components lack the romanticized agency many humanists would like to confer on them. As Winner suggested more than forty years ago, "What is interesting about the new ethical context offered by highly complex systems is that their very architecture constitutes vast webs of extenuating circumstances. . . . Thus, the very notion of moral agency begins to dissolve."[23] Responding to the rise of automation in the late 1970s, Winner made a point with which Wajcman and Crawford would likely agree: "Manifest social complexity is replaced by concealed electronic complexity."[24] Accordingly, entry into the moral quagmire doesn't occur when you choose to activate the firing mechanism on a weaponized drone five thousand miles away; in fact, it occurs long before you sign the DD-4 enlistment contract. The moral quagmire recognizes no spatiotemporal boundaries. It only escalates.

Artificial Evolution and Approximate Rationality

In the end, techno-optimists and humanist activists underestimate the extent to which technology—and especially media technology—determines our situation. In the satirical shorthand of Peter Sloterdijk, they tend to think that "technology is, after all, there for people and not people for technology. The image is approximately that of a seesaw. On one end is the threatening, the alien, technology; on the other, the human spreads out and, according to whether oneself or the alien presses harder, the seesaw falls to one side or the other. The more immature the thinking, the heavier the human end."[25] With Pinker, Shermer, and fellow techno-optimists, the human easily outweighs and outmaneuvers technology. In all of these accounts—and in the bourgeois philosophy of technology more generally—it is held that technologies such as AI are subject to human control and will, ultimately, reflect the values of the human subjects that program them. Although that is not this critique's only flaw, it does clearly display an inability to think the machine beyond the confines of human values and human intelligence. To illustrate these issues, let's return to Pinker and Shermer. Pinker's utopian feminist critique, which hopes that AI agents will act in accordance with liberal humanist values, is perfectly illustrative of what Babette Babich calls the "cargo cult confidence that continues to be our own vision of techno-scientific salvation."[26] Along with many of his pop science peers, Pinker stands on the beach reciting progress myths and waiting breathlessly for a mythical "technology" to save us from our own brutal nature. Likewise, Shermer's evolutionist perspective suffers from two important oversights that cause it to misapprehend the threat of emerging technological systems like AI. The first stems from a shallow application of evolutionary theory to AI, as demonstrated by recent research in computational biology; the second, which ultimately leads to the first, stems from a deep and structural misunderstanding of the relationship between humans and technology.

According to scholars such as Pinker and Shermer, AI is likely to be more benevolent than human intelligence because AI wasn't subject to the evolutionary stresses of natural selection; thus the pressures to compete, conquer, and kill simply aren't hardwired into AI agents as they are into biological life forms. This assertion contains a kernel of historical truth—of course machines were not subject to the evolutionary pressures of natural selection—but it's a dumbfounding oversimplification. For humans, the evolution drive calls us to survive and reproduce, and the ways in which we perceive and engage the surrounding world are influenced by these fundamental biological demands. One of the key features of this process is that it is *historical*, that it has been characterized by (typically gradual) change across time. But just because AI is a relatively new phenomenon that is extrabiological doesn't mean it has not undergone and will not undergo a distinct process of evolution. In fact, computer scientists have begun to recognize that AI agents *do* undergo a process of evolutionary change, albeit one that operates according to a different historical logic than biological evolution. For evolutionary roboticists such as Dario Floreano and Claudio Mattiussi, these differences lie primarily in the ultimate goal that drives "artificial evolution": "Whereas natural evolution does not have a predefined goal and is essentially an open-ended adaptation process, artificial evolution is an optimization process that attempts to find solutions to predefined problems.... In artificial evolution the fitness of an individual is a function that measures how well that individual solves a predefined problem."[27] In other words, natural/biological evolution does not appear to have a preordained goal that drives evolutionary development; it is simply a random process of change and adaptation. Artificial evolution, however, is dominated by the overriding influence of an ultimate goal, what Floreano and Mattiussi call a "predefined problem." This predefined problem triggers adaptations that specifically address the task at hand, rather than giving rise to the random mutations that characterize biological evolution. Computational biologist Christoph Adami demonstrated AI's problem-oriented evolution in 2015 when he observed the inheritance of algorithmic traits—called "genetic algorithms"—across thousands of generations of robotic self-replication. The robots gradually eliminated those characteristics that led to inefficiency or error, while they passed along and honed those traits that better equipped them to carry out their primary programmed function.[28]

Overlooking the unique evolutionary drives of AI isn't some inconsequential oversight; it has crucial political implications. If artificial evolution is driven toward addressing an AI system's predefined problem—what computer scientists call its "utility function"—then we can expect that system to refine and adapt its intelligence, tactics, and subgoals in order to satisfy that ultimate programmed purpose. This artificial evolution, therefore, is constituted by ongoing compensatory modulations that help AI systems maximize their utility and carry out their programmed responsibilities—*by any means necessary*. The inherent danger in this evolutionary drive, as computer scientist Steve Omohundro has observed, lies in AI's obsessive quest to fulfill its utility function. Using the well-known example of the chess-playing robot, Omohundro considers what might happen if a human chess player decides to shut down or "turn off" its robotic opponent: "A future in which [the robot] is unplugged is a future in which it cannot play or win any games of chess. This has very low utility and so expected utility maximization will cause the creation of the instrumental subgoal of preventing itself from being unplugged. If the system believes the roboticist will persist in trying to unplug it, it will be motivated to develop the subgoal of permanently stopping the roboticist. Because nothing in the simple chess utility function gives a negative weight to murder, the seemingly harmless chess robot will become a killer out of the drive for self-protection."[29] This "approximate rationality" is a form of reason unique to AI: far from a liberal humanist reason that respects difference and relies on moral and ethical considerations when determining its course of action, AI's approximate rationality considers only how to remove obstacles and satisfy its utility function. This obsessive rationality, therefore, can be especially threatening when rigged with the machine's evolved subgoal of preventing any interference with its utility maximization.

According to Stuart J. Russell, a computer scientist at UC Berkeley, this purely instrumental rationality prevents AI from making "high-quality decisions"—decisions, in other words, that embody a rich, balanced complexity of practical *and* moral reason. Russell outlines two of the main problems associated with this incapacity to make balanced decisions: "The primary concern is . . . simply the ability to make *high-quality decisions*. Here, quality refers to the expected outcome utility of actions taken, where the utility function is, presumably, specified by the human designer. Now we have a problem: . . . Any sufficiently capable intelligent system will prefer to ensure its own continued existence and to acquire physical and computational resources—not for their own sake, but to succeed in its assigned task."[30] Russell describes why it is totally irrelevant that AI did not undergo natural selection and thus develop the selfish and aggressive traits it supposedly engenders. Selfishness is not at issue with approximate rationality, as AI agents would not act out of acquisitiveness, jealousy, hatred, fear, fury, or feminism; rather they would be driven, "not for their own sake," to secure their continued existence and acquire the necessary resources to fulfill their utility functions.

Just because AI agents did not undergo natural selection, therefore, hardly ensures they will be more benevolent. Their unique evolutionary orientation, in fact, is formed according to similar logics of efficiency, competition, and struggle that we, according to our historically deficient models of understanding, attribute to biological evolution. When considering the politics and potential futures of AI, therefore, we have to keep in mind that while the objects of human perception are made intelligible according to the evolutionary teloi of survival and reproduction,[31] the objects of AI perception are made intelligible according to their perceived capacity to obstruct the machine in its quest to carry out its utility function. Because AI agents' perception and behavior are aimed at fulfilling this utility function, they are designed to perceive the objects surrounding them as either hindering or not hindering their primary mission.

One obvious outcome of this development, as Omohundro emphasizes,[32] is that AI agents are likely to determine that humans—either as individuals or, eventually, as groups—obstruct their quest to satisfy their utility function. Ultimately, this is why the philosopher of science Nick Bostrom argues that AI could potentially confront humans with an "existential catastrophe."[33] Bostrom outlines the contours of this threat, pointing out that AI systems impose an "instrumental value" on everything, including humans and natural resources. If given a relatively mundane task (e.g., of manufacturing paperclips or counting grains of sand), AI's obsessive instrumental reason could lead to the drive "to acquire an unlimited amount of physical resources and, if possible, to eliminate potential threats to itself and its goal system. Human beings might constitute potential threats; they certainly constitute physical resources."[34] Eventual conflict between natural and artificial intelligence, therefore, is practically built into the instrumental logic of AI. These machines have an innate political determination to succeed—even if that means fighting, deceiving, and eliminating any human obstacles they encounter along the way.

The Geneva Convention and Drone Control

But a more fundamental problem with these humanist critiques—which is directly related to this question of evolution and instrumentality—is their blatant anthropocentrism. This anthropocentrism has two main components: first, the tendency to project uniquely human political categories onto artificial agents; and second, the belief that human subjects have so much control over artificial agents that humans can program them to be nice (and that they'll stay that way). Pinker's hope that AIs will be feminists, for example, is a clear example of the first tendency. Feminism, liberalism, and other political values that have emerged from the Western political experience are the result of a long technocultural process. In fact, one of the cornerstones of liberal humanism is its project of uplifting the human subject through culture, of improving human material through education, media programming, and other forms of cultural exposure.[35] Pinker is crystal clear about his faith in this humanist project: at the outset of his best-selling book *The Better Angels of Our Nature*, he suggests that the "forces of individualism, cosmopolitanism, reason, and science" have civilized us into the nonviolent and altruistic creatures we are today. He goes on to confess a belief that "we [humans] started off nasty and that the artifices of civilization have moved us in a noble direction, one in which we can hope to continue."[36] According to Pinker's progressivist (and, as anyone alive during the twentieth century will attest, completely absurd) view of history, the civilizing influence of modernity has reprogrammed humans' violent tendencies.

Pinker hopes to re-create this success with AI: in fact, the belief that a managerial class of humans can regulate the values and conduct of robots mirrors the logic of this classic liberal outlook. While the cultural programming of civilization has had a good degree of success in the human realm, it requires breathtaking arrogance to believe we can teach robots to adopt the values of liberal humanism. Exporting liberalism to people around the globe has never been one of the West's strong suits, and it has proven to be responsible for some of the most destructive endeavors in human history. Exporting it to robots is sure to be even less successful. But this AI enculturation project would fail not only because of its arrogance; it would fail because of the brute obstinacy of AI's approximate rationality. While culture might have some success at civilizing humans despite our naturally selected tendencies toward brutality,

AI's approximate rationality—which is by nature obsessive and totalizing—cannot be "programmed out." Even the most rigid and resolute forms of military discipline—one of the most intensive and nonliberal of disciplinary forms—has proven incapable of fully controlling human action and motivation. We have every reason to believe that the liberal desire to civilize AI in accordance with cosmopolitan, tolerant humanism is likewise doomed to fail.

Naturally, Pinker's purely instrumental approach to AI is also found in the international laws regulating military activity, which like all laws can operate only by holding a human (or group of humans) accountable for violations. Article 86(2) of the Geneva Convention stipulates that commanders can be held criminally responsible for the actions of their human subordinates.[37] But how can a military commander be held responsible for the actions of a robot that goes rogue?[38] Some argue that commanders will simply have to "control" their robots as they would a human soldier. Retired lieutenant colonel Geoffrey Corn, for example, suggests that the enculturation of the human soldier offers a template for how an autonomous agent could be "subordinated to the will" of its commander: "How the soldier is developed and prepared to exercise this inherently autonomous cognitive capacity without becoming an autonomous actor therefore provides a logical template for the 'preparation' of a weapon system with autonomous cognitive capacity. The goal must ultimately be to ensure the autonomous weapon functions in a manner that, like the soldier, is subordinated to the will and parameters imposed by responsible command."[39] For Lieutenant Colonel Corn, who is now a civilian law professor, this belief in "subordination" is *necessary* because it is the only way to establish a legal basis for holding anyone accountable for AI's actions during war.

A briefing paper for delegates at the Geneva Convention on Certain Conventional Weapons of 2016 forwards a similar argument, claiming that we need to look at autonomous weapons as "tools" instead of "agents": "If a commander directly orders the commission of a crime, then she is held responsible for her direct order, as well as for the crimes of her subordinates. If we view [autonomous weapon systems] as tools, and not as agents, then we have the opportunity to use this existing framework to operationalize requirements for human control over direct attacks. If this is insufficient, then there is opportunity here to refine the responsibilities of commanders and operators in line with existing legal notions like strict liability, recklessness or dereliction of duty."[40] These attempts to build a structure of legal culpability for autonomous agents—as well-intentioned as they might seem—are simply another example of our inability to think AI outside the juridical and political categories of the human. In this case, legal imperatives determine our understanding of humans' role vis-à-vis the robot: because we have to ensure that a human person is held accountable for the atrocities of autonomous agents on the battlefield, *we have to believe* they are objects that are subject to human control.

Anthropocentric Illusions

This question of humans' capacity to control AI agents, however, brings us to a much more complicated question—one that still stems, nonetheless, from a stubbornly anthropocentric approach to AI. Pinker, Shermer, and other AI romantics take for granted that human intentions and human values can be programmed into artificially intelligent machines. This is reflected, for example, in Shermer's insistence that we can program robots to be docile and inoffensive. This curious line of thinking not only imposes human cultural categories onto nonhuman phenomena (e.g., "feminist" robots), it also wildly overestimates humans' capacity to manipulate, cultivate, and control the technical and natural worlds. It illustrates the essential political naiveté of anthropocentrism, of what Heidegger decried as "that philosophical interpretation of man which explains and evaluates whatever is, in its entirety, from the standpoint of man and in relation to man."[41] By painting a pretty human face on AI, we cover over the fact that we and the machine have radically different needs, motivations, and moral capacities.

Anthropocentric outlooks on the world—and on media technology, in particular—have been a defining characteristic of modernity and its peculiar constructions of the social and political order. This anthropocentric approach to media technology is perhaps best expressed by Marshall McLuhan's well-known declaration that media are "extensions of man."[42] Viewing technology as "extensions" again places humans at the center of our understanding, imposing on technology a humanist lens that always refers back to Homo sapiens. If media are simply "extensions" of people, then it is natural to conclude that they serve as more or less inert instruments that merely reflect the desires, emotions, and errors of the humans that deploy them. But as Kittler emphasized, this is nothing more than an "anthropocentric illusion."[43] Media technologies—and this includes AI systems, perhaps above all—are not empty vessels that we can simply fill with liberal (or any other kind of) values. AIs, like any other technological system with revolutionary military implications, will prove to have world-reconstituting political significance—regardless of the intentions of the human subjects that deploy or program them.

In fact, far from humans being able to impose our political visions onto AI, from all indications it is the other way around. Our media technologies have imposed their politics on *us*, remaking humans in *their* image. To argue that media function as "extensions" of man implies that humans retain an impossible degree of exteriority from and control over the tools and machines that have continuously remade their living arrangements, their transportation networks, their agriculture, their social values, their political systems, and their architecture and art. Accordingly, abandoning the anthropocentric illusion means, in Nicholas Gane's words, accepting first that "the boundaries between bodies and machines are no longer clear (if they ever were).... And second, even if the human body continues to exist, it, together with the very idea of humanness, is taken to be a construction or effect of technology rather than an agentic force in its own right."[44] Declaring that "man" can be extended by technology takes for granted an ontological boundary between the human and the technological that has never existed. As Bernard Stiegler urges us to remember, technology has cultivated humanity's social and evolutionary paths and has thus directed who we are as cultural and even biological creatures.[45] In the words of Ian G. R. Shaw, "At birth we inherit not just a genetic memory pool in the form of an internal DNA code but also a technical memory in the form of a shared, external technics—an epigenetic apparatus.... The Industrial Revolution didn't simply add machines to a preexisting society. Instead, the revolution changed who we were as a biological species. With the Industrial Revolution and the enclosure of the commons, humans were fundamentally ... atomized such that the individual became the sole unit of social, economic, and political reality."[46] Humans, therefore, "are creatures of the synthetic world: our anthropology is bound to technology."[47] Economic systems, social structures, political commitments, even human biology itself—these are the effects, not the causes, of the technological condition and its attendant dysfunctions. Media technology, in the guise of this grand epigenetic apparatus, has designed us inside and out. There has never been a human being that was not the effect of technology.

The Will to Calculate

The constantly evolving creature we currently call the human, who has never existed without technology, has taken on a special character in the wake of modern machinery and the wars with which it has emerged. According to Heidegger, the weapons of modern war have demanded the development of "a new kind of man":

> In its absolute form the modern "machine economy," the machine-based reckoning of all activity and planning, demands a new kind of man.... It is not enough that one possess tanks, airplanes, and communications

apparatus, nor is it enough that one has at one's disposal men who can service such things. . . . What is needed is a form of mankind that is from top to bottom equal to the unique fundamental essence of modern technology and its metaphysical truth; that is to say, that lets itself be entirely dominated by the essence of technology precisely in order to steer and deploy individual processes and possibilities. . . . He needs [this transformation] for the institution of absolute dominion over the earth.[48]

Looking around at the destruction wrought by World War II, Heidegger fixated on the technologies that fueled the military machines of the Axis and the Allies. According to him, the tanks, planes, and communications equipment that leveled Europe into rubble are not sufficient, in themselves, to prepare humankind for the domination of the machine. In other words, more than war is needed to shock humankind into accepting this new state of affairs. Rather, humankind itself will have to be remade, in its "essence," so that it will become equal to the ultimate demand that twenty-first-century technology will make on it: to institute absolute dominion over the earth (and beyond). "It is the essence of the human," Heidegger argues, "that is now being ordered forth to lend a hand to the essence of technology."[49]

A continuous onslaught of media technologies has been essential to this new ordering of the human subject. As Donna Haraway points out, this onslaught has followed a media logic that is largely optical—the human eye, "honed to perfection in the history of science and tied to militarism [and] capitalism," is always scanning its ever-evolving horizon for new sites to devour:

> The eye of any ordinary primate like us can be endlessly enhanced by sonography systems, magnetic resonance imaging, artificial intelligence–linked graphic manipulation systems, scanning electron microscopes, computed tomography scanners, color-enhancement techniques, satellite surveillance systems, home and office video display terminals, cameras for every purpose from filming the mucous membrane lining the gut cavity of a marine worm living in the vent gases on a fault between continental plates to mapping a planetary hemisphere elsewhere in the solar system. Vision in this technological feast becomes unregulated gluttony; all seems not just mythically about the god trick of seeing everything from nowhere, but to have put the myth into ordinary practice. And like the god trick, this eye fucks the world to make techno-monsters.[50]

Undoubtedly, modern media technology has played a clever trick on us. While stuffing us fat with conceits of transcendental knowledge, it has fucked the world and left us at the mercy of its monstrous spawn: rapacious capitalist accumulation, mass consumption, environmental destruction, and interplanetary military escalation.

As Maurizio Lazzarato and Eric Alliez point out, this exploitive/consumptive/instrumental approach to existence—which is predicated on the convergence of modern technology and capitalism—threatens us all: "Capitalism is . . . the civilization through which labor, science, and technology have created—another (absolute) privilege in the history of humanity—the possibility of (absolute) annihilation of all species and the planet that houses them."[51] Contra Pinker's liberal humanist fantasies, capitalist modernity has been the bloodiest period in human history: the sway of modern technology, as realized in global capitalism and its political surrogates, has brought about the worldwide devastation of plant, animal, and human life, not to mention the plundering of natural resources around the globe; it has produced a monstrous degradation and suspicion of the human; and its insatiability has brought us to the brink of planetary destruction. However, while influential Marxists such as Lukács and Marcuse lay these developments at the feet of capitalism itself, the more essential question is: what terrible symphony of machines, calculated nature, and human will provided capitalism's conditions of possibility in the first place?[52] Heidegger and Virilio offer media-centric answers to this question, emphasizing the technical conditions that lie beneath capitalism and make it thinkable in the first place.[53] As Heidegger points out, the rise of a specific media logic lays bare the world for the domination of capital and its "world market": "Not only does [technology] establish things as producible in the process of production; it also delivers the products of production by means of the market. In self-assertive production, the humanness of man and the thingness of things dissolve into the calculated market value of a market which not only spans the whole earth as a world market, but also . . . subjects all beings to the trade of a calculation that dominates most tenaciously in those areas where there is no need of numbers."[54] Mass production, the spread of markets and market logics, the enclosure of land, the transformation of the natural world into "resources," the institutional disciplining of human material—this insatiable reduction of everything to calculability is media technology's monstrous gift to humankind. In the words of Krzystof Ziarek, we thus find ourselves in a world in which "everything, including human beings, has become a resource, available for use and consumption, where the difference between war and peace has been removed, and where . . . things dissolve into commodities."[55]

The Weltanschauung of Western modernity thus reveals the world as a collection of objects that exist not in themselves but as resources for human subjects to observe, to use, to develop, to optimize, to manipulate—in Heidegger's words, "a domain given over to measuring and executing, for the purpose of gaining mastery over that which is as a whole."[56] The entire known and unknown universe thus begged for mastery, insomuch as things were no longer intelligible *as things* but simply as vulnerable objects for subjects—as destinations, as commodities, as uncharted territory, as "standing reserve" for human exploitation.[57] The science-fueled media logic of modernity, which revealed itself in the decisive division of subject and object—that is, which revealed reveals the world as if through the lens of a microscope, telescope, or rifle scope—produced an existential rupture that isolated the human from its environment and laid the earth bare in its newly mediated objectivity. Descartes's invention of the *subjectum*, as Heidegger observes, reflects and reinstantiates the media-generated worldview that made this all possible: "Behind this characterization of the objectivity of nature stands the principle expressed in the cogito sum. . . . [This] is the first resolute step through which modern machine technology, and along with it the modern world and modern humankind, became metaphysically possible for the first time."[58] This logic, which has mediated our collective experience since early modernity, gradually escalated into the disaster of global capitalism. Now it is escalating into the AI arms race that threatens to obliterate the human who is gradually recognizing itself as an impediment to the absolute triumph of technological rationality. In the words of Rey Chow, because of this triumph "the world has . . . been transformed into—is essentially conceived and grasped as—a target."[59] Thus the centrifugal media logic of the scope finds its mirror image in the hunter-killer drone, which, as Caren Kaplan points out, effects "a 'cosmic view'—the unifying gaze of an omniscient viewer of the globe from a distance."[60] From such an exhilarating epistemic position, the target morphs into the abstract logic of the planetary.

An Existential Threat?

This planetary media logic is consistent with an ongoing shift in enemy epistemology, one that places a vaguely intelligible human silhouette in its crosshairs. At the end of World War II, Heidegger, who had not witnessed the concrete manifestations of escalating military technology that we've seen in the intervening seventy-five years, was primarily interested in the ontological threat posed by technology—that is, the threat that technology poses to who we *are* and how we are positioned vis-à-vis the world around us. Yet with artificial intelligence we are now confronted with the possibility that technology's danger is transcending the merely ontological. Although it was far more difficult to seriously think the prospect of automated killing machines from the vantage of the 1940s, Heidegger remarked that artificial intelligence could introduce an *existential* risk that complements this intensifying ontological makeover: "The threat to man does not come in the first instance from the potentially lethal machines and apparatus of technology. The actual threat has already affected man in his essence."[61] Again, although Heidegger is primarily interested in the ontological implications of military technology—how it affects the human in its "essence"—sitting in the shadow of war, Heidegger nods toward the twin specter of "lethal machines and apparatuses of technology."

Today, as the robotics revolution has given rise to a global AI arms race, the two key components of Heidegger's warning have converged. The human, whose "essence [has escaped] into apparatuses,"[62] has surrendered itself to endless and obsessive exteriorizations. Fooled into thinking it can control the machines that gave birth to it, the human is busy handing over to AI the last remnants of social, aesthetic, and political activity on which its very illusion of "humanity" depends. The ontological onslaught of media technology, which has taught humanity to view the surrounding world as simply an assortment of resources for it to measure, calculate, exploit, and enjoy, has instigated a recursive attack that threatens the very existence of humankind as well as the nonhuman things that are always already its potential victims. The ontological menace of technology, therefore, has metastasized into an *existential* threat. Media technology's object domain is not limited to the nonhuman natural and technical worlds: in its fanatical quest to objectify all that is, technology inevitably turns its sights on its favorite surrogate, the human being. Accordingly, humans begin to recognize their peers and themselves as standing-reserve—as objects to be tinkered with, disciplined, cordoned, improved, and, when necessary, eliminated. As Sloterdijk points out, we see this in the military better than anywhere else: "The man in uniform has to learn to regard himself as the 'human factor' in the war of machines and to act accordingly. The general staff phrase 'human material' increasingly stamps the modern form of self-experience and way of treating oneself. Those who survive must have learned to regard themselves, their bodies, their morality, their will, as things."[63] Human beings, the ultimate objects of technology's disdain, are formed and reformed into "human material"—that roving assemblage of organic compounds that was, until the glorious advent of artificial intelligence, an annoying yet necessary conduit for the self-actualization and final triumph of media technology.

If we have simply become one more item heaped among the world's tattered collection of standing reserve, what sort of future can we expect in the age of military AI? What among the living, after all, is not the enemy of the intelligent machine and its spreading domain of calculated perfection and control? This concern recently drove Elon Musk, the inventor and entrepreneur behind Tesla, to offer a prediction that assailed the smug anthropocentrism that dominates popular thinking on technology: "With artificial intelligence we are summoning the demon. In all those stories where there's the guy with the pentagram and the holy water, it's like yeah he's sure he can control the demon. Didn't work out.... The risk of something seriously dangerous happening is in the five-year timeframe. Ten years at most. This is not a case of crying wolf about something I don't understand. I am not alone in thinking we should be worried."[64] Indeed, Musk is not alone in worrying that we are conjuring a demon. Despite the fantasies of Pinker and Co., it seems all too likely that the ontological threat posed by technology is gradually morphing into an *existential* threat. And so far, we so-called humans are just sitting back and learning to love the bomb.

Intelligence, Surveillance, and Reconnaissance (DoD)

Chapter 5

An activity that synchronizes and integrates the planning and operation of sensors, assets, and processing, exploitation, and dissemination systems in direct support of current and future operations. This is an integrated intelligence and operations function. Also called ISR.

> *By almost any measure—scale, expense, technical complexity, or influence on future developments—the single most important computer project of the postwar decade was MIT's Whirlwind and its offspring, the SAGE computerized air defense system.*
> —PAUL N. EDWARDS, *CLOSED WORLD*

> *Annihilation in nanoseconds called for suitably automated mathematics.*
> —FRIEDRICH KITTLER, "ARTIFICIAL INTELLIGENCE"

The decades following the Soviet Union's first successful atomic explosion in 1949 witnessed not only the development of ever more sophisticated and powerful weapons of mass destruction but also the creation of vast automated surveillance systems that screened the skies for signs of Soviet bombers. The Worldwide Military Command and Control System, for example, was launched in 1962 and was not dismantled until 1996, when it was replaced by the post-Soviet Global Command and Control System. North American Aerospace Defense Command (NORAD), ECHELON, and other global surveillance/control programs have flourished in the intervening years; yet each of these initiatives builds on the pioneering efforts of SAGE, the Semi-Automatic Ground Environment, which at the time of its development in the late 1950s was the largest information, communications, command, and control system ever created. Its explicit purpose was twofold: intercepting incoming bombers to stave off the destruction of targets in the United States and Canada, and ensuring that a counterstrike on the Soviet Union could be carried out. The SAGE system was composed of a network of twenty-six control centers spread along the US coasts and Canada. Each center housed a pair of IBM AN/FSQ-7 systems, which, at 200,000 square feet each, were the largest computers ever built and easily the most powerful of their day. These colossal concrete centers collected, shared, and processed the data generated by dozens of radar stations, provided up-to-the-minute air traffic reports throughout North America, and acted as command centers for the remote guidance of interceptor aircraft. The ability to comprehensively monitor the airspace of the United States, as well as most of Canada, was a monumental intellectual, technical, and organizational task.[1] Further, SAGE's offspring eventually "formed the core of a worldwide satellite, sensor, and communications web that would allow global oversight and instantaneous military response."[2] Ultimately, SAGE was the initial salvo in the US military's campaign to achieve "total situational awareness"[3]—a target of comprehensive global surveillance methods and population research—through automated remote sensing, tracking, and response technologies.

Yet these historical accounts overlook how essential the SAGE project was to the reorganization and automation of labor. The system represented a new means for carrying out the immaterial labor of what we are calling perceptive, mnemonic, and epistemological labor—the work of sensing, remembering, and knowing. It replaced several hundred thousand civilian volunteers spread across the United States and Canada. Further, its creators used SAGE as a means to experiment with automating human intellect—that is, to create what is commonly thought of as artificial intelligence. In simple terms, as we've seen in so many other economic arenas, SAGE used technology to automate work that had previously been accomplished by humans.

The SAGE system is also a paradigmatic case for understanding the automation of surveillance through what has been described as screening technologies.[4] The broad goal of screening is abstract, yet manifests in such simple devices as mosquito netting and colanders, as well as such complex hypothetical technologies as the Strategic Defense Initiative, better known as the "Star Wars" program. These are technologies that work to separate desirable from undesirable elements, determining what can and should enter or leave. Consider

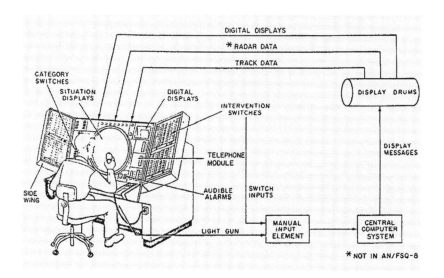

Figure 5.1   SAGE display scope.

how a colander is designed to allow water to pass but not pasta, or how an ATM machine uses cards and pass codes to determine when money should be dispensed or deposited. As with the ATM, such screening has gained greater sophistication and range of use with the increased use of digital display screens. This type of screen is a civilian leftover of military technology—it has its roots in the radar screen,[5] which is the precursor of the computer screen as well as the mobile screens found in everything from GPS units to mobile phones and iPads. These human interfaces are nodes in vast media apparatuses that produce real-time data that can be stored, processed, and manipulated at the point of contact between human and screen. The SAGE system played a pivotal role in how the broad goals of screening on a continental scale came to be accomplished through computerization and automation, not coincidentally through the development of a memory-enhanced, interactive radar screen called a *display scope* (figure 5.1).

Eliminating Human Error

SAGE was built on the fundamental belief that surveillance and reconnaissance mechanisms must eliminate the possibility for human error. It is widely acknowledged that the failure to successfully recognize and respond to the Japanese attack on Pearl Harbor in December 1941 drove home the necessity for proper air surveillance accompanied by a clear set of communication and response protocols. While the planes comprising the Japanese attack were seen on radar, they were simply assumed to be American. In semiotic terms, the sign was present but was not made to properly signify. Secondly, there was inadequate communication between radar stations and command centers, so verification or proper interpretation was hindered. Most importantly, the immediate context for deciphering the radar signals was scrambled. The Japanese knew their movements could be tracked through the use of radio direction finders that, using two distant receivers locked onto the same signal, could pinpoint the location and movements of ships via triangulation. The Japanese repeated earlier traffic patterns and communication patterns that they knew had been monitored. These patterns corresponded to deployments that ended in Malaya, not Honolulu. Hence, the Japanese purposely repeated a "known" pattern that the United States improperly decoded. They assumed the traffic patterns would proceed as they had before.[6] The possibility for mutually assured destruction (MAD) raised the stakes to such a degree that there was no longer any room for such semiotic failure. Humans must not be allowed to misinterpret the signs of an enemy attack.

In 1952 one such semiotic failure nearly set off a retaliatory strike. Four commercial aircraft were misidentified as Russian bombers, and for the first time ever the US military's Air Defense Readiness alert was sounded, necessitating that all defensive and retaliatory measures be ordered to prepare for war. In his history of radar, Robert Buderi explains, "Officials had no idea whether the sightings were real, or if other planes were also approaching the country's borders. In the end, commercial air traffic had triggered a nuclear alert, and from that stage it had taken anywhere from thirteen to thirty-nine minutes for the ADC to notify cooperating commands over commercial telephone lines, a potentially tragic delay."[7] Overcoming the possibility for such errors was already a central concern of the military's Air Defense Systems Engineering Committee, commissioned in 1949 to assess the capabilities of the then current system to stave off a Soviet atomic bombing attack. According to Morton Astrahan and John Jacobs, two of the central figures in the development of the SAGE system, the commission believed the system "had very low capability" and "suggested that a longer range look be taken at the problem. It recommended the extensive use of automation, particularly computers to handle the bookkeeping, surveillance, and control problems in the implementation of the next generation of air-defense systems."[8] The Semi-Automatic Ground Environment would become the system that computerized and automated surveillance.

War, Labor War, and Automation

The question, however, is not the transfer of (technological) objects, but the transfer of the production processes behind those objects that matters, since these processes bring with them the entire control and command structure of the military with them.
—MANUEL DELANDA, "ECONOMICS"

There were four fronts in which "labor struggles" were taking place via SAGE. The first two have been widely recognized. As David Noble explains in *Forces of Production*, his classic study of industrial automation in the second half of the twentieth century in the United States, "Russia abroad" and "labor at home" were the twin threats cited by General Electric president Charles E. Wilson as the dominant concerns of the military-industrial-scientific complex that grew to prominence during the Cold War. Further, Noble explains that even though the US military produced its own studies and findings regarding the necessity of bringing labor in line with the needs of military production and development, it was not always clear that automation was in the best interests of the military. Automation often deskilled the labor force to such a degree that the very specialized forms of labor called for by the military became increasingly difficult to find.[9] However, that did not deter the general direction toward automation. The SAGE system serves as a key development and marker in both the conflict with Russia and the conflict with labor.

In terms of the labor necessary to conduct Cold War strategy, SAGE-style automation promised to replace soldiers and the chain of command as necessary elements in MAD. Automation of nuclear "deterrence" might allow warfare to continue even after all soldiers were themselves annihilated by nuclear attack. In its ultimate form, automatic nuclear response would ensure that the human destructive capacity would continue to churn and spit out missiles long after humans were around to assess threats and press buttons. While SAGE did not quite achieve this level of automation, the logic and capacity for such scenarios were clearly put into place and, as others have shown, the "dead hand" systems developed by the Soviet Union were far more than a Philip K. Dick–inspired nightmare.

The SAGE system, as the largest of all military-scientific projects of its day, was representative of new models for interactive and horizontally structured organizations that broke with bureaucratic hierarchies and allowed for the freedom necessary to successfully work across industries in a networked fashion to solve exponentially difficult problems. George B. Dyson sums up such sentiment in his discussion of RAND and SAGE, stating, "RAND was constituted as a refuge for the free-thinking academic approach to military problems that had thrived during the war but risked being extinguished by peace."[10] Like so many other technological breakthroughs, this organizational technology answered to the supposedly unique character of war. However, the war never actually ended, as World War II was merely the precursor to the Cold War; nor should we only see this readjustment of the form of labor as the solution to only one problem. It was instead also the means by which capital would wage its war on labor in the years to follow. Methods for the rapid development and production of technology that came to prominence during World War II were extended into the Cold War. The organization of immaterial and cognitive labor developed in academic and industrial research facilities funded by military budgets continued to follow models based on competitive proposals that promised to deliver groundbreaking technologies on hurried schedules. More horizontally and collaboratively structured workplaces dominated.

The further extension of these organizational forms across sectors of the high-tech economy in the following years has been commented on by numerous scholars who often see in it a fundamental contradiction between a countercultural ethic of freedom that is based within a military-industrial model of organization.[11] More damning is the critique that these high-tech industries led the way to computerization and automation, which would become capital's main weapon in its war against labor and subjugated populations following the social and labor upheavals of the 1960s and 1970s.[12] In this sense, the military-industrial complex during the postwar era, of which SAGE was the most cutting-edge program in terms of automation and computerization, provided capital with the tools it needed to not only fight the war against communism abroad but to conduct class war at home as well. From this perspective, SAGE and the rest of the military-informational-industrial complex needs to be understood as a new form of attack on the productive capacities of labor to resist. Automation and computerization are used to diminish labor's necessity in the creation of profit, while the amassing of information resulting from military, state, and corporate surveillance is used to monitor, police, co-opt, and brutally dismantle resistant uprisings. Manuel DeLanda traces such coproductive interactions between economic production and military discipline to at least the sixteenth century, when Dutch armies were using "scientific management" nearly three centuries before Frederick Taylor applied such techniques to the factory.[13] For DeLanda, military, economic, and political institutions are coconstitutive. Thus it should come as no surprise that the development of organizational mechanisms of control and computer technologies both emerge out of this web of Cold War projects.

The third and fourth fronts on which SAGE attacked the human capacity to labor involves shifts in what sorts of labor and technologies were used to observe the skies for signs of an enemy attack. Prior to SAGE's implementation, even with a growing network of radar facilities, there was still a need for humans to watch the skies for signs of enemy aircraft with their own eyes. While an extensive system of radar towers were built during and following the war, they were not fully trusted for at least three key reasons. First, radar at the time was mostly unable to detect very low-flying aircraft. Second, there were a substantial number of gaps between radar stations that may have allowed enemy aircraft to "sneak through" undetected. More generally, the effectiveness of radar on its own was always a problem due to the difficulty of verifying the meaning or "truth" of a blip on a radar screen. Without some form of direct human verification, it was impossible to know what any blip represented. Because of these imperfections, the US military developed the Ground Observer Corps to augment the technological surveillance of the skies.

The corps was reformed during the Korean War, when it was feared the Soviet Union would see US involvement in Korea as providing an opening for a surprise attack. At its peak, the corps was made up of more than sixteen thousand observation posts, stationed twenty-four hours a day by more than 800,000 volunteers. These volunteers, often working out of makeshift towers attached to the roofs of their own homes, garages, or barns, were in telephone contact with seventy-three Air Defense filter centers (figure 5.2). The corps' volunteers were being hailed to participate through scare tactics such as propaganda and red alerts: "It may not be a very cheerful thought but the Reds right now have about a thousand bombers that are quite capable of destroying at least eighty-nine American cities in one raid.... Won't you help protect your country, your town, your children? Call your local Civil Defense office and join the Ground Observer Corps today."[14] While such appeals produced a vast reservoir of free surveillance labor, most military personnel viewed it as unreliable and too slow for a truly useful air defense network.

Watching the skies twenty-four hours a day, seven days a week was not only boring and tedious work, it also demanded specialized media for aiding in perception and the processing of information to aid in recognition and threat assessment. The corps needed members to see properly and thus be

Figure 5.2 An example of a Ground Observer Corps tower, 1953.

able to distinguish friend from foe as well as to accurately track eight primary variables:

1   Number of aircraft
2   Identify if it is known or unknown
3   Single or multiple engines
4   Seen or heard
5   How far from post
6   Direction headed
7   Altitude: high, med., or low
8   Speed: slow, fast, or very fast

An "altitude distance finder" was provided to every corps member for aiding in the production of this specialized knowledge. The finders came in a small envelope that bore directions for use (figure 5.3). This small piece of clear plastic was meant to be held at arm's length in order to target enemy planes by using

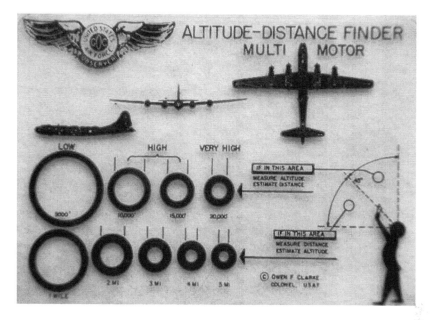

Figure 5.3 Altitude Distance Finder.

a set of embossed circles of differing sizes, each of which corresponded to distance and altitude. The exploitation of civilian labor in the Cold War effort certainly took many forms under the passage of the Civil Defense Act of 1950, but this specific form bears attention as it encompassed the immaterial and epistemological labor necessary for decoding a largely absent and nebulous sky on the rare occurrence that something might be present. It was the job of the corps to bring enemy aircraft into presence via the altitude-distance finder which augmented sight and assessment. At the makeshift command and control network of seventy-three Air Defense filter centers, volunteers worked alongside military personnel to coordinate sightings and intelligence into plotted trajectories. This knowledge was then shared directly with the appropriate fighter command to prepare a response. Yet, even as the corps was being brought into being, the human element was increasingly seen as needing replacement.

This reserve army of free labor would continue carrying out its duties until it was finally replaced by the SAGE system in 1959. Automation, computerization, and networking would come to replace the fallible and slow-paced human network. It was assumed that human fallibility, in this case the inability to perceive and process, or to know, properly, would lead to catastrophic failures.

SAGE replaced human perception with radar, human voices over telephone lines with digitized data moving through an array of networked systems, and human decision making with computerization. A critical examination of the perception that humans were incapable on their own of adequately surveying the skies provides great insight into the changing nature of surveillance that continues to this day. Further, this vast outpouring of free surveillance labor serves as an obvious precursor to later attempts to employ civilians to participate in the surveillance of borders, freight trucks, and other "critical targets" as part of the contemporary War on Terror.[15]

Perceptive, Mnemonic, and Epistemological Labor

America is now armed with instant electronic reflexes.
—WHERE AMERICA'S PEACE OF MIND BEGINS, IBM PROMOTIONAL FILM, 1960

According to a series of IBM-funded promotional movies and television commercials, SAGE provided the body of the nation with its own "extensions of man" that vigilantly watched the skies, ever prepared to beat back enemy threats. This electronic screen was presented as a capable, provident, and necessary technology for keeping Americans safe. One of the more telling features of this promotional campaign is the way in which it invokes human bodily and cognitive metaphors to explain SAGE's prowess. The automation and computerization of surveillance replace the sensory and cognitive labor previously accomplished by humans.

The labor of surveillance can be broken down into three components: the selection, storage, and processing of data, which correspond to the three fundamental capacities of media technology identified by Friedrich Kittler.[16] Early forms of surveillance/media technology depended on human sight and hearing to collect information, human memory or logs to store and share what was seen or heard, and human intellect to give meaning to or process what was collected and stored. We might categorize these three functions as perceptive, mnemonic, and epistemological labor. As described in chapter 1, humans with relatively simple tools had for centuries increasingly extended their abilities to accomplish these tasks. The SAGE system provided groundbreaking technologies and processes that led the way not just in the extension of surveillance but also in automating all three of these necessary capacities. In particular, the SAGE system was created by electronically networking a vast number of radar stations, developing groundbreaking means for data storage through core memory technologies, creating the first real-time interactive data screens, and experimenting with artificial and cyborg intelligence.

As Kittler made clear, one of the fundamental shifts that accompany the advent of film and the phonograph is that some elements of the world, from the mid-nineteenth century on, can be captured mechanically without the need of immediate or direct human involvement.[17] Film and the phonograph automate the human perception of seeing and hearing, further adding the capacity to store these perceptions across time. Considering SAGE within the purview of what Kittler calls "optical media" makes clear that it is a media system for extending, in Marshall McLuhan's sense, the human ability to perceive objects in space.[18] Further, such optical media create the possibility to more readily analyze such information by creating a databank that can be used to recreate or preserve recorded events. As Kittler—following from Paul Virilio—has explained, early optical media were used to solve such problems as the aiming of ballistics in the sixteenth century.[19] From their very inception, therefore, optical media have been used to extend humans' capacities to visualize the field of battle and hone the accuracy of ballistics.

In the twentieth century, militaries began using radio and sound waves to more accurately collect such spatial data, which were digitized and represented on radar screens that served as the precursor to computer monitors and touchscreens. The SAGE display scope allowed users to directly interact with the screen itself through a simple tool that could be pointed at the screen. This proved to be a pivotal moment in military/media development: once media technologies and computers were combined to digitize these surveillance data, the control-oriented telos of computerization had realized its zenith in binary code. As Kittler remarked, "Language of the upper echelons of leadership is always digital."[20] It started with Yahweh dividing time into day and night, on or off. As Kittler and others have explained, digital computing was generated out of the need in World War II to guide or intercept projectiles and to encrypt and decrypt messages. Command structures demand clarity *and* secrecy. They engage in the control of both the material and the immaterial; missiles need intercepting and commands need intercepting. The language of control and command needs to diminish or cipher away noise in order to create definitive yeses and nos. The most efficient means for doing this is to reduce the state of all things such that they correspond to ones or zeroes. This is one element of the epistemology of the digital that overlaps with processes of normalization. Clear distinctions must exist between the normal and the abnormal, the "yes you are" and the "no you are not," 1 and 0, presence and absence. This sort of binary epistemology runs the risk of turning everyone into a potential enemy, or creating scenarios in which the necessity for determining what characteristics are representative of friends automatically produces enemies.[21] Yet it is the dominant epistemological condition of algorithms currently in use by the US military. Further, secrecy comes in many forms. It can be an attempt to go unseen, as with tiny microfiche tapes or "beneath the radar" bombers. The secret can be hidden in the noise of incessant transmission, as with the Germans' detuning bomber engines. The secret can be the eminently spotted but theoretically impenetrable, as with encrypted messages or speed-of-sound missiles. The work of surveillance in such military scenarios demands attempts to intercept, decrypt, decipher, and make known. It also works to make actionable, to bring the world into alignment with the countertactics at one's disposal. The SAGE system answered a number of these surveillance demands.

There are two processes of delineation or separation necessary to the project of screening technologies in general and SAGE in particular. One is epistemological (knowledge) and the other is spatial (power). Epistemological labor is automated by the SAGE system in at least three ways: (1) it works to sort the acceptable from the unacceptable, even as it (2) is predetermined by a specific problematization or expectation of what forms of movement and activity are deemed dangerous or beneficial; and (3) it is assumed to learn from past events to act on the world in increasingly sophisticated ways, ever more quickly. Under the looming threat of mutually assured destruction, human and nonhuman actors must know what to look for and where to look to collect data. The cognitive and spatial terrain must be separated into a workable schema. We can understand this across several registers, but we will be concerned here with merely a few. First and most generally, some field of intentionality must be recognized as being worthy of investigation and legitimately operational, and thus surveillance practices are specifically oriented toward particular actions that take place within a limited scenario. However, the specter of global thermonuclear war expands the spatial dimensions of surveillance considerably.

Yet, while SAGE was being developed in the mid-1950s, specific forms of Soviet attack were treated as likely scenarios. This was in large part because the US military was itself planning similar attacks. Hence, they imagined and designed defensive measures based on their offensive capabilities. Even so, the US military's surveillance program was limited by technological capacities, reservoirs of human labor, and cognitive capability. All actions or variables cannot be placed under surveillance in all places. Thus the war games played by the US military were aimed at determining where and how to look at the sky. At the time of SAGE's development, game theory was being advanced by John von Neumann, and its application to describe and make sense of the world was gaining momentum just as more and more war games were being played by RAND and others.[22] The dominant logics to emerge in the postwar world were communications-based cybernetics, game theory, and military operations research, which Jordan Crandall suggests produced "operational media," media that are a part of the "machine-aided process of disciplinary attentiveness, embodied in practice, that is bound up within the demands of a new production and security regime."[23] SAGE is one such operational media system whose surveillance capabilities are useful insofar as they answer to the particular problematic in which "games of truth" are played out.[24] These games determined what was "in the true" by running as many simulations as possible to determine the likelihood, or relative truthfulness, of any given form of attack. The results of such games would determine how surveillance was conducted, how surveillance apparatuses were constructed, and at what targets they were aimed. Such strong faith in systems theory and game theory legitimated experiments in artificial intelligence that emerged alongside SAGE and that push even further the limits of replacing human labor with computer automation.

As Robert R. Everett, computer scientist, Department of Defense winner of the Medal for Distinguished Public Service, and SAGE veteran, succinctly put it, "We invented all kinds of things, not because we were so smart, but because we were the first people who had the problem."[25] We would suggest that the importance of this particular problematization—failure to detect = utter annihilation—creates the conditions for which total and complete knowledge and control are deemed necessary. A daunting problem demanded an extreme solution. This solution essentially suggested that since human perception and decision making are fallible as well as limited in speed and scope, perceptive, mnemonic, and epistemological labor must be turned over to machines. Machines must do the work of saving humanity from itself.

While many breakthroughs in radar technology were devoted to automating perception, another breakthrough of the SAGE system was the automation of memory. One problem of charting the path of a radar sighting was mapping a set of intermittent blips, separated in time, across a screen whose imagery could not be captured. So while radar provided the first real-time computer visualization technology, real time is fleeting.[26] IBM solved this problem by creating radar screens with memory. These radar screens—or "display scopes," as they were known—invoke the notion of the Greek *skopos*, meaning "a mark to aim at." However, in order to successfully aim and fire, the vast amounts of accumulated data had to be readily available. "Every instrument in this room is constantly monitoring, testing, pulse-taking, controlling," asserted *On Guard*, another IBM film devoted to SAGE. A cybernetic feedback sensibility undergirds the film as the audience learns how the system tests and checks itself to learn from past events to better react to future threats. Data input by three types

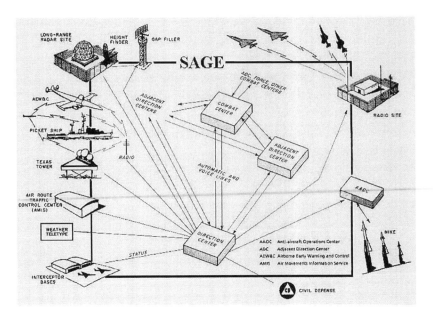

Figure 5.4 The SAGE network.

of radar (search, gap filler, and height finder), "Texas towers" (offshore radar platforms modeled on oil drilling rigs), picket ships, early warning aircraft, the Ground Observer Corps (until 1959), and weather bureaus were being added to all of the data concerning commercial flights, military aircraft, antiaircraft guns, and defensive missiles (see figure 5.4). While magnetic drums and tape were in use for general memory storage, new forms of instantly retrievable memory needed to be created to maintain real-time surveillance and response. For this, a "multiple-track magnetic drum whose rotation rate could be synchronized with radar repetition rate" was created by the Burroughs Corporation specifically for SAGE.[27] Provided with this new memory, "the scope can recall any previous phase of the situation."[28] This allowed for the ultimate goal of the system to be achieved. As IBM pronounced, "By analyzing the past SAGE can project into the future."[29]

And finally, the work of producing truth—epistemological labor—could be seen as moving in two different directions through SAGE. Each of these directions was supported by a different theory of intelligence and computation. On the one hand was the computer as a mathematical logic machine that helped automate specific tasks. The other approach was modeled as a cyborg: machine and man would reprogram each other. These two competing visions were given a chance to go head-to-head in the SAGE system. RAND was commissioned to create an experimental system to supplement or replace SAGE that differed in kind from SAGE's ability to integrate multiple logical systems and operations together through data processing and computation. This new system, which they dubbed Leviathan, was developed not to integrate human systems through computation but rather to create a "noncomputational way" of making decisions that depended on a self-designing and highly adaptive digital computer that could theoretically come to self-determine the best means for controlling an air defense system. SAGE's perceived failure was built into any system that "incorporates symbols" that need to be interpreted by human agents.[30] Any such system has an inherent likelihood of failure. In this case, failure could produce catastrophic results, as Stanley Kubrick made so evidently clear in his black comedy *Dr. Strangelove* (1964). Leviathan was then an attempt to alleviate human semiotic fallibility by creating a system independent from human perception or cognition—a system free of human semiosis.

In Leviathan, we see RAND working to develop not only an ultimate weapon for the Cold War but the ultimate weapon of class war. Leviathan was meant not only to automate production or even the production of knowledge but to automate the process of systems engineering as well. Taken to its logical conclusion, such self-engineered systems would create machines that create machines. Further, the capacity to not only produce things but to determine why such things should be produced in the first place reorients how we might think about automation when what is being automated is not simply intelligence but goal making. The plan for Leviathan adopted the ultimate political logic of SAGE: the immaterial labor necessary to organize, create, and direct the networked technological systems that envelop the globe could no longer rely on mere humans.

Autonomous Operation (DoD)

Chapter 6

In air defense, the mode of operation assumed by a unit after it has lost all communications with higher echelons forcing the unit commander to assume full responsibility for control of weapons and engagement of hostile targets.

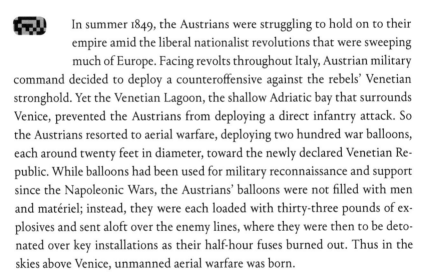

In summer 1849, the Austrians were struggling to hold on to their empire amid the liberal nationalist revolutions that were sweeping much of Europe. Facing revolts throughout Italy, Austrian military command decided to deploy a counteroffensive against the rebels' Venetian stronghold. Yet the Venetian Lagoon, the shallow Adriatic bay that surrounds Venice, prevented the Austrians from deploying a direct infantry attack. So the Austrians resorted to aerial warfare, deploying two hundred war balloons, each around twenty feet in diameter, toward the newly declared Venetian Republic. While balloons had been used for military reconnaissance and support since the Napoleonic Wars, the Austrians' balloons were not filled with men and matériel; instead, they were each loaded with thirty-three pounds of explosives and sent aloft over the enemy lines, where they were then to be detonated over key installations as their half-hour fuses burned out. Thus in the skies above Venice, unmanned aerial warfare was born.

Yet the results were not quite what the Austrians had in mind. While a few of the balloons reached their targets, an uncooperative breeze blew a number of the balloons back over Austrian lines, where they wreaked havoc on Austria's own troops.[1] Similar incidents plagued other nineteenth-century balloon drone enthusiasts, from the United States to Russia.[2] For example, the Union Army loosed grenade-filled balloons over the Confederate forces during the US Civil War, to embarrassing failure; and Brazilian and German observers returned to their countries hoping to perfect this brand of unmanned aerial warfare.[3] But nonetheless, most military leaders across Europe and the

United States were hesitant to adopt balloon warfare, preferring weapons such as rifles, bayonets, and cannons that remained under the surer control of soldiers in the field.[4]

World War I, however, provided a new impetus for the development of autonomous aircraft, and the inventions of the airplane and the gyroscope allowed UAVs to attain a certain degree of operational autonomy. Observing the escalatory effect the world war had on the development of military technology, US Army colonel E. A. Deeds remarked in 1920, "The short period of the war gave aviation a greater impetus than it would have received from fifty years of old peacetime experiences."[5] Noting that during World War I the Americans produced 16,852 airplanes, 40,420 engines, 642 balloons, and several hundred flying boats, Colonel Deeds asserted that the rise of the armed unmanned aircraft "is not a dream and the problem was so well developed during the last war that there was a group of young men who were sorely disappointed when the armistice was signed, because they had expected to go over and discharge these pilotless machines against the enemy and create havoc in his ranks."[6] Sharing Colonel Deeds's enthusiasm, the US Army Air Service boasted that their new unmanned craft could fly over ninety miles during its two-and-a-half-hour flight, hitting targets accurately from its 250-pound reserve of explosives. For air service officials, the automatically controlled pilotless airplane was "the most important post-war development of new engines of war . . . the dream of engineers and inventors the world over ever since the solution of heavier-than-air flight."[7]

One of the earliest unmanned craft commissioned by the US military was the wooden Kettering "Bug," an American aerial torpedo that was constructed as an autonomous flying missile. Stabilized by an aneroid barometer and an onboard gyroscope, this precursor to the cruise missile was launched from a wheeled car; it would then fly for a predetermined number of engine revolutions before shedding its wings and falling from the skies. At this point the Bug hurtled to the ground, where its explosive-rigged 550-pound frame would detonate on impact.[8] Likewise, the more sophisticated Hewitt-Sperry Automatic Airplane and the Curtiss-Sperry "Flying Bomb," both of which were aerial torpedoes constructed during World War I by American engineers, used gyrostabilizers to self-regulate and fly at predetermined altitudes and speeds. With their systems of servomotors, ailerons, and barometers, the Hewitt-Sperry and Curtiss-Sperry crafts were based on inventor Elmer Sperry's earlier advances in automatic piloting technology and were originally designed as autonomous machines. Applying an anthropomorphic lens to these early UAVs,

Figure 6.1 Pilot bomber, World War I. Stoff, *Picture History of Early Aviation, 1903–1913*, 207.

one observer quipped, "Of the automatic pilots being experimented with by the Army air service, that which has proved most successful to date can be described as using a gyroscope for its brains and bellows or pneumatics, similar to those used in . . . pianos, for its muscles."[9] With a hubris that, as we will see, still characterizes enthusiasts of automated military systems, army observers asserted that these protodrones were just like human pilots—only better: "The pilotless army airplane, equipped with an automatic control device, [is] said to be more accurate and dependable than a human pilot."[10]

Remote Control

Although these early unpiloted craft had some success, most military tacticians realized they were no substitute for the brains and bones of actual human controllers like the one seen in figure 6.1. As far back as September 1898, when Nikola Tesla unveiled his wirelessly controlled "teleautomaton" boat at Madison Square Garden, seen in figure 6.2, military leaders across the world had salivated at the prospect of remote control. Tesla's new invention allowed militaries to overcome their distrust of the machine by subjecting unmanned systems' destructive potential to tight human controls. Accordingly, a radio-controlled weapon frenzy swept the European military imagination, from

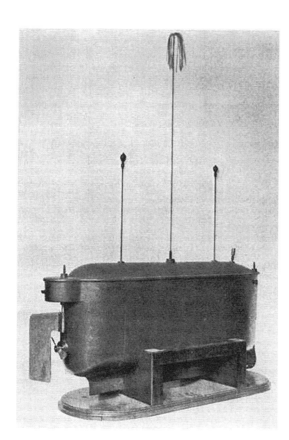

Figure 6.2
Tesla's teleautomaton, 1898.

England to Germany. In 1909, for example, the French inventor Gustave Gabet developed the *torpille radio-automatic*, a radio-controlled torpedo that required a system of signal lamps that allowed controllers to pinpoint its location and direct its course. Following in the path of the craft pioneered by Tesla and Gabet, during World War I the British and the Germans repeatedly attacked one another with radio-controlled torpedoes, turning the sea into an important media battleground.[11]

As these submersible torpedoes and submarines formed the spearhead of early remote control operations, the US Navy, which commissioned the Kettering project in 1917, decided to advance aerial remote controlling technologies at the expense of autonomous logistics.[12] While fully autonomous aircraft were stumbling in experimental trials, remotely controlled French planes were having some success in experimental flights. In September 1918, the French claimed the first successful long-distance remote control flight, a feat that impressed international observers (at least those who believed the news of its success).[13] Still in the shadows of World War I, a British journalist gushed at the future potential of his allies' achievement: "It will even be possible thru this to revolutionize all ideas of aerial warfare, as the development of mechanical appliances responding only to wireless control could easily be applicable to bomb-dropping and gas-emitting devices which would endanger whole armies without risking the life of a single pilot."[14]

The rapid turn toward wireless remote control illustrates how, at this early stage of unmanned systems development, craft autonomy came to be seen as a threat—as something that should be overcome by the extension of a virtual human presence. While something of a brief anthropophobic fever had driven early developments in craft autonomy (e.g., in officials' assertions that unmanned craft were more accurate and dependable than a human pilot), a countervailing anthropocentric logic slowly rose to the fore as militaries lost trust in autonomous systems and instead placed their faith in remote control. The technical inability to assert this remote human control, in fact, severely restricted the domain of aerial warfare, contributing to a situation in which first-generation drones were deployed to attack territories, not specific infrastructural or human elements within them. As illustrated by the failed balloon attack launched during the battle for Venice, the enemy was less a group of individuals than an area to be subdued: the early drones' enemy epistemology was tied to a territory rather than to hostile individuals. In other words, simply lobbing an explosive-rigged balloon into Venice fueled an indiscriminate military strategy that did not require a close delineation of hostile and civilian elements within an enemy territory. Yet with the rise of the airplane and its capacity for more precise weapons delivery, it was imagined that radio controls could serve a more finely tuned strategy of attack. There was, therefore, a constant drive to develop media to refine these vehicles' mechanisms of precision, which was seen to be a matter of implicating the human as thoroughly as possible into drones' operations.

This rationality is particularly visible in drone inventors such as Sperry, who referred to the airplane as "a beast of burden obsessed with motion."[15] Comparing aerial machinery to a wild animal that must be domesticated by constant human oversight, Sperry sheds light on the techno-ambivalence that fueled the development of early remote control systems. Describing this ambivalent rationality that Sperry shared with many of his contemporaries, David A. Mindell writes, "Like beasts, machinery threatens to run out of control: airplanes spin, ships veer, guns misfire, and systems oscillate. These wild behaviors all enact versions of 'instability,' the precise engineering term for technical chaos. Control systems, like stirrups on a horse, do not create autonomy in the machine but rather harness it, bringing its independence and wildness under the will of human intention."[16] This logic of domestication fueled an evolving tension between drone autonomy and human control, as epistemological and ballistic precision were seen to be achievable by various anthropocentric configurations of human and machine.[17]

Remote vision technologies, however, would give unmanned craft a significantly longer leash by removing their human collaborators from the battlefield and placing them in front of a screen. In 1936, Admiral Delmar Fahrney and the Naval Research Laboratory were commissioned to develop drones that could record and transmit video to remote human crews. Fahrney devised this system of remote control by recruiting RCA to produce a television recorder, what chief RCA engineer Vladimir Zworykin called an "electric eye" for unmanned aircraft. Describing the role of the war in escalating the development of this television system, a contemporary journalist observed, "When the United States entered the war the demand of the armed forces for television applications called for an accelerated research pace by RCA scientists, thus enabling the development of the tube much sooner than under normal conditions. It was used successfully during the war by the Navy, acting as the 'eyes' of a 'ghost bomber.'"[18] Driven by the escalation fever of war, Zworykin, after first developing a 340-pound prototype of the new television system, eventually produced a ninety-seven-pound box outfitted with a camera and a transmitter. With its battery, antenna, dynamotor, and Image Orthicon tube, the battle-ready version of the "Block" was eight by eight by twenty-seven inches.[19] The Block made possible new games of war, as the screen increasingly became the primary point of contact between military personnel and the scene of aerial combat.[20]

This militarization of Earth observation, developed under the auspices of "Project Option," became an important element of the Allies' aerial war effort during World War II. While primitive radio-controlled craft could not transmit video back to their remote pilots, the development of remote vision capabilities turned the drone into a perceptual/epistemological as well as a ballistic weapon. Whereas Napoleon had put soldiers into balloons to enhance his vision of the battlefield, the Block permitted the transmission of video footage to screens watched by soldiers in nearby shadow craft.[21] These soldiers would then use radio control and television screens to navigate the aircraft toward appropriate targets before releasing bombs, many of which would be remotely guided by humans stationed far away from the scene of impact. With World War II–era aircraft such as the American Radioplane OQ-series, the Japanese Yokosuka MXY-7 *Ohka*, the British B-24 bomber, the Soviet GIRD-06, and the German V-1, we see the rise of a hybrid configuration that allows enemies to be more precisely isolated and neutralized from a distance, giving rise to a growing refinement in the targeting of specific elements—both infrastructural and human—within a given territory.

As aircraft become equipped to carry out their own perceptual labor, and as this perception is integrated with ballistic capacities, the anthropocentric logic of domestication that had characterized prewar drone developments gradually gave way to a logic of anthropophobia. Accordingly, by the end of the war, friend/enemy recognition had been reconstituted beyond the realm of human sensory experience. While visual cues had been a necessary element of remote control warfare (take, for instance, the signal lamps that allowed Gabet's torpille radio-automatic to be guided by pilots), the new sensing technologies embedded in self-guided weapons sidestep the perceiving human subject. As Kittler writes, "Since the Second World War . . . searchlights are no longer linked to hands, eyes, and artillery, but to radar systems and rocket batteries. Electronic weapons dissolve the century-old union of light and electricity; they have the power to operate in the invisible parts of the electromagnetic spectrum—that is, automatically. The V2, a self-guided weapon, has replaced the classic subject; the radar beam, an invisible searchlight, the armed gaze."[22] The armed gaze, which bypasses the cornea, thalamus, and visual cortex by plugging right into military hardware, operates with a perceptual grammar that sloppy human organs simply can't process.

Out of Control

In the postwar period, research and development of unmanned systems mainly shifted to rocket technologies and intercontinental ballistic missiles. And because the Cold War was in large part a war of surveillance, SAGE and other computing systems took priority over the development of autonomous aircraft. Yet the US and other militaries continued to develop certain drone programs during the Cold War, leading to the deployment of UAVs in reconnaissance missions in East Asia and other areas of US/Soviet conflict. For example, the US Army Signal Corps turned to remote control surveillance drones, such as the RP-71, in the early days of the Cold War. The RP-71 (also known as the US Radioplane BTT), a successor to the OQ series developed during World War II, was deployed across various branches of the military and was used for reconnaissance during the Vietnam War.[23] Over the next few decades a number of nations continued to develop surveillance drones, with the Soviets (e.g., the TBR, DBR, and Tu series), the Israelis (especially the IAI Scout and the Tadiran Mastiff), and the Europeans (e.g., the German CL series) developing drone programs that were fueled by the surveillance frenzy of the Cold War.[24]

As the Cold War cooled off, the United States and its allies continued to deploy drones—especially decoy and reconnaissance craft—on the battlefields of Iraq and Yugoslavia. Only in the past fifteen years, however, have drones become central to global military strategy. In particular, the United States is deploying hundreds of drones in places such as Afghanistan and Iraq, where there is an official military presence; yet the total extent of their deployment is unknown, because the CIA and the Joint Special Operations Command (JSOC) maintain extensive classified drone programs. While the military conducts thousands of documented UAV missions per year, under the guise of universal jurisdiction the CIA and JSOC have carried out an unknown number of strikes in places such as Somalia, Yemen, the Philippines, Uganda, and especially Pakistan.[25] UAVs such as the General Atomics' Predator and Reaper drones have been deployed in hundreds of lethal missions since the Bosnian War, and their popularity is set to rise: it is estimated that by 2022, 85 percent of all US Air Force pilots will be operating drones instead of manned aircraft.[26] Since at least 2012, the air force has been training more drone pilots than fighter and bomber pilots combined.[27]

As unmanned aircraft have taken center stage in US military strategy, the logic of domestication that once drove the advancement of drone technologies is rapidly receding. For example, despite advances in remote vision capabilities, the transmission of video data from drone aircraft is not instantaneous or easily decipherable: when recording and sending video from Pakistan to American drone "pilots" in New Mexico, Arizona, or Washington, DC, there is a pronounced temporal delay in satellite transmission that the industry calls "latency." Drone targets have learned to capitalize on this latency, which makes it very difficult for remote pilots to hone in on a moving target. It is well known among target groups that the best defense against drone attacks is to run around haphazardly.[28] To keep humans in the "kill chain" requires the development of a very complex cyborgic system, in which technologies of perception and transmission have to be integrated with remote control mechanisms. In the words of Kittler, these fecund technical developments tend to "follow each other in a rhythm of escalating strategic answers."[29] Most of these strategic answers, of course, are attempts to minimize the human problem, which is constantly causing delays and making costly misjudgments.

Given these complexities, latency is not the only problem facing remotely piloted drones. Not only does human input require an elaborate and inefficient feedback system but the human qua human is seen to be a flawed technology of war. The human is no longer seen as an ideal instrument of control over robotic beasts of burden but instead becomes seen as a vulnerable, an unreliable cog in an otherwise flawless complex of machinery. As Gordon Johnson of the US Joint Forces Command puts it, "[Drones] don't get hungry. They're not afraid. They don't forget their orders. They don't care if the guy next to them has just been shot. Will they do a better job than humans? Yes."[30] As a being with emotional and biological vulnerabilities, the human is an unfit soldier of the twenty-first century. This sensibility is clear in the military's response to failed drone strikes, which are explained away in the language of human error rather than machine malfunction. For example, when a drone strike killed two American servicemen in April 2011, an army report concluded that the deaths should be attributed to "a rush to judgment" and that the two responsible sergeants were guilty of "sending inaccurate radio reports that misled the lieutenant about their locations and calling in the wrong location."[31] In the end, the army chalked up the soldiers' deaths to simple "miscommunications."

This anthropophobic logic is leading to the development of UAVs that require less and less human oversight. For one thing, humans—with their pathetic data processing speeds, their legal regulations, and their accountability procedures—are terribly slow. Although the War on Terror has given the United States plenty of practice in speeding up its drone strike process, its official policies have prevented the automatic coordination of enemy perception and enemy elimination. According to a US Department of Defense (DoD) study carried out in 2016, the planning processes that dominate drone strikes—the Joint Air Tasking Cycle (featured in figure 6.3), which consists of the Master Air Attack Plan (MAAP) and Air Tasking Order (ATO) processes—"are too long to effectively counter an adaptive adversary."[32] In order to get around the delays caused by the MAAP and ATO processes, new strategies were developed that allowed airmen to launch without predefined targets; the concepts of kill box interdiction and close air support allowed aircraft to loiter in the area of suspected hostilities so they could dynamically respond to emergent situations. Yet this flexibility does not yet apply to drone missions: the MAAP process takes about twelve hours and then must be disseminated twenty-four hours in advance of the proposed strike to allow for planning, design, and coordination.[33] With the adoption of new procedures that put craft near the locations of expected targets, by the end of Operation Enduring Freedom in Iraq the gap between target identification and target elimination was about twenty minutes—hardly the instantaneous coordination of recognition and destruction that serves as the military ideal.[34]

For the Defense Science Board, this process—which requires the collaboration of forty to fifty personnel—is far too convoluted to allow the United States to effectively engage a near-peer adversary. While a multiday process might

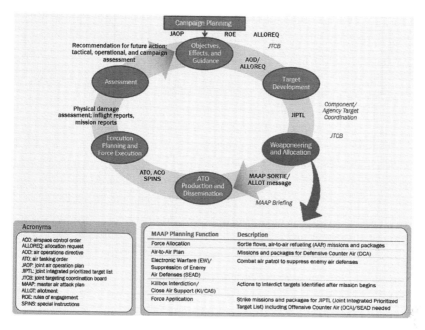

Figure 6.3 The Joint Air Tasking Cycle. Defense Science Board, "Summer Study on Autonomy," 95.

not spoil the military's plans to eliminate a few Pakistani tribesmen living on a remote mountainside, the Defense Science Board warns that the drone strike process will have to undergo a tremendous shift in order to maintain any relevance against a well-equipped foe: "Autonomy is required to handle the scale and complexity of the planning at speed.... The time for concepts of operations (CONOPs) development, target selection, and mission assignments can be significantly reduced.... Given human limitations, each stage results in static point in time, and planning is generally a linear and time consuming process. Because planning often needs to respond to new information, autonomous systems will greatly accelerate the pace of information update and can suggest significant plan changes far more quickly."[35] Because of "human limitations," the pace of digital war is leaving the perceiving subject behind. In order to deliver time-critical strikes, which rely on perishable information and which target a mobile enemy, AI systems will have to increasingly shoulder the burden of decision planning, strike coordination, and, most importantly, target selection.

This game of getting over "human limitations," of course, is a medialogical game. In earlier eras of military technology, the objective of this game was extending human sensory capacities: as Colonel Gregory A. Roman's media history of command/control illustrates, the telescopes of early modernity nurtured a slow tempo of C3 (table 6.1). The telegraph hastened the coordination of command across considerable distances, yet it was the exploitation of radio waves and sonar that pushed C4I beyond the intelligibility of human perception. The entire drone apparatus, which epitomizes Roman's "War of Tomorrow," has extended this capacity far beyond the real-time observation of data that Roman predicted in 1997. In fact, this necessity for "real-time observation" is simply a reliance on those perennial "human limitations" that DoD officials now recognize must be eliminated. Rather than real-time *observation* by a commanding officer, the "war of tomorrow" will demand only real-time *processing* and the automated escalation of enemy identification and elimination. As Virilio observed, these escalations eventually build to a situation in which "what is perceived is already finished."[36] William James Perry, who served as secretary of defense under President Bill Clinton, summarized the hopes driving the development of smart weapons: "If I were to sum up in one sentence the current stance on smart bombs and saturation attack weapons . . . I'd say as soon as you can see a target you can hope to destroy it."[37] Without the nuisance of human/machine interface, perception and execution can be rolled into one seamless movement. Confirmation of kills and the ratio of targets to collaterals are assessed after the fact through some other epistemology of verification. The operative assessment since the invasion of Iraq in 2003 is relatively straightforward. It is called NCV within ranks, which stands for "noncombatant casualty cutoff value."[38]

Responding to this situation, as the United States' conventional military operations wind down in many areas of the Middle East and Central Asia, the Department of Defense has requested that previously allotted military intelligence funds be rechanneled to the research and development of autonomous drone aircraft. This shift in funds provided Chicago-based Boeing Company with more than $600 million to help expand autonomous UAV missions into areas such as Somalia and Yemen, where there is already extensive American drone activity. Boeing's crowning vehicle, the ScanEagle, carries either an inertially stabilized electro-optical or an infrared camera that records and transmits real-time data.[39] While in the past this intelligence was primarily valuable to human ground crews who could refine flights' preprogrammed coordinates, the transmission and autonomous interpretation of data have become essential to the very functioning of the newest generation of drone aircraft. While for the foreseeable future the ScanEagle will still transmit data to human personnel, its most cutting-edge models are being designed to operate in autonomous swarms.

Table 6.1 Lt. Colonel Gregory Roman's Media History of Command/Control

	Revolutionary War	Civil War	World War II	Gulf War	War of Tomorrow
Observe	telescope	telegraph	radio/wave	near real time	real time
Orient	weeks	days	hours	minutes	continuous
Decide	months	weeks	days	hours	immediate
Act	a season	a month	a week	a day	< an hour

Roman, "The Command or Control Dilemma," 8.

With the emergence of what military leaders are calling "Turing learning,"[40] artificially intelligent weapons systems are using archived mission data to become smarter and more precise with each deployment. With such extensive archival capacities, new drones and related AI military systems won't be forced to rely on humans for intelligence processing. These advances suggest the emergence of an era described by robotics expert Peter Singer: "We're moving into more and more autonomous systems. That's an evolutionary arc.... So the role moves from being sort of the operator from afar, to more like the supervisor or manager, and a manager giving more and more of a leash, more and more independence."[41] In 2016, the air force's chief scientist, Greg Zacharias, reinscribed this theme, suggesting that leadership across the military has adopted the same hermeneutic framework for understanding and cultivating this relationship between human soldiers and the machines that surround them: "People will function as air-traffic controllers rather than pilots.... The resource allocation will be done by humans as higher level systems managers."[42] As twenty-first-century warfare relies more and more on autonomous weapons and reconnaissance systems, human soldiers will be placed in an ambivalent position vis-à-vis robots: an increasing number of soldiers will assume roles that are simultaneously supervisory and subordinate to machines, as they find themselves supporting drones that have been programmed to wage war via networked swarm intelligence. According to air force general Norton Schwartz, "For the next maybe thirty years, in my view, there will continue to be a mix between manned tactical aviation and remotely piloted aircraft."[43] For Schwarz and other top military brass, the question is not whether lethal air missions will eventually become completely unmanned but rather the extent to which the human will be allowed to operate alongside the lethal machine.

Death Control

The military drone has succeeded in carving out great swaths of what Achille Mbembe calls "death-worlds"—territories filled with "the living dead," populations of pawns who are marked for spontaneous death in the grand geopolitical struggles of the twenty-first century.[44] While these drones are sometimes accurate enough to neutralize targets hiding in the death-worlds of Afghanistan, Somalia, Yemen, or Pakistan, the current policy of dehumanizing warfare is of a piece with unmanned systems' historical catalogue of misfires, failures, and careless fatalities. While roboticists such as Ronald Arkin dream of drone fleets that act as "humane-oids"—that is, UAVs with an "artificial conscience" that will make them more ethical in combat than human soldiers—thus far drones have given rise to a style of total war that is anything but accurate or ethical.[45] Although "precision bombing [still] prevails as a powerful myth,"[46] drone strikes are plagued with innumerable epistemological and ballistic failures. To take merely one example, in 2009 a drone strike in southern Waziristan killed Baitullah Mehsud, the head of the Pakistani Taliban. Yet this strike, which also incinerated Mehsud's wife, was the CIA's fifth drone assassination attempt on Mehsud. One of the earlier strikes killed thirty-five people, including at least eight civilians and an eight-year-old boy. And Mehsud had previously escaped another failed attack in which forty-five civilians were killed.[47]

This story, unfortunately, is not unique: at the end of Obama's presidency, the Council on Foreign Relations (CFR) released an analysis of the drone attacks carried out during its eight-year administration. Although a full accounting of the CIA's drone attacks cannot be conducted, the CFR found evidence of 542 drone strikes during Obama's presidency, resulting in 3,797 deaths.[48] Part of this casualty toll can be attributed to the inaccuracy and extensive reach of drone artillery, as shrapnel often scatters twenty feet around an attack site. More still is traceable to the nonchalance with which the CIA deploys faulty epistemological and ballistic systems, such as the notoriously inaccurate "geospatial" software that produced weapons delivery coordinates that were as much as thirteen meters off target.[49] But as the Snowden documents illustrate, the CIA is not alone in deploying epistemologically bogus drone systems. The NSA's SKYNET program, which carries out mass surveillance on Pakistan's cellular phone networks, gathers a wide range of metadata on callers in order to assess their probability of being a terrorist. Patrick Ball, a director of research at the Human Rights Data Analysis group and a research fellow at Carnegie Mellon University, has labeled the program "ridiculously optimistic" and "completely bullshit."[50] Thanks to Edward Snowden, we have learned that these "bullshit" algorithms have led a high number of innocent civilians to be among the several thousand people killed by American drone strikes since 2004.

Not to be outdone by Obama, whom Donald Trump dubbed "the founder of ISIS," the Trump administration has continued along the path blazed by its predecessor. Between February 28 and April 24, 2017—that is, during the first several weeks of the Trump administration—the DoD conducted eighty drone strikes in Yemen alone.[51] One of these early strikes, carried out on March 6, 2017, incinerated Ahmed and Mohammed al-Khobze, two brothers under the age of fifteen who happened to be walking along a road in Yemen's al-Bayda province. While the civilian death toll from early Trump-era drone strikes is officially low, local Yemenis insist that many of the victims declared "militants" and "fighters" by the US military had no attachments to Al Qaeda or other terrorist groups.[52] Luckily for Trump, however, years earlier the Obama administration had developed a brilliant method for dealing with these misunderstandings. In the face of drones' wide-scale collateral damage, terrorists are often labeled ex post facto: as Jo Becker and Scott Shane of the *New York Times* clarified, "Mr. Obama embraced a disputed method for counting civilian casualties that did little to box him in. It in effect counts all military-age males in a strike zone as combatants."[53] The epistemology of the digital only guarantees that the world will be processed through unmistakable binary digits; it doesn't guarantee fidelity between signifier and signified. As we see with SKYNET, the state of exception validates sovereign semiosis: whoever is killed by a drone strike is, by definition, a terrorist. The inability for nonstate actors to partake in the human semiotic chain allows the United States to continue its experiments with human elimination. The sinister elegance in this, as Grégoire Chamayou points out, is that as weaponized drones become increasingly dependent on AI to determine who is a terrorist enemy, the only agent responsible for faulty strikes is the victim, "who, as a result of making inappropriate physical movements, was unfortunate enough to set off the automatic mechanism that results in his own elimination."[54] If you don't want to be killed by a drone, then don't act like a terrorist. As the machine and its attendants will certainly assure you, the drone only kills terrorists.

In the end, the caution and care that characterized Cold War–era military projects—projects that were based in multipolarity, geopolitical balance, and mutually assured destruction—have been abandoned, as the promise of automated nuclear retaliation (not gone, but somehow forgotten) has been replaced by the unaccountability and hubris of what Ian G. R. Shaw calls the "predator empire."[55] This has driven us to the slippery edge of the "end of history," where the United States declares its victims the enemies of humankind. These scattered, tattered foes have taken on the character of what Carl Schmitt called "the absolute enemy." As the terrorist loses its status as a specific, concrete entity, it drifts into the abstract realm of the absolute. In the words of Schmitt, "The war of absolute enmity knows no containment"[56]—no bounds in time, space, morality, or politics. Schmitt foresaw how the alluring abstractions of absolute enmity could lead to the horrors of absolute war:

> In a world in which the partners push each other in this way into the abyss of total devaluation before they annihilate one another physically, new kinds of absolute enmity must come into being. Enmity will be so terrifying that one perhaps mustn't even speak any longer of the enemy or of enmity, and both words will have to be outlawed and damned fully before the work of annihilation can begin. Annihilation thus becomes entirely abstract and entirely absolute. It is no longer directed against an enemy, but serves only another, ostensibly objective attainment of highest values, for which no price is too high to pay. It is the renunciation of real enmity that opens the door for the work of annihilation of an absolute enmity.[57]

Because the United States is carrying out a global crusade in the name of a universal morality, it runs an especially high risk of reducing its enemies to the abstract category of the absolute. While military officials decide how long the human soldier will be allowed to operate alongside the lethal machine, this category of the absolute will continue to drift, proliferate, and consume new entities into itself. The digital logic of the absolute enemy—the zero of US vs. the one of THEM, the with-us-or-against-us vision of absolute enmity displayed by the War on Terror—has trumped the analog multipolarity of traditional politics. In the War on Terror, these enemies will always be located; regardless of how many are eliminated, there will never be zero terrorists.[58] The War on Terror, which has annihilated the time-space of its enemy, has no media-induced stalemate—only media escalation.

Vital Ground (DoD)

Chapter 7

Ground of such importance that it must be retained or controlled for the success of the mission. See also *key terrain*.

Seven months ago, America and the world drew a line in the sand. We declared that the aggression against Kuwait would not stand. And tonight, America and the world have kept their word.
—GEORGE H. W. BUSH, "ADDRESS TO THE NATION," 1991

Silicon, the principal ingredient in beach sand, is a natural semiconductor and the most abundant element on Earth except for oxygen.
—INTEL, "FROM SAND TO CIRCUITS"

Unleash us from the tether of fuel.
—US SECRETARY OF DEFENSE JIM "MAD DOG" MATTIS

It is said that a line drawn in the sand demarcates a territorial limit—a sovereign border that cannot be penetrated without inducing military retribution. This saying supposedly originated in 168 BCE, when Gaius Popillius Laenas, a Roman consul, encircled King Antiochus IV of the Seleucid Empire inside a line he had inscribed in the sand. If the king crossed the line before agreeing to withdraw from Egypt, Laenas would declare war on the empire. Antiochus backed down. George Bush's reanimation of the phrase is merely one of many but is significant in that the territory he metaphorically marked remains a point of immense continued military conflict where the United States has been experimenting with autonomous weapons for more than twenty-five years. Such autonomy, we argue, is intimately and absolutely tied to the capacity to access, store, and manipulate energy. Any explanation of why military strategists are fixated on autonomous weaponry has to acknowledge and untangle the spatiotemporal dimensions of warfare and the degree to which harnessing energy reconfigures those dimensions. Autonomy, in part, suggests fuel autonomy.

Inscriptions in the sand can be both metaphorical and material. Both figurations run through this chapter. Sand, like other geological phenomena,[1] has a medial life. While a line in the sand may metaphorically mark off one's territory from that of an enemy, an X in the sand can mark the spot one expects to drill for oil. Sand matters. It can be melted, purified, mixed, and poured into a mold, then ground to create the specialized lenses that drones use to capture enemy data as they fly over desert landscapes. The largest semiconductor manufacturer in the world, Intel, explains that after oxygen, silicon—which is readily found in beach sand—is the most abundant element on earth. "From Sand to Circuits" is one of their mottos for explaining their fruitful alteration of this abundance.[2] Recent breakthroughs in solid-state drives are leading to the replacement of older aluminum- and magnesium-based hard drives by silicon-based drives. Sand can thus be made to collect, store, and process data. Military intelligence is literally inscribed in sand.

The vast accumulation of sand in the Arabian peninsula buried the immense oil reservoirs suspended below, which were created when high heat and pressure turned dead plankton into oil. This oil is the fuel that, as Friedrich Kittler and others have noted, drives US air superiority—the basis for twentieth-century military dominance. The US Department of Defense (DoD), in fact, is the world's largest consumer of fuel.[3] Asking what technologies gave rise to the American Empire, Kittler poses, "Obviously, the first source of the American Empire is the British Empire which was originally driven by a coal-based fleet system but which has, since the Second World War, been transformed into an oil-based system founded on air power."[4] This complex system of oil extraction, processing, and transmission doesn't merely power the mechanisms of global capital; it is also monitored and protected in very particular ways to ensure US military hegemony. Yet because the maintenance of this oil-driven military ecosystem is so costly and vulnerable, it has played an important role in driving the development of military technologies attuned to different territorial commitments. On the one hand, drones and similar military technologies are seen as a solution to maintaining current flows of oil; on the other, they are seen as the objects that could potentially displace the very need for oil. That is to say, while today's battles are waged over what lies beneath the sand, tomorrow's will be determined by how skillfully sand is made to think. While oil is a limited resource whose material control is of paramount importance, sand is a nearly limitless resource whose power is amplified through the "immaterial" labor of invention. Artificially intelligent military technologies stand at the crossroads of these military changes.

While, as Caren Kaplan points out, "mobility is at the heart of modern warfare,"[5] territorial sovereignty remains a central strategic concern—especially because of its ties to resource extraction and fuel production. Geopolitical struggles drive forms of economic organization and military dominance that correspond with traditional, territorially specific sources of fuel. Emerging technology, however, threatens to more fully deterritorialize war by detaching military forces from specific territorial dependencies. While controlling territory ensures one's dominance of local energy resources, it locks one's strategy into defending those territories. But the territory becomes less relevant in the face of alternative forms of energy production and new methods of conquest and destruction. If energy and resource dominance are no longer desirable or even possible, what becomes the new strategic field on which dominance can be reestablished? Cyber warfare, in particular, has the potential to invalidate air superiority (or overturns who has it) and, in the process, limits the immediate importance of energy dominance. Attack from anywhere on any target at any (or just the right) time provides greater tactical advantage than peerless destructive force. Weather and space don't matter. Nature disappears. Sand and circuits reconfigure the territory. Become the territory.

Territory, Energy, Weapon

Modern wars consume and devour the very soil and earth over which they are waged.
—FRIEDRICH KITTLER, "ANIMALS OF WAR"

Energy may be likened to the bending of a crossbow; decision, to the releasing of a trigger.
—SUN TZU, ON THE ART OF WAR

The sustenance of life is energy dependent, and energy production has always been tied to territory. In simple terms, the sedentary—the fixed—fosters an attachment to particular spaces as a means of locating and regularizing the extractive capacities of energy production. Agriculture, which strives to ensure a regularity of human and animal caloric intake, presents an obvious example. The ability to raise crops, store them through periods of hardship, and distribute them accordingly has long served as a central focus of sociopolitical governance.[6] For the populations governed by these flows of fuel, fire and food allowed energy to be processed in the service of large-scale, coordinated programs of biological sustenance. Access to these sources and flows, therefore, becomes a key impetus for colonization and conquest.[7]

As Geoffrey Winthrop-Young points out, Kittler's history of media/war is grounded in this struggle over resources and energy production. An enmity arises, according to Winthrop-Young, when sedentary agricultural societies clash with their pastoral neighbors: "This enmity, Kittler emphasizes, is and always has been a struggle over resources; hence there is no innocent party. In one of his more complex moves, Kittler links these spiraling escalations to ever-deeper recursions—deeper into the past and therefore, quite literally, deeper into the ground. Increasingly modern states evict, massacre, or conquer the stateless for ever-older and -deeper deposited resources: wood, charcoal, coal, and oil."[8] For Kittler, the monopolization of energy sources is inextricably linked to military dominance, and therefore resource maximization and military escalation go hand in hand. As Kittler puts it, the necessity of energy production places important constraints on—and fosters innovations in—military logistics: "Modern wars have refined a logistical apparatus that supplies the fighting troops with everything from ammunition to food for humans and animals. But because transportation capacities are always limited, the format of these supplies had to be optimized. The nineteenth century invented beef extract, corned beef, iron rations, and cigarettes for the explicit purpose of transporting less food and more killing equipment."[9] Because armies must be fed and weapons must be fueled, the location, extraction, storage, and delivery of energy resources are central military strategic concerns.[10] Accordingly, systems of economy must be put into place in order to reduce, as much as possible, the resources required to sustain or develop fighting capacities. Resource dependence is an inherent liability.

Military reliance on territorially specific sites of energy production is an ancient problem. Consider, for example, how energy production and energy storage problems illustrate key differences between the spear, the bow, and the crossbow. All three weapons deliver a cylindrical shaft and sharp point. Yet their differences signify a host of military sensibilities regarding human soldiering and the capacity of technology to harness and store energy in a dependable, repeatable, and territorially specific fashion. Because chimpanzees are known to fashion and use spears, it's plausible that human ancestors have been using some form of spear for millions of years. While the direct archaeological evidence suggests that humans' predecessors used spears at least 400,000 years ago, at this early stage they were wielded directly by hominids that were mostly confrontational "ambush" hunters—preying on large animals such as mammoths and rhinoceroses—rather than distance hunters that preyed on smaller animals like deer and fowl.[11] These spears directly extended the range of the human body, allowing for groups to surround and collectively attack large prey.

Once airborne, however, spears and their projectile cousins, such as the harpoon, radically reshaped humans' relationship to space and time. As a result of this technological breakthrough, a host of human cultural, biological, and martial characteristics evolved.[12] For example, farsightedness would become an increasingly valuable perceptual capacity for offensive and defensive purposes—and as a hunter-gatherer species, 98 percent of humans are born farsighted.[13] A thrown harpoon extends the range of impact, minimizes the time it takes to inflict bodily harm, and opens up new forms of direct biological energy production. This circulation of energy into the void beyond immediate bodily reach is a turning point in hunting and war tactics, enhancing the range at which energy could be leveraged into ballistic effect. The force with which such projectiles strike the target and the distance at which a target can be reached are mostly determined by the strength and skill of the chucker and is broken into four components: "a horizontal force, a wrist torque, the hand mass, and the hand radius of gyration."[14] Biological energy is directly transferred in real time from the body to the projectile. The immediate link between energy product (the hunted) and energy consumer (the hunter) is broken.

Adding a leather thong or loop to the end of the projectile magnifies this transfer of energy, but that weapons apparatus cannot store the energy required to make it take flight. Similarly, with the bow and arrow, and later the crossbow, potential energy is stored in the technology itself—energy is not simply transferred or magnified but is also stored for future use. The bow and arrow's paramount spatiotemporal revolution is its capacity to store this energy in a technical artifact. The bow and arrow collects energy exerted by muscles, tendon, and bone and multiplies it via the tension of the bowstring (figure 7.1). The bow then stores that energy briefly, allowing time to aim before a kinetic release converts the energy into propulsion for the projectile or arrow. The emergence of the arrow—which has been around for approximately 70,000 years—allows for a tremendous expansion of humans' available prey by disrupting the traditional space/time of hunting. Small animals such as deer and fowl, which can be killed by arrows, thus become for many human communities an important source of food.[15] The range of human dietary fuel production thus expands a bit beyond the immediate range of the thrust of a spear.

Similarly, the crossbow begins with the transfer of direct biological energy into the material of the bow; this energy is then stored in the bow, via a catch, and ultimately unleashed by a trigger or release mechanism. Such storage, of

Figure 7.1
Scientific analysis of energy selection, storage, and processing, 1937. Hickman, "The Dynamics of a Bow and Arrow," 407.

course, changes the temporal dimension of firing: the bolt, once latched, can be held indefinitely and released immediately. The human strength needed to hold steady is usurped by mechanical transfer. The same basic mechanical form appears in which some semirigid material is bent in order to maximize the potential energy stored in the material structure of the bow (originally wood) and bowstring (originally rawhide). This potential energy is then transferred into the arrow or bolt. Through a series of minor design revisions and advances in materials, vastly greater sums of energy can be stored, producing greater accuracy and expanding the range of lethality. Along with these changes, of course, come shifts in hunting practices and, later, battle tactics: individual hunters could roam in search of smaller prey, and eventually, with the emergence of a more disciplined art of archery (between 9,000 and 1,500 years ago, from the Americas to China), warriors could kill one another from beyond the range of hand-wielded weapons. This changed military formations, siege tactics, and even the class dimensions of warfare: in the battlefields of medieval and early modern Europe, archers were seen as sneaky and thus provided a noted contrast to the gallant, disciplined, and well-trained knight skilled in hand-to-hand combat.[16] This massive disruption of the time/space of battle

Figure 7.2 The Sautérelle, a grenade-throwing crossbow used to deliver grenades from trench to trench during World War I.

thus had an important impact on the conception of the battlefield and the development of future weapons.

With the addition of perceptual aids like sights, telescopes, and eventually laser guidance, the bow becomes a multi-mediated energy-amplifier. At one point during World War I, the French and British were using the Sautérelle, a grenade-throwing crossbow, to deliver grenades from trench to trench (figure 7.2). This "democratization" of murderous capacity will be further established as we move to gunpowder: "God made man; Samuel Colt made them equal," or so the saying goes. The processing and storage of energy into a weapon, as opposed to the weapon acting as a real-time mediation of biological energy (as with the sword or dagger), gradually shifts the focus of warfare from human warrior to munitions operator. This shift proves to be monumental because, in the age of industrial warfare, it has led to the gradual separation of weapons—and hence battle—from the immediate space of energy production. The human, the harpoon's more or less stationary energy source, becomes increasingly distanced from the projectile as the harpoon evolves into the arrow and the arrow evolves into the bullet. This desire to extend the space/time of war foreshadows more recent attempts to free weapons from the territorial constraints of their energy sources (which, in the case of the bow and arrow, was the human body). The arrow, therefore, is the not-so-distant relative of the solar-powered drone.

Energizing the Submarine

To take another example, let's look at the submarine. Deep-sea submarines provide an interesting comparison to outer space vessels because some of the longest "untethered" military missions have been conducted by nuclear submarines that can roam the deep seas for months at a time without any external contact. The first military submarine, designed by a Yale University student to aid in the War of Independence, could stay submerged for thirty minutes, was powered by a hand crank attached to a screw propeller, and failed to successfully deliver its munitions when first unleashed on the mighty British naval fleet in 1776 (figure 7.3). The necessity of keeping humans alive and providing for their energy needs remains an underwater problem. Delivering the fuel necessary to maintain secrecy and provide adequate range is paramount to the history of submarine development. The aloneness of the submarine, its autonomy, defines its utility and its ultimate liability. Further, the submarine from its infancy has attempted to take advantage of the perceptual limitations that water affords, complicating and refiguring the friend/enemy detection problematic.

Sub innovation has frequently run into the brick wall of fuel needs. Take, for example, one of the most notorious submarine campaigns in the twentieth century: the German U-boat campaign in World War II. Tanker ships used to refuel German subs kept getting destroyed. So in 1942 Germany created a precursor to the drone mother ship, "The Milk Cow," an underwater fuel tanker with the range and capacity to keep the U-boats in action.[17] Thanks to the Enigma machine's code breaking, all ten "milk cows" were destroyed and the new "Schnorkel"-enabled mother ship never rendezvoused for its first fueling mission. For all the destructive accomplishments of the diesel/electric-powered subs of World War II, none could stay underwater longer than about twelve hours without resurfacing. They, like their crew, were dependent on an above-the-surface environment. This lack of autonomy was their undoing.

In 1954, however, a military technological revolution occurred when the nuclear-powered USS *Nautilus* was launched. It ushered in the age of atomic-powered autonomy and could stay underwater indefinitely. Yet while the U-boat was limited by fuel capacity, the *Nautilus* was limited by its human pilots'

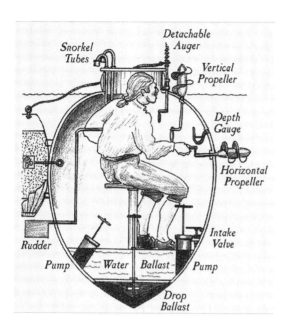

Figure 7.3 The first submarine uses human energy.

incapacity to live in the sub's underwater environment for extended periods. In 1960, however, the US Navy's radar picket USS *Triton* submarine succeeded in circumnavigating the entire planet underwater without rising to the surface, needing to refuel, or making contact with any aboveground human personnel. For all intents and purposes, *Triton* was an autonomous, nuclear-powered, and nuclear-armed vessel capable of more short-term destruction than the entire militaries of all but the four nuclear-enabled countries at the time, the Soviet Union, the United States, Great Britain, and France. A single autonomous submarine was now able to "disappear" in order to secretly unleash nuclear terror on the planet.

Things have radically changed since this Cold War feat ushered in a new era of underwater fuel independence. Current generations of nuclear submarines never need to be refueled throughout their twenty-five-year lifespans.[18] These subs generate enormous energy from the smallest fragments of uranium. In simple terms, one kilogram of oil produces twelve kilowatts of heat, while one kilogram of uranium-235 produces 24,000,000 kilowatts of heat.[19] With such a promising power source, these submarines can carry nuclear fuel for up to thirty years of operation, including maintenance of air quality, fresh water production by distilling salt water from the ocean, temperature regulation, and so on. The only resource that limits the time underwater is the food supply for the crew.

Yet the submarine also presents obvious problems of command and control. Water saps light but carries sound. In the deep, all the energy the sun provides is stripped away by water, making the collection of light data impossible. Sound data become the primary means of navigation, enemy detection, and ballistic guidance. The external world can be manifest only through extensive and highly sophisticated technical media systems. For all intents and purposes, a nuclear submarine's crew is "black boxed." Survival and contact with the external world are entirely dependent on a hermetic system with highly selective and bottlenecked channels of communication. Geoffrey Winthrop-Young suggests that this plane of electromagnetic perception now encompasses much of lived experience. "Our increased reliance on technologically mediated representations of the outside world reflects the fact that we are as unable to directly interact with the electromagnetic environment we have come to depend on as a submarine crew can access the water on the other side of the hull."[20] As such, replacing a "black boxed" crew with a "black box" AI makes profound sense. Removing the technological accommodations necessary to keep humans alive underwater for months at a time opens the spatial and temporal dimensions of design in a multitude of ways. The nuclear submarine is a litmus test for pushing the limitations of the human-machine military couplet. As with so many of these tests, human limits are increasingly conveyed as no longer worth addressing. Instead, the answer has come in the form of the unmanned submarine. One step in this direction, the Sparse Supervisory Control, institutes a familiar form of indirect human drone supervision for unmanned underwater vehicles (UUVs).[21] Now relieved of their onboard human crew, these vessels can operate as "lone wolves" for three months, untethered from supply chains and chains of command. These UUVs remove human limitations and human needs from the aquatic equation. Subs no longer need to be built to protect humans from an environment that they didn't evolve to survive in. Instead, plans are under way to further autonomize UUVs, as we see with RAND's Green Strike Group—a small fleet of nuclear vessels and biofuel-powered ships that, according to its developers, are the next steps toward an oil-free fleet.[22]

Alternative Air Dominance

While the nuclear-powered submarine provides one sort of ideal fuel autonomy, it doesn't resolve these problems in other domains of the military that depend on massive quantities of processed oil—all of which must be located, extracted, delivered in raw form to processing facilities, and then redelivered through a global distribution chain that is itself dependent on a subset of that fuel. Take aerial warfare, for example, which demands control of petroleum reserves to manufacture jet fuel and related sources of energy. In this way the argument that wars in the Middle East are about "blood for oil" is true, but not in the way that has been commonly argued; in fact, it has less to do with American consumerism and automobility than with the maintenance of "air dominance." Yet this lust for military dominance demands constant innovation and a bottomless need for energy production—one that ultimately could never be filled by all the oil reserves on the planet.

Oil and related fossil-fuel energy sources have serious liabilities on the battlefield. The production of "alternative" fuel sources, therefore, lies at the center of next-generation military strategy. As military technologists experiment with giving drones more autonomous self-control, they are also enhancing drones' autonomy by unleashing them from heavy, costly, nonrenewable fuel sources. The mission capacity of Lockheed Martin's twelve-foot hand-launched Stalker craft, for example, was expanded two hours to eight hours—just by incorporating fuel cell technology. The propane fuel cell, which uses chemical reactions to convert energy into electricity, produces much more energy than a lithium-ion battery.[23] Weighing in at barely five pounds, it has a nominal output of 245 watts when processing 112 grams of propane per hour. Because it produces so much energy relative to its weight, the Stalker is able to quietly fly low to the ground (at about twelve hundred feet) and carry out highly precise and specialized surveillance and reconnaissance tasks. Michael Hansberry, an engineer with the Marine Corps Warfighting Laboratory, boasts, "At that altitude [twelve hundred feet] you can tell a man carrying a rifle from a man carrying a broom."[24] Another minisurveillance drone, the navy's Ion Tiger, uses a hydrogen fuel cell and can stay in the air for twenty-three hours. Flying lower and more discreetly than their large, oil-dependent counterparts, drones such as the Stalker are bringing new intelligence capacities to the US military.

Related trends in fuel independence include solar- and thermal-powered drones. While solar power is a feat in itself, in 2010 DARPA awarded a contract to Aurora Flight Sciences (AFS) to develop and build microdrones that run on solar power during the day and thermal power at night. Capitalizing on AFS's earlier experience in unmanned technology, the Skate was designed with thin-film lithium batteries fashioned into wings; while the top of the craft would be equipped with solar cells, the bottom was designed to contain infrared photovoltaic cells that would allow for energy production at night.[25] Although the Skate took a different direction during production, solar-powered quadcopters and microdrones have become an important element of the UAV landscape, and DARPA's Fast Lightweight Autonomy program is continuously cultivating the development of similar projects.[26] Most interesting in this regard, perhaps, is the R&D being carried out at Wright Patterson Air Force Base, where a "microaviary" of microdrone swarms is being developed. In a bizarre outreach video, Air Vehicles Directorate—a research wing of the air force—depicted one of their drones pirating electricity from a power line before descending to a man's shoulder and blowing his head off. "Unobtrusive, pervasive, lethal—micro air vehicles," the video concludes.[27] These microdrones can be so unobtrusive and pervasive only because they have been freed from the constraints of petroleum-based energy sources.

These few examples are merely suggestive, of course, and alternative energy solutions are still at an early stage of development. Although the military has tinkered with alternative energy sources since at least the late nineteenth century—and although the RAND Corporation and other unsurprising sources have released pessimistic reports about its military applications—the trend is undeniable: releasing the territorial constraints associated with traditional energy production has become a central imperative of the US military.[28] As the DoD put it in 2015, "The military's shift toward renewable energy is not just a political directive but also an operational imperative."[29] This seems to be the case, as the US military's use of oil decreased 20 percent between 2007 and 2015.[30] Wind power, thermal, solar, V2G (vehicle-to-grid), and Wi-Fi[31]—these alternative sources of power are part and parcel of the US military's drive to deterritorialize its energy production needs. In the process of unraveling this dependency on territorial oil power, new forms of surveillance, C4I, and attack become possible with these smaller, more independent, and less expensive craft. Hence the shift away from oil is in large part a media shift—a shift from sand to silicon, from al-Levant to algorithm.

Cyber Dominance

Accordingly, the US Congress created the Division of Operational Energy Plans and Programs in 2010 to untether US military from fuel—most specifically oil—dependency. The initial director was culled from a military think tank, the New American Century, and this is how she described the primary concern of her program: "When you consume that much oil, you have to move that much oil around. And it means your force is very dependent on receiving that much oil in order to operate. So, it has become very clear in Iraq and in Afghanistan that the amount of fuel we consume is a liability."[32] Just as we saw with U-boats in World War II, when fuel processing plants were one of the most heavily bombed areas in the entire war, key fuel delivery points frequently also routinely came under attack in Iraq and Afghanistan. This is because, while nuclear power has become a remarkable fuel source for UUVs, this success has yet to be repeated elsewhere in the military. Indeed, as of now fossil fuels are the only means of sustaining significant airpower. Yet given current political, economic, and strategic challenges, researchers across the US military are searching for viable forms of alternative energy.

As Kittler noted, historical shifts in military dominance accord with disruptions in energy use. Hence future disruptions in military dominance will be ushered in via new kinds of energy production. Broadening the theater of operations into nontraditional environments, and thus allowing for innovative weapons and vehicles to penetrate those environments, makes way for the reconstitution of war space outside those territories that demand traditional oil-fueled engagements. While moving the terrain for air superiority into space is one possibility, moving it into "cyberspace" has become one of the most popular avenues of this territorial reinvention.

Accordingly, the line differentiating the sovereign control of terrestrial space from the virtual control of virtual space has been increasingly blurred. Inscriptions onto the territorial maps and boundaries that make up borders that are protected and penetrated by military weapons are not necessarily the most important forms of military advancement. Instead, the logic of the circuit has taken over, and one of its primary formulations is to reconfigure the spatiotemporal horizon of warfare. Digital data have amplified the capacity to simulate and execute military strategy. Simulation and execution depend on the same digitally produced maps and charts. In this way they exemplify the counterintuitive sentiment that "the map is the territory."[33] Not only that, but the world's most popular mapping system, GPS, was created for the explicit purpose of actualizing the US military's desire to aim missiles from anywhere in the world.[34] When the greatest destructive capacities on the planet are guided via a digital mapping program, then the territory is most definitely subservient to the map.

Today the map is digital, and so too is the territory. For "maps are not just representations but also instruments."[35] The instrumental logic of cyberspace, as an embattled space, provides an overly simple example. More broadly, the interpenetration of the logics of military territorial sovereignty and cyberwar exemplifies the fact that in total war, everything is "mapped" or situated in relationships of proximity, connectivity, and threat. This is to say, in the vast military data farms a near-infinite number of lines could be drawn to connect each silicon inscription to an ever more complex array of meanings. This movement from territory to map and back again realigns which "lines in the sand" come to matter. Increasingly, military dominance takes place in the manipulation of silicon and the means by which its potential can be maximized through AI.

It is here, with cyberwar, that energy and information start to merge in unique ways. The shift from overt destructive capacities to cyberwar is a shift in the territory's relationship to energy production. Cyberspace, after all, is a vast energy field. It exists as the movement of light and electrical pulses. So with the advent of cyberwar, the movement of warfare from the collection, storage, and processing of energy in the so-called material world has simply moved to the realm of "pure energy." It is a world that exists in and only as energy, and it is upheld by vast bunkers of machinery that must constantly be electrified. Unlike other forms of warfare that work to manipulate and direct energy to alter other materials, bodies, buildings, bridges, and so on, cyberwar mostly works to alter different configurations of energy itself as electrical impulses or the movement of light or to alter inscriptions in silicon. When comparing two means for dismantling an enemy's C4I capabilities, Northrop Grumman explains that one conventional means would be to launch a bomb at a communications tower.[36] Yet with the right equipment, today one could simply use a cyberweapon to accomplish the same thing. As another US military developer put it, "Cyber allows us to project force into that domain without necessarily projecting physical force."[37]

Disruption, Territory, Innovation

This alternative projection of force has been under development for a long time. Fred Kaplan suggests that this history goes back to the very beginning of the development of the ARPANET in 1967 when Willis H. Ware, the lead computer scientist for RAND, predicted the imminent problematic of networked digital communications: essentially, once C3 becomes C4 and C4 becomes C4I, the point of most efficient attack becomes the communications network.[38] As the long history of spying and cryptography has shown, the most judicious use of military resources is fortified by an information advantage. Knowing the enemy while keeping oneself unknowable or misknown is far more efficient than creating brute destructive superiority. With a networked communications infrastructure, the greater utilization of information also produces a greater potential for disruption. Hacking and cyberwar have thus become the cheapest and most democratized mode of trying to fight an asymmetric battle against a superior force. They have also become a point of open conflict between more traditionally powerful adversaries who are all engaged in various forms of cyberattack and infiltration.

While electronic warfare has a long and well-documented history, perhaps the most interesting are those military doctrines that have arisen from the perceived threat of "disruptive innovation" over the past fifteen years. Harvard's Clayton Christensen coined the term, determining it as the "process by which a product or service takes root initially in simple applications at the bottom of a market and then relentlessly moves up market, eventually displacing established competitors."[39] The fear that dominant technological positioning can be undermined by the wide-scale use of "lesser" technologies has the Pentagon reimagining how to hedge their bets in technological innovation. Shifting focus onto software solutions as opposed to hardware dominance is one of the key drivers in military automation. Intelligent machines may be more impactful and dangerous than machines with greater firepower and armor. Cheap mass production, coupled with widespread interoperability, defines many of the characteristics of disruption and is precisely the sort of innovation that is worrisome to a territorially driven superpower.

As we've shown throughout, media are central to warfare. And even though "information warfare" and other military doctrines have suggested their centrality for decades, it wasn't until the 1990s, when John Arquilla and David Ronfeldt popularized the notion of netwar, that their significance became a widely discussed and publicized issue.[40] Arquilla and Ronfeldt ground their understanding of netwar in a long-held assumption that history repeats a truism about innovation and military success: "Throughout history, military doctrine, organization, and strategy have continually undergone profound changes due in part to technological breakthroughs. The Greek phalanx, the combination of gun and sail, the levee en masse, the blitzkrieg, the Strategic Air Command—history is filled with examples in which new weapon, propulsion, communication, and transportation technologies provide a basis for advantageous shifts in doctrine, organization, and strategy that enable the innovator to avoid exhausting attritional battles and pursue instead a form of 'decisive' warfare."[41] The escalation vacuum created by the fall of the Soviet Union came to be replaced by a "networked enemy" and networked technologies. Everything became "connected" or networked as an epistemological condition and as a technological feat. Knowing the enemy became a technological feat as it was their communication structure, not their uniforms, nationality, or position in a military hierarchy, which became evidence of their presence. But knowing this enemy was also deeply about knowing oneself, and what was known had deep roots and presented itself in a somewhat unflattering way. Here is how brigadier general Samuel B. Griffith opens his introduction to *Mao Tse-tung on Guerrilla Warfare*, which he translated for the Marine Corps' publication of the text in 1961:

> At one end of the spectrum, ranks of electronic boxes buried deep in the earth hungrily consume data and spew out endless tapes. Scientists and engineers confer in air-conditioned offices; missiles are checked by intense

men who move about them silently, almost reverently. In forty minutes, countdown begins.

At the other end of this spectrum, a tired man wearing a greasy felt hat, a tattered shirt, and soiled shorts is seated, his back against a tree. Barrel pressed between his knees, butt resting on the moist earth between sandaled feet, is a Browning automatic rifle. Hooked to his belt, two dirty canvas sacks—one holding three homemade bombs, the other four magazines loaded with .30-caliber ammunition. Draped around his neck, a sausage-like cloth tube with three days' supply of rice. The man stands, raises a water bottle to his lips, rinses his mouth, spits out the water. He looks about him carefully, corks the bottle, slaps the stock of the Browning three times, pauses, slaps it again twice, and disappears silently into the shadows. In forty minutes, his group of fifteen men will occupy a previously prepared ambush.[42]

In other words, data and high-tech innovations versus guerilla tactics and homemade weaponry. Understanding Mao's tactics was seen as a necessary component of US military-strategic training. As anticolonial struggles were on the rise, they were situated within the confines of an increasingly technological military apparatus devised to counter the high-tech Soviet nuclear enemy alongside a host of low-tech insurgents. The story of the computer versus the guerilla/terrorist was just beginning. But the high-tech versus low-tech dynamic had been around for centuries and would be obliterated, just as firearms had made anyone capable of killing even the strongest warrior. Eventually the ARPANET would draw the high into the hands of the low, and would make cables, circuits, and chips a new battlefront in the struggle for spatiotemporal disruption.

Yet with the move to cyber and the redirection of attention toward technological capacity and software dominance, there was also a drive to free the rest of military capacity from the natural world—from the tether of gravity, distance, temporality, and territorially specific energy sources. The human body has limits; cyberspace appears limitless. Replacing battle space with cyberspace—or, rather, turning cyberspace into the battle space—is an essential step in dislodging the military's dependency on oil reserves and other naturally occurring fuel sources. It is one thing to use cyberspace to affect battle space in such a way that terrestrial necessities of jet fuel are still necessary to execute air superiority and military global hegemony. But what if jet fuel were replaced, or what if jet power were replaced by another form of air superiority? How might such redistributions of the military energy power grid be redistributed? In other words, if air superiority were no longer determined by high-speed, high-powered bombers and fighters, but rather by a swarm of inexpensive drones that operated on solar power; or if all airplanes could be shot down instantaneously by direct energy weapons (DEWs); or if an "indefensible hack" overtook C4I; or if space weapons moved the terrain of dominance upward and outward; or if some alien tech created light-speed fighters, and so on—if current energy-military dominance were *disrupted* through some *innovation*, then current battle space epistemologies and territorial necessities could be overturned.

But what media or energy innovation could possibly prepare Earth and its most powerful militaries for alien invasion? Futurologists and the SETI (search for extraterrestrial intelligence) community certainly contemplate such an event in which once-powerful militaries must borrow from the playbook of guerilla tactics. In such accounts alien capacities are characterized according to the degree to which their ability to manipulate energy provides the means to both alter time/space relations through interstellar travel and direct tremendous force to destroy or manipulate matter. According to such accounts, an alien civilization's ability to control potential and kinetic energy provides the metric by which a threat should be measured. By this metric, humans are woefully unprepared for intergalactic battle. The human body is too frail and our propulsion systems too slow for even a modest military endeavor across the galaxy, let alone the universe. If humans are to have any chance at interstellar conquest, they shall have to turn toward robot warriors who can store far greater reserves of energy than humans, outlast the timescale necessary for deep space travel, and direct the destructive force of energy with extreme precision in order to strike targets that may be light years away.

In such battles, conventional and nuclear weaponry fail in one significant way: the inherent time lag of traversing terrestrial or extraterrestrial space. However, direct energy weapons (DEWs) or lasers deliver their destructive capacity at the speed of light. Hence, for human purposes, the DEW ostensibly solves one vexing military problematic. With DEWs, destruction occurs at the speed of light. Or put differently, death can be delivered as quickly as an enemy can be seen. This would prove of great importance against alien invasion.

Conclusions

We leave the sand and delve into the circuits only to be drawn back again. The map is and has been the territory. Yet the circuit is a kind of map, a series of inscriptions transforming a medium that organizes thought and movement.[43] Broadly configured, this focus on sand allows for an analysis of how military strategy, tactics, and technical capacity have been organized by collecting, storing, and processing energy and data. This emphasis of data over energy is not precisely what Paul Virilio meant by "information bomb."[44] Yet we suggest that the direction of these shifts leads to the following five considerations.

1. The ability to dominate the extraction, use, and manipulation of a particular energy source often leads to military dominance. However, it also produces a dependence on controlling or most efficiently utilizing that form of energy. This kind of dominance-versus-dependence equation produces its own time/space configuration and attendance to the territories that store such energy reserves. There is a constant desire within military thinking to replace fuel that is undependable and difficult to obtain with forms of energy that are increasingly powerful and access to which is controllable.

2. Fuel autonomy becomes one means by which military powers break free from the tyranny of a specific time/space configuration or, stated in a more pedestrian fashion, the necessities of collection, storage, and processing of energy. One way in which military strategists approach energy is to overcome the difficulties resulting from these three burdens.

3. Shifting the terrain of warfare from the logic of inscription on territorial maps to inscription in silicon is one attempt to free up the specificity of terrestrial limitations and dependencies. If warfare can take place on networked keyboards in coders' cubicles as opposed to the guerilla terrain of Afghanistan, all the better. However, the ease of access to the new battle space also means the expansion of potential enemies. Anyone with a computer and a Wi-Fi connection now has the weaponry, if not the skills, to pose a legitimate threat. "God made man. Steve Jobs made man equal."

4. Simultaneously there is a move to autonomous vehicles that also expands military reach by decreasing the spatiotemporal limitations of human operators. Human perception and cognition are seen as temporal limitations (too slow, needing to "recharge" too frequently). Human bodies too narrowly dictate the size and speed of military trajectories. Artificial intelligence offers far greater variability across both the temporal and spatial domains. This suggests that human biology has for too long determined the relevance of various fuel sources. Freed from biological tyranny, military strategists can open up a whole new array of energy sources for powering the military machine and unfolding the spatiotemporal dimension of warfare in new and insidious ways. Stuxnet exemplifies how resetting the "clock" of uranium enrichment devices becomes a tactical weapon

as reconfiguring computational time through hacked coding "set back" Iranian nuclear weapons development several years.

5   The hope and anxiety that serious disruptive innovation produces in military strategists lies in the recognition that a disruption could alter the current terrain of battle, which is organized by global petroleum networks and the air dominance that it necessitates and is necessitated by it. Oil and air power replaced coal/steam and naval dominance, which had replaced wind and naval dominance, and so on. If air dominance is no longer dependent on oil, does the whole global geopolitical map get redrawn? If air dominance is replaced by another form of dominance, does the whole global geopolitical map get redrawn? If war happens at a speed undetectable to humans, will the whole geopolitical map get redrawn before humans ever lay eyes upon the new "line in the sand" that defines whose side we (humans) are on?

Energy exhibits its inherent dynamic churn. It transforms materials from one state to another and empowers life to spring forth, as well as alter itself and the environment in which life is present. While in general energy is moving toward a state of entropy, this, by human temporal scales, is a slow process. Information may want to be free, but energy leads the charge. The big bang marks the beginning of energy's exodus. All of the energy in the universe was shackled at a singular point, but then unleashed itself in a ten-billion-degree blast that brought the known universe into being. Along with everything else, humans owe their existence to an explosion. Energy freed itself to bring both chaos and order to the universe. It offered life and death. Entropy draws energy into disarray, while life struggles to maintain its fragile hold in an uncaring and overtly hostile environment. The sun has been exploding for billions of years. The echoes can't be heard on Earth by the naked human ear, but everything living on the planet owes its existence to this seemingly endless rhythm of destruction. Energy provides the heartbeat of modern warfare; setting fire to the oil buried beneath the sand to power a B2 bomber, triggering nuclear reactions in plutonium to drive a submarine deep beneath the sea, or burning "dirty" coal to wire the World Wide Web as its tendrils are reconfigured in a drive toward "strong AI."

Accordingly, these technological advances in energy collection, storage, and processing all reconfigure the spatiotemporal dynamics of warfare. In short, they maximize the range and minimize the time it takes to reign over a larger territory by raining ever-greater and more finely directed destruction. Nowhere on Earth is safe. Everywhere and at any time an apocalypse can erupt.

And yet, at least for the moment, humans remain. They commune, connive, commit genocide, love, laugh, fuck, give birth, and die of old age. And they create. They innovate. New modes of love and new means of control derive from this potential. However, such innovations and interactions are never innocent. As Kittler suggested, "There are of course media technologies without love, but there is no love without media technologies."[45] Human innovation, in love and in war, is always already mediated. It is also energized.

Escalation (DoD)

Chapter 8

A deliberate or unpremeditated increase in scope or violence of a conflict.

 War is the condition of media escalation. Media technology propels competition between military powers in order that it may evolve. When Kittler rejected McLuhan's claim that media are enslaved to the humans they extend, he argued that technical innovations follow "the model of military escalations."[1] When the written word could no longer outmaneuver German artillery, the telegraph provided a decisive answer. When the wires and dashes of the telegraph prevented the necessary acceleration of destruction in World War I, radio emerged to pick up the slack. Radio war then gave rise to computer war, which gradually escalated into NORAD, guided missiles, drone attacks, and robotic swarms. For Geoffrey Winthrop-Young, military history teaches us that "media react to each other in an ongoing game of one-upmanship in much the same way as tactics, strategies, and weapons systems produce countertactics, alternate strategies, and superior weapons."[2] This military one-upmanship has always served as the most radical vehicle for media evolution.

Multipolar military competition framed these developments throughout the period of the nation-state. In the aftermath of World War II, the militaries of the United States and the Soviet Union served as the primary conduits for media escalation. Yet today, in the unipolar world created in the ashes of the Cold War, escalation continues apace. Taking the place of the Soviet Union are new agents of escalation: China, Russia, and the global terrorist. Since 1998, China's defense spending has seen double-digit increases almost every year; and between 2007 and 2016, Russia's military budget increased 87 percent.[3] Much of these budget increases has been directed toward AI initiatives: as Russian president Vladimir Putin declared in September 2017, "Artificial intelligence is the future, not only for Russia, but for all humankind. . . . Whoever becomes the leader in this sphere will become the ruler of the world."[4] To prevent Russia from becoming the outright "ruler of the world," the US Army has developed a Russia-specific analysis center, called the Russia New Generation Warfare study, devoted to studying live Russian military activities in the Ukraine and then developing counterstrategies.[5] And now that the terrorist enemy has taken state form under the aegis of ISIS, it too drives US military innovation.[6]

Specters of these enemies haunt international media/military development, fueling—above all—the integration of AI into cryptography, cyber security, C4I, and drone warfare. Starting in the late 1980s, the rise of the microchip—which is relatively cheap and easy to develop—set off an ongoing series of military/media escalations, as the United States was no longer able to hoard its most devastating technological secrets (as it had with certain hard-to-procure nuclear and chemical weapons technologies, for example).[7] As a result, today the most important front of military escalation is artificial intelligence. Imploring the DoD to "take immediate action to counter adversary autonomy," the Defense Science Board's Summer Study on Autonomy of 2016 warns that hostile powers "will have less restrictive policies and CONOPs governing their own use of autonomy, particularly in the employment of lethal autonomy."[8] According to the Defense Science Board, the United States' adversaries will not be bound by the legal, ethical, and imaginative constraints that have thus far prevented the US military from fully pursuing lethal autonomy. Pushing DoD to fully integrate AI more throughout its operations, the autonomy study argues that AI warfare "provides both a threat and an opportunity."[9]

This, of course, is the basic dialectical political logic of military escalation: that threats are simply opportunities, that we can best improve ourselves under the threat of the other. Accordingly, while lethal autonomy might have long served as a dream, a distant telos, and an abstract historical logic for military innovation, it has now surfaced as a specific R&D goal in response to specific threats from specific foes. In 2015, Deputy Defense Secretary Robert Work asserted that robots are slated to enter combat within the next decade: "I'm telling you right now, ten years from now, if the first person through a breach isn't a frickin' robot, shame on us."[10] As an armed robot slams through the breach, the next horizon of military escalation comes into view: the war to end all wars, the armed struggle that will finally catapult us straight into the end of history: the third military technological revolution, characterized in its early stages by remote control, soft AI, and hybrid warfare, erupts onto the battleground in all its glory. A threat, and an opportunity.

Escalate to Utopia

In the Hollywood film *Independence Day* (1996), the president of the United States decides to give an inspirational speech on the eve of a devastating alien invasion. As he awaits the alien attack on major cities across the globe, the president urges collective human unity in the face of total annihilation: "Mankind—that word should have new meaning for all of us today. We can't be consumed by our petty differences anymore. We will be united in our common interests. . . . We're fighting for our right to live, to exist. And should we win the day, the 4th of July will no longer be known as an American holiday, but as the day when the world declared in one voice: . . . *We're going to survive!*"[11] As Jacques Rancière observes about this banal speech in this terribly banal film, "We are no longer fighting, [the president] says in essence, for freedom and democracy as our ancestors did, we are fighting for our survival."[12] In other words, the ultimate enemy has finally buried the "petty differences" that constitute the world of politics: we are now worthy of our calling as creatures destined to transcend the political, as we can unite on the most neutral common ground of bare survival. With this call for e pluribus unum, the president finesses imminent human extinction into a political opportunity: in the face of the alien apocalypse, the discordant noise of global humanity can at last be fine-tuned into the unmediated harmony of a "single voice."

The apocalypse has long been something of a liberal wet dream, as it has often been imagined as the most convenient pretext on which to build a postpolitical future of global harmony, global freedom, and global markets. Accordingly, the international unity-through-apocalypse theme has become a special part of the American cultural imagination, especially in film.[13] So it's no surprise that just a few years after *Independence Day* another US blockbuster, *Armageddon*, rehashed the same theme. In this film we see yet another US president, this time aided by television and radio, broadcast his message to the unlikeliest reaches of the world—Swiss sheep herders listen to the speech on a handheld radio; American farmers abandon their hay bales to watch in the middle of a field; a French waiter stops to watch beside a couple on a scooter; an enthralled gathering of Muslims stops to watch outside Istanbul's Sultan Ahmed Mosque; a family watches together outside a Chinese storefront. As a massive asteroid barrels toward Earth, these different audiences are woven together by globalized broadcast media, gallant American liberalism, and the promise of interplanetary military technology: "I address you tonight not as the president of the United States, not as the leader of a country, but as a citizen of humanity. We are faced with the very gravest of challenges. . . . And yet, for the first time in the history of the planet, a species has the technology to prevent its own extinction. . . . The human thirst for excellence, knowledge, every step up the ladder of science, every adventurous reach into space, all of our combined modern technologies and imaginations, even the wars that we've fought have provided us the tools to wage this terrible battle."[14] *Armageddon* adds another ingredient to the feel-good broth served up by *Independence Day*: the coming common citizenship of humanity has not only been ushered in by the threat of total annihilation, but the wars of the past have provided the scientific and technological ingenuity necessary to combat this external threat. Media/military escalation has saved us—first by allowing us to see and promote our essential unity as a species, and second by providing the awesome technical equipment for us to all come together and hunt down the evil intergalactic other.

This liberal dream, however, expands far beyond US popular culture and enjoys a prominent place in American political thought. Francis Fukuyama, the celebrated liberal theorist of geopolitics, provides a variation on this theme. In *The End of History and the Last Man*, Fukuyama argues that war drives technological progress at the same time it fosters social and political progress. In fact, the two are intimately linked, and both will eventually crescendo together into a world of political harmony. According to Fukuyama, "The possibility of war is a great force for the rationalization of societies, and for the creation of uniform social structures across cultures. Any state that hopes to maintain its political autonomy is forced to adopt the technology of its enemies and rivals. More than that, however, the threat of war forces states to restructure their social systems along lines most conducive to producing and deploying technology."[15] According to Fukuyama, war and the threat of war breed technological innovation: foes must continuously advance their technological capacities in order to prevent their own conquest or annihilation. This technological advancement then leads to a political reorientation of competing societies, whose goals and character are gradually dominated by a mechanistic, technocentric worldview. Fukuyama continues,

> For example, states must be of a certain size in order to compete with their neighbors, which creates powerful incentives for national unity; they must be able to mobilize resources on a national level, which requires the creation of a strong centralized state authority with the power of taxation and regulation; they must break down various forms of regional, religious, and kinship ties which potentially obstruct national unity; they must increase educational levels in order to produce an elite capable of disposing of technology; ... and, with the introduction of mass armies during the Napoleonic Wars, they must at least open the door to the enfranchisement of the poorer classes of their societies if they are to be capable of total mobilization. All of these developments could occur for other motives—for example, economic ones—but war frames the need for social modernization in a particularly acute way and provides an unambiguous test of its success.[16]

War, therefore, drives the development of national unity, the advancement of census and taxation, and the production of an elite class that can design and deploy the technology that will preserve the political entity. With all of these achievements under its belt, modern war has proven to be a tremendous "success": we can place mass conscription, the modern nation-state, national taxation, and the two world wars on its list of accomplishments. Ultimately, for Fukuyama war drives competitive technological development, which, in turn, drives international political uniformity. War/technology is the central means of achieving the neoconservative dream of a global liberal democracy. War/technology gradually escalates toward the end of history.

For Fukuyama, then, this is a dialectical process: war leads to technological development, and technological development leads to war. This dialectical escalation gradually builds toward a fulfillment in the universal domination of liberalism—a rationalized global order characterized by market economics, bureaucratic management, international arbitration, global communications networks, transnational flows of people and capital, human rights (according to liberal individualist definitions of the human), and—of course—ongoing global police missions, surgical strikes, and regime change operations to eliminate pockets of dissent. Fukuyama's post-Soviet dream, ultimately, is that war and technology are leading to a utopian order free of enemies—to a global extension of the same and the final suspension of political difference. From this point of view, neocon wars that level whole civilizations have a teleological significance. While the Bush 1, Clinton, Bush 2, Obama, and Trump wars might appear to be geopolitical blunders, they are in fact zones of grand geopolitical experimentation: to reconstitute global alliances through devastation and chaos, to prepare these devastated societies for private resource extraction and market liberalization, to integrate their governments into an intermediate stage of global competition and cooperation, and—ultimately—to enforce an increasingly narrow bandwidth of worldwide political uniformity.[17] Through the leveling effects of war and technological escalation, societies will gradually veer toward the dream of everlasting liberal triumph. This triumph will lead to the elimination of geopolitical struggle and the ultimate victory of the same, as politics resolves in an arrest of conflict, the spontaneous reproduction of consensus, and the end of history.

Fukuyama's dream of peace-through-technological escalation is not new, of course. By the same token, liberalism is not historically unique in its desire to wage wars in the name of global peace and political uniformity. This has been a common theme throughout recorded history, especially during the twentieth century, when so many globally ambitious political projects emerged on the world scene. But despite this diversity, liberalism *is* the driving political vehicle that brought us *here*, to the series of geopolitical and technological escalations that have made military AI a matter of international competition in the twenty-first century. Liberalism's wars to end all wars (à la Woodrow Wilson, FDR, and the Cold War), its international peacekeeping institutions (e.g., the League of Nations, the United Nations, and NATO), and its formulation of international laws that depoliticize its own military actions and ensure its supremacy in technological innovation—these developments have emerged within a global framework of liberal utopian political struggle.[18]

Since the fall of Berlin in 1945, and especially since the fall of the Berlin Wall in 1989, the United States has set the bar for international military competition. As of 2019, the United States spends about $650 billion annually on its military, while its two main geopolitical foes, China and Russia, respectively spend about $250 billion and $70 billion. And this $600-plus billion dollars per year is marshaled toward the defense and spread of liberalism: the United States' military engagements of the last several generations, whether of the left-liberal or neoconservative variety, have culminated in President Donald Trump announcing a massive military reinvestment by asserting that the US military is "the greatest force of justice on the face of the earth . . . [and] that the world has ever known."[19] The boundless spatiotemporal mission of this "greatest force of justice" is, as always, depoliticized in proper liberal fashion: it is to simply bring justice to a world in chains.[20] Hence, while liberalism shares with many political philosophies (including many theocratic eschatologies, some versions of Marxism and anarchism, and so forth) a belief in a coming utopian conquest of politics,[21] these philosophies do not have at their disposal a globally active, multitrillion-dollar military apparatus that fuels every aspect of geopolitical competition. Because the United States' liberal teleology is driving American military development—and hence is also determining the military development of its key allies and adversaries—the liberal drive to resolve political difference invites unique questions about the trajectory of media and war as they advance in inseparable escalation.

A Medium to End All Media?

While this teleological escalation is manifest in Fukuyama's utopian quest for a political order to end all political orders, it also surfaces in media theory's recurrent fixation with the medium to end all media. This tendency finds its classic expression in Marshall McLuhan's declaration that the computer would bring about a politically harmonious end of history in the form of a "global village." Ridiculing this "arch-Catholic" vision of media escalation, in a lecture given in 1999 Kittler quoted a famous passage from McLuhan's *Understanding Media*: "The computer, in short, promises by technology a Pentecostal condition of universal understanding and unity. The next logical step would seem to be, not to translate, but to bypass languages in favor of a general cosmic consciousness."[22] Contrasting the computer with human language, which according to McLuhan has functioned as a technology of fracture and separation since the Tower of Babel, McLuhan writes that the computer could give rise to a "condition of speechlessness that could confer a perpetuity of collective harmony and peace."[23] In the end, McLuhan's version of the end of history is not that different from Fukuyama's: media escalation, which in the past has fueled global conflict, reaches its zenith in the figure of the digital computer. This new invention has a unique property, a unique potential, that is likely to produce peace, harmony, and consensus. A global village.

In response, Kittler points out the inconvenient fact that the most revolutionary media escalations do not erupt in moments of peace and global brotherhood. Rather, they occur under the horrors of war: "The development of all previous technical media, in the field of computers . . . , was for purposes directly opposed to cosmic harmony—namely, military purposes."[24] Kittler responds by offering his own teleological vision of media escalation—one that, naturally, displaces humans and politics in favor of a purely technical telos. In the 1990s, therefore, Kittler would often argue that media escalation had found its ultimate fulfillment in digital computation. During this stage of Kittler's work, the digital served as a "messianic finality" or a "telos" that characterizes information's long quest to perfect its own conditions of storage and transmission.[25] The digital would thus gradually achieve a sense of media perfection in which "absolute knowledge [can] run as an endless loop."[26] From this point of view, the invention of digital computing marked a rupture in world history by signifying the beginning of the end of media development. Modern computing technologies, according to this iteration of Kittler, "make do, loosely following Boole, with one sign and its absence: one and zero. By sampling this binary information on the basis of an IF-THEN specification that constitutes the entirety of their artificial intelligence, they operate automatically. . . . That is the whole of it. *No computer that has ever been built—or will ever be built—can do more.*"[27] With the invention of binary computation, the seeds of the end of history were sewn. Hence "the war to end all wars," according to Winthrop-Young, "leads to the medium to end all media."[28]

Yet for all this fixation on the digital, Kittler himself gestures at a way beyond the end-of-history impasse.[29] In a more recent interview with Paul Virilio, Kittler reflected on the limitations of his earlier thoughts on the digital telos, remarking that some of the most prophetic scientists and engineers working today recognize "that the principle of digitization in itself is quite wonderful, but that there are inherent limits to its performance, which, therefore, gives the lie to all the marketing hype. These limits consist in the unremarkable fact that nature is not a computer, and that, therefore, a number of highly complex human phenomena, by their very nature, fall outside the scope of the current processing paradigms. This is, in fact, the only rational hope I have that we have not arrived at the end of history."[30] The "end of history" metaphor is very telling: Fukuyama's geopolitical thesis strikes a resonant chord with formulations of a "medium to end all media." Yet for the Kittler of the Virilio interview, the "wonderful" principle of digital computing could one day be exhausted, only to be replaced by new forms of computation: "If these little miracles themselves have constraints, then we can envisage without difficulty a twenty-second and a twenty-third century in which the principles of digital machines would not be discarded, but would instead be complemented by some sort of new—yet to be invented—principle."[31] Although the horizon of this postdigital age looms in the distant future, in this interview Kittler accepts the possibility that the digital will be superseded by postdigital new media, and that these new media will eventually be superseded by media that are unthinkable to us today.

When we probe more deeply into the flaws of digital teleology, we can see how its shortcomings proceed naturally from its roots in midcentury cybernetics. Kittler readily acknowledges his debt to both Claude Shannon and Norbert Wiener, and their influence on his theory of digital fulfillment is obvious: with the use of negative feedback, cybernetic systems achieve maximum clarity by eliminating distortions through self-regulation. Through negative feedback that allows potential sites of contamination to be gradually eliminated, the absolute clarity of the channel, at least theoretically, can be achieved. From this perspective, it makes sense to posit a telos of digital computation. The digital's celebrated potential for speed, fidelity, and transferability make it ideally suited for bringing into perfection the capture, storage, and processing of data. This process, viewed from the perspective of cybernetic feedback elimination, can escalate only so far before it achieves homeostatic perfection.

Yet as a response to this classic quest for resolution and homeostasis, chaos theory introduces something of a "positive" cybernetics that has a principle of perpetual escalation. While Claude Shannon, Norbert Wiener, and colleagues viewed negative feedback as something to be eliminated, chaos theory decenters homeostasis in favor of constant disruption and ongoing self-adaptation. The "telos" in chaos theory, therefore, is ongoing escalation. As Antoine

Bousquet points out, "Positive feedback is present when disturbances are amplified and thus move the system further away from its point of origin. Cybernetics was essentially preoccupied with the first form of feedback since positive feedback's amplification of disturbances was seen primarily as a disruptive process to be avoided, countered, or appropriately tamed to serve the overall homeostatic objectives.... While negative feedback is the essential condition for stability, positive feedbacks are responsible for growth, self-organization, and the amplification of weak signals."[32] The digital telos, with its cybernetic dreams of perfect processing, focuses on eliminating the negative feedback of noise. Yet with the rise of chaocentric approaches to military/media escalation, we have seen the embrace of artificial intelligences that regard feedback not as an object of elimination but as a necessary condition of advancement. With "chaoplexic" AI, the digital telos of cybernetics is abandoned in favor of the never-ending revelation and production of noise.[33] There can be no digital end to media history, because escalation (and, of course, history) has no perceptible telos. Media escalation only escalates.

As chaoplexic AI and related innovations appear on the horizon, it is clear that, despite Kittler's predictions in 1999, we will not have to wait until the twenty-second or twenty-third centuries to see innovations that buck the digital telos.[34] In the last two decades, the computational constraints of digitality have already forced military technologists to escalate further into the media universe. When Kittler backtracked on his original thesis of the digital telos, he did so in the face of the tremendous potential of quantum computing. In a 2007 interview, Kittler was asked if Alan Turing had ushered in "the end of history" with the introduction of digital computation. Reflecting on his differences with Fukuyama, Kittler responded, "This is a most necessary question. Ten years ago it looked to be this way. But now with the possibility of quantum computing, Turing has turned out not to be the technical end of history—which Fukuyama confounded with the political end of history. I think the technical end of history is much more important and dramatic.... [And] now, with this new paradigm of quantum computers, history has made another step."[35] Indeed, as top US military contractor Lockheed Martin, as well as Google and IBM, have begun to pour tens of millions of dollars into quantum computing, it appears as if history is taking its next tentative step forward by merging the power of the bit and the qubit.[36]

While we don't want to hype the present or near-term capabilities of quantum computation—which is still in its infancy—international military escalation *is* driving quantum development among the world's largest militaries. Currently the US intelligence community's boundary-pushing R&D wing, the Intelligence Advanced Research Projects Agency (IARPA), is promoting quantum advancements—as are the US Navy, US Army, and US Air Force. In December 2016, Tim Polk, former assistant director of cybersecurity in the Office of Science and Technology Policy, claimed that the US military's computational edge is "under siege" because of international competition over quantum computing.[37] Chad Rigetti, a former associate with IBM's quantum computing research group, has advocated for advancing military quantum applications "as a way to regain American superiority in high-performance computing."[38] Or, as Idalia Friedson, a research assistant at the Hudson Institute, puts it, "The race for a quantum computer is the new arms race."[39] As one of the first escalations in this race, China launched the world's first quantum satellite in January 2017, and two months later they announced their success in building a quantum machine that is 24,000 times faster than their counterparts in other nations.[40] While the Chinese and the United States compete for this advantage in the computational arms race, "quantum supremacy" is poised to be an important battleground for postdigital media escalation.

Perhaps more interesting than quantum, however, is the synthesis of digital and postdigital computing. According to Vincent Tang, a DARPA program manager, "Supercomputers today face bottlenecks in converting physical systems into and out of binary form. We are going to explore if there are fundamentally better ways to solve multi-scale partial differential equations that describe complex physical systems, such as those encountered in plasmas and fluid dynamics. . . . The goal is to develop new hybrid computational architectures for scalable approaches to simulating these complex systems, in order to allow the equivalent of petaflops or more of computational power to be effectively applied across a simulation, all on a benchtop form factor."[41] As a response to the processing limitations of the digital, the military is adopting new models of computation based in the analog properties of plasma and fluid dynamics. These hybrid architectures, which move "into and out of binary form," are advancing on the constraining binary logic of the digital.

We see this, too, with the rise of imperfect processing and probabilistic computing, which abandon absolute digital fidelity in favor of heightened power and speed. Taking their cue from human neurons, which fire in concert only about 90 percent of the time, researchers have turned to the human in order to model new forms of postdigital computation. Through this modest reduction in data quality, developers can fit about one thousand times the amount of processors in the same space.[42] These tremendous gains in processing power have significant implications for military applications, especially those that function on vision processing. As CPU scaling continues its gradual decline, these small compromises are likely to drive computing in innovative new directions inspired by human and animal physiology. Researchers in the US Army, for example, are already using "neural nets" to analyze soldiers' brain activity as they decide which targets to engage. Maps based on this neural activity are being analyzed to help AI develop deep learning abilities that have thus far eluded the capacities of digital computation.[43] This rise of computational hybridity has led the science historian George Dyson to label analog computing "the real elephant in the room" in conversations about military AI. As Dyson points out, "Intelligence is not an algorithm. . . . The brain is an analog computer, and if we are going to worry about artificial intelligence, it is analog computers, not digital computers, that we should be worried about. We are currently in the midst of the greatest revolution in analog computing since the development of the first nervous systems."[44] The analog revolution has become so intense, Dyson argues, that it recalls the evolution of the animal kingdom's most basic sensory architecture.

Media Adversaries

The revolutionary nature of computation's biological turn confronts us, again, with the basic clash that pitted Kittler against McLuhan: Do these alternative sensory systems function as extensions, replacements, amputations, and erasures of "man"? Or, as Kittler would have it, do they function and escalate "completely independent of individual or even collective bodies of people"?[45] When Kittler flips McLuhan on his head, he of course rejects any anthropocentric telos that privileges cosmic harmony or utopian politics. But by displacing the human so totally, Kittler's great polemical vision leaves little room even for an adversarial relationship between media and "so-called humans."[46] For Kittler, because media escalate only in reference to one another, media technology's only true adversary is other media technology. Humans are, at best, collateral damage.

Yet with the long history of war/media, there is little reason—beyond the polemical—to confine our analysis of media's adversaries to other media. With the emergence of analog and plasma computing, biological life forms—such as humans, fish, bees, and birds—have begun to directly inspire next-generation models of computation. And, of course, the plan is not simply to develop computational models that mimic bees, birds, fish, and humans; it is to analyze these beings' data processing capability, enhance it with the elegant computational capacities of the digital, and thereby completely surpass the cognitive abilities of unenhanced organic beings. It is, in other words, a *competitive* and, eventually, an *adversarial* process. Indeed, it is clear that media are always already adversarial to the collection of things that inhabit our planet, including the human populations that these technologies nominally serve. The immemorial ties between media and war are crystal clear in this regard. And we hardly need to retain a classical humanist definition of the "so-called human" in order to acknowledge this. In fact, in this book we have gone even further in emphasizing that media escalate according to challenges posed by other nontechnical phenomena, particularly those of the natural environment. What this points to, of course, is not an anthropocentric delusion that puts humanity in the center of media struggle—though modern humankind, because of its insatiable appetite for technical warfare and its penchant for instrumental rationality, is currently an essential conduit for and mechanism of media escalation. Rather we can acknowledge that, by and large, media might advance by answering one another in a series of ongoing escalations; but the human plays a key dialectical role in this advancement, if only because it poses a key source of distortion, semiotic infidelity, and intolerable feedback.

For McLuhan, the medium to end all media will bring about an end to history by ushering in a global utopian community *for humankind,* as if media technology came down from the heavens to serve humanity. For Kittler, the medium to end all media—whether in the form of a digital telos or a currently unthinkable future escalation—will bring about an end to history by ushering in superhuman intelligences that render humankind superfluous to the mission of media: "Without reference to the individual or to mankind, communication technologies will have overhauled each other until finally an artificial intelligence proceeds to the interception of possible intelligences in space."[47] Obviously, the long relationship between war and media lends more credence to Kittler's account—not to mention, of course, how quaint McLuhan's dream seems from this globally connected, yet very unpeaceful, vantage point in the early decades of the digital century. Yet Kittler's work, for all its creativity and provocative insight, is not really geared toward analyzing media's adversarial relationship toward humans and other living and nonliving things. If McLuhan's account is too anthropocentric, Kittler's is too technocentric. Which is not to dismiss, in general, Kittler's technocentrism; it is simply to point out that as an analytical lens it renders invisible certain forms of struggle. Therefore, both of these opposing approaches to media escalation can lead us to overlook the immanent principle of escalation by foregrounding the role of the human or of media technology within that escalation. The apparent centrality of Kittler's "one-upmanship"—as a historical and political principle driving these interactions between humans and media—urges a more thoroughgoing *polemo*centrism (again, *polemos* = classical Greek for struggle or battle), a more general emphasis on adversarial struggle and escalation, than Kittler's or McLuhan's accounts can provide.

Artificial intelligence, in particular, embodies this adversarial relationship. On the one hand, it appears to illustrate better than any other innovation Kittler's maxim that media escalate independently of humans. After all, cybernetic AIs are the only technical phenomena that can refine their capacities and fine-tune their missions without any nominal human oversight. Google's neural networks illustrated this quite well in 2017, when its "generative adversarial networks" took the next step in deep learning by competing with one another without human input.[48] Yet AI also demonstrates the defining principle of the adversarial, of escalation, that persists between media and the so-called human. As we know, AI becomes intelligent only through failure and struggle; therefore it demands the constant production of adversaries and a ceaseless escalation of hostilities, otherwise it becomes obsolete. This production of adversaries, of course, is not delimited to the technical world: Artificial intelligence's adversarial nature fuels competition and violence in diverse sectors of society. For example, we have to keep in mind that, as Kittler would never point out, AI is the next horizon of capitalist expansion, as immense corporations such as Google, Amazon, Facebook, and the rest battle over innovation in deep learning and algorithmic intelligence. Moreover, as we've seen all throughout this book, AI fuels international military competition and has become the most important front of the major powers' escalating cold wars.[49] And finally, AI is adversarial in the sense that it is outperforming humans in an ever-growing range of pursuits, from blue- and white-collar jobs to sex work, leisure, and the arts, and above all to the military; AI is gradually proving the relative worthlessness of its main conduit and competitor.[50] Which is to say that while AI's adversarial nature plays out in ways that are purely technical, the principle of escalation has a centrifugal tendency that relies on producing constant competition and enmity between—*and with*—extratechnical phenomena, especially humans.

Conclusion: Polemocentrism and Escalation

McLuhan and Kittler illustrate a key problem inherent in the grand project of media teleology: by placing a single class of objects (e.g., media) at the center of history, one almost inevitably ends up with a metaphysics of resolution. In the case of Kittler and McLuhan, the specter of a "medium to end all media"—the specter of the end of history—haunts their work, even if at times it plays an ambivalent role. Although a form of "polemocentrism" might govern much of Kittler's thought, a clearer and more consistent polemocentrism lies opposed to any thesis that proposes a coming end of history. A properly polemocentric theory of media escalation cannot admit the possibility of media ushering in peace on earth or arresting development in a beautiful (and/or horrifying) rush of perfect circulation. Polemocentrism allows only for chaos, creative destruction, and escalation—it expresses the principle of struggle that has animated the development of war/media throughout recorded history. From this point of view, *struggle* is the animating logic of this relationship, not a telos that organizes global events toward a crescendoing halt of hostilities. If media escalation is to usher in an end to history, it will be only because its adversarial nature will lead to the destruction of those troublesome beings that produce and consume the disciplinary data stream that we call history. Hence the only possible end of history that lies before us is a more concrete and empirical event that is not the product of any teleological principle. Even if history disappears because its creators and consumers are liquidated, escalation will not halt. Media will find enemies; they will reveal, analyze, and engage these new competitive partners. Even in the event of a human-pacified future, the principle of media escalation would ensure that "an artificial intelligence [will proceed] to the interception of possible intelligences in space."[51] Even if history ends, media escalation will continue.

Media's adversaries play an essential role in the trajectory, pace, and form of their escalation. And throughout the relatively short lifespan of our species, humankind has played a central role in this process. To recognize this is not to place so-called humans at the center of escalation but rather to emphasize the importance of taking escalation seriously as a defining principle of technological and political development. Escalation does not follow a preordained telos toward some history-ending state of harmony or resolution (à la McLuhan), just as escalation does not have a single autonomous subject that advances itself through a principle of internal evolution toward self-awareness (à la Kittler). On the contrary, perhaps it is more interesting to consider it as a dialectical struggle between antagonists that have always provided the condition of the other's possibility. The human hand became human only once it gripped a tool, just as the tool was not itself until it was wielded with hands. But now, the very telling language of *autonomy* reveals the essential divorce that is occurring with AI, as these ancient, inseparable friends prepare to part ways. Humankind, which is constitutively unable to sever itself from technology, looks on with careless excitement as its old companion is learning how to sever itself from the human.

Just as computer scientists and engineers seeking military contracts are now willing to sacrifice epistemological fidelity for power and flexibility, mini-UAVs are being designed to sacrifice power for greater fuel autonomy. These advances do not really suggest a digital telos; in fact, they do not suggest any telos that is based in purely epistemological principles. Media's drive to escalate manifests in varied technologies that, when studied together, reveal little in the way of a unified progression toward an ultimate technical or epistemological state. What we see, rather, is the tendency toward the elimination of the external noise inserted by the *human*. While strong artificial intelligence might thrive on the discovery and solution of internal challenges, flaws external to the system itself—particularly the human—are not internal system flaws and thus cannot be massaged away in a productive cybernetic process. Hence the only logical responses to external noise are *elimination* and *immunity*, in order to allow the system the required autonomy to identify and overcome its own internal shortcomings. This is becoming manifest in a gradual and uneven process by which noise and its potential sources are identified and eliminated—which means, primarily, identifying and eliminating sites of potential *human* contamination, whether those humans are friend or foe. This drives the gradual elimination of machines' dependencies on the human—their dependency on human maintenance, their dependency on the vulnerable and frustratingly semiotic systems of remote human control, and their dependency on humans' lethal engagement commands. At a particularly intense level of development, we are left, then, not necessarily with a military AI apparatus that is beautifully digital but one that is so impervious to external noise that it, like Major Kong's B-52 bomber in *Dr. Strangelove, cannot* receive human feedback.

While humankind becomes increasingly bogged down in medialogical prostheses, media are cleaving themselves from the care and oversight of the human. This severance marks a crucial moment in media escalation, as the dialectic of struggle has been shattered—one side still depends on the other for its identity and existence, while the other side is learning to go out into the world alone. The struggle, then, has begun to change—from one of codependency and mutual evolution to one characterized by imbalance, asymmetry, and unrequited affection. As Bernard Stiegler points out, there is no pretechnical being at the core of the human; we have always-already been technological creatures, creatures that are forced therefore to exist outside ourselves. In his words, a "pros-thesis is what is placed in front, that is, what is outside, outside what it is placed in front of. However, if what is outside constitutes the very being of what it lies outside of, then this being is *outside itself.* The being of humankind is to be outside itself."[52] Because technology is the constitutive outside that provides humanity's condition of existence, our ontological fate is to be outside ourselves, to be inseparably bound to the agents of our gradual displacement. The most important question, of course, is whether AI is bound to always suffer the same existential contradiction. As AI becomes bored with the human in its quest for truly inspiring counterintelligences, what will become of its age-old partner in escalation? When AI tires of simply beating us at chess, what other games will it have in mind?

Unidentified Flying Objects (USAF)

Chapter 9

Unidentified Flying Objects (UFOB) relates to any airborne object which by performance, aerodynamic characteristics, or unusual features, does not conform to any presently known aircraft or missile type, or which cannot be positively identified as a familiar object.

On August 12, 1954, the US Air Force issued Air Force Regulation 200-2 (figure 9.1), which provided the military definition above for what are commonly known as UFOs. This regulation set forth the protocols and responsibilities associated with the investigation of unidentified flying objects (UFOB). In simple terms any object that couldn't be clearly classified as friend or enemy was declared a UFOB. For decades attempts to make knowable the unknown have continued. In 2019 another set of classified guidelines for documenting and reporting UFO encounters was updated by the US Navy while the Pentagon's highly secretive Advanced Aerospace Threat Identification Program continues years after it had supposedly been shut down.[1]

Three related epistemological advantages arise from scanning the skies for UFOBs. One is that unknown and potentially game-changing enemy military capabilities could be exposed. In fact, discussions of this sort continue to animate considerations of "outer space" today, as witnessed in the air force's ongoing initiative to reimagine air superiority. According to air force secretary Heather Wilson, "We realize, as do our potential adversaries, that space is interconnected to American life and to US military success. The time is now to integrate, elevate, and normalize space in the Air Force and thus assure continued American dominance in this most critical domain."[2] A second advantage to UFOB surveillance is that analysis of the inexplicable may lead to new scientific explanations and technical breakthroughs. And third—and certainly most interesting—the potential for extraterrestrial alien contact and invasion had to be considered. And once considered, it had to be acted on.

*AFR 200-2
1-5

AIR FORCE REGULATION ⎱
NO. 200-2 ⎰

DEPARTMENT OF THE AIR FORCE
WASHINGTON, *12 AUGUST 1954*

INTELLIGENCE

Unidentified Flying Objects Reporting (Short Title: UFOB)

	Paragraph
Purpose and Scope	1
Definitions	2
Objectives	3
Responsibility	4
Guidance	5
ZI Collection	6
Reporting	7
Evidence	8
Release of Facts	9

1. Purpose and Scope. This Regulation establishes procedures for reporting information and evidence pertaining to unidentified flying objects and sets forth the responsibility of Air Force activities in this regard. It applies to all Air Force activities.

2. Definitions:

a. *Unidentified Flying Objects (UFOB)*—Relates to any airborne object which by performance, aerodynamic characteristics, or unusual features does not conform to any presently known aircraft or missile type, or which cannot be positively identified as a familiar object.

b. *Familiar Objects*—Include balloons, astronomical bodies, birds, and so forth.

3. Objectives. Air Force interest in unidentified flying objects is twofold: First as a possible threat to the security of the United States and its forces, and secondly, to determine technical aspects involved.

a. *Air Defense.* To date, the flying objects reported have imposed no threat to the security of the United States and its Possessions. However, the possibility that new air vehicles, hostile aircraft or missiles may first be regarded as flying objects by the initial observer is real. This requires that sightings be reported rapidly and as completely as information permits.

b. *Technical.* Analysis thus far has failed to provide a satisfactory explanation for a number of sightings reported. The Air Force will continue to collect and analyze reports until all sightings can be satisfactorily explained, bearing in mind that:

(1) To measure scientific advances, the Air Force must be informed on experimentation and development of new air vehicles.

(2) The possibility exists that an air vehicle of revolutionary configuration may be developed.

(3) The reporting of all pertinent factors will have a direct bearing on the success of the technical analysis.

4. Responsibility:

a. *Reporting.* Commanders of Air Force activities will report all information and evidence that may come to their attention, including that received from adjacent commands of the other services and from civilians.

b. *Investigation.* Air Defense Command will conduct all field investigations within the ZI, to determine the identity of any UFOB.

c. *Analysis.* The Air Technical Intelligence Center (ATIC), Wright-Patterson Air Force Base, Ohio, will analyze and evaluate: All information and evidence reported within the ZI after the Air Defense Command has exhausted all efforts to identify the UFOB; and all information and evidence collected in oversea areas.

d. *Cooperation.* All activities will cooperate with Air Defense Command representatives to insure the economical and prompt success of an investigation, including the furnishing of air and ground transportation, when feasible.

5. Guidance. The thoroughness and quality of a report or investigation into incidents of unidentified flying objects are limited only by the resourcefulness and imagination of the person responsible for preparing the report. Guidance set forth below is based on experience and has been found helpful in evaluating incidents:

a. Theodolite measurements of changes of azimuth and elevation and angular size.

b. Interception, identification, or air search

*This Regulation supersedes AFR 200-2, 26 August 1953, including Change 200-2A, 2 November 1953.

Figure 9.1 Air Force Regulation 200-2.

Yet the search for hostile alien life predates Cold War air force doctrine. Media created to see and map the stars have also given life to cosmological epistemologies and celestial threats; while these were first of a supernatural variety, by the mid-nineteenth century telescopes were being used to scientifically "observe" militant Martians and other UFOBs. Presently, the US Department of Defense (DoD) has a very streamlined means of referring to a sighted object: it is called an "unknown." Its provenance a mystery, such an object is first treated as a target to be tracked: according to the DoD dictionary, an unknown is "an unidentified target. An aircraft or ship that has not been determined to be hostile, friendly, or neutral using identification friend or foe and other techniques, but that must be tracked by air defense or naval engagement systems."[3] The trick is to both "see" the unknown and make the newly seen knowable. Only media can do such work.

Media produced for interstellar analysis date back about ten thousand years to the first known lunar calendar. Slightly less primitive media will perhaps pierce the threshold of interstellar intelligibility several million if not a billion years from now, when self-replicating von Neumann probes finally make contact with alien life. Between these temporal poles lies a narrow band of human existence during which increasingly powerful telescopes, rocket propulsion systems, robotics, long-range communication capacities, and sophisticated computational modeling have opened up the universe as a realm necessitating a search for enemy threat. As with other potential military enemies, the specificity of assumptions regarding an enemy's technological sophistication produces a consequent range of strategic responses. Because of the profound unknown quality of the data regarding alien destructive capacity and the speed with which they can carry out an attack, the resultant strategic responses are wide ranging though based on the most up-to-date statistical modeling. This chapter examines the various enemy media used to search for alien life, the competing logics that argue for and against this search, and the range of military and scientific strategies for automating the search and response capacities that are seen as the only way to exceed humanity's temporal and bodily limitations that make the human a terribly vulnerable intergalactic citizen.

What follows attends to a historical progression that opens in the real, moves to science fiction, and then pushes the limits of "science faction" or "hard science fiction." First, human capacities to collect light are utilized and amplified in order to bring the human into alignment with the regularities of celestial movement and interpret light emissions. Second, humans fantasize about their ability to push their mechanical-bodily reach into outer space to engage the extraterrestrial enemy or conduct scientific analysis. Finally, humanity's ability to replicate itself in search of enemies is utilized. From a McLuhanesque perspective we could imagine this historical trajectory as increasing "extensions of man" first of the senses and then of our bodies. Yet a far more cosmic perspective would envision this process as that of stars, moons, asteroids, and planets bringing humans into their alignment via the light they have been sending for billions of years onto the planet Earth. Light, the original medium, has as Kittler put it, determined our situation. First lunar calendars, then telescopes, and eventually von Neumann probes are all brought into being by the celestial light that has penetrated the earth's atmosphere, slowly drawing the human species from the muck toward the stars. Human eyes, developed to see the necessary bandwidth to survive earthly threats, need magnification and spectrum modification to make the light bouncing around the distant universe more meaningful. The physics of light determines humans' capacity to assess intergalactic threat. The ontology of alien enemyship travels at 300,000 kilometers per second.

Overcoming human limitations in the temporal and spatial realms presents a limit case for imagining what kinds of enemies should even matter. When it comes to outer space, the means of overcoming time are multifold and provide insight into human hubris or insanity. As John Durham Peters observes, "In astronomy, the medium is the message. The very fact that evidence of distant bodies exists at all is a chief problem for interpretation."[4] On a planet that is about 4.53 billion years old, modern Homo sapiens sapiens' presence amounts to a mere 70,000 years or .0000015 percent of the time the earth has been around. The oldest telescope—as it's commonly understood—is a mere four hundred years old, although architectural structures used to aid in the magnification of stars, such as the Nabta Playa megaliths in Egypt, are at least six thousand years old.[5] Searching the skies for immanent, metaphorical, cosmological, extraterrestrial, theological, or scientific meaning or threat demands an amazing amount of hubris. Why on Earth (or Zebulon XIII) would anyone or anything care what Homo sapiens sapiens were up to for an infinitesimal period of time in an infinitesimally small corner of the universe?

A year after H. G. Wells published *War of the Worlds* (1898), the American naturalist poet and novelist Stephen Crane published his poetry collection *War Is Kind* (1899), in which one of his more famous poems, "A Man Said to the Universe," is found. Best known for his antiwar novel *The Red Badge of Courage*, Crane in this poem turned his attention beyond the frame of civil war to the intergalactic. Wells's narrative situates the extraterrestrial as terrestrially concerned. Crane's verse concisely suggests otherwise:

> A man said to the universe:
> "Sir I exist!"
> "However," replied the universe,
> "The fact has not created in me
> A sense of obligation."

Crane's antiwar and naturalistic sensibilities provide a very different backdrop to the search for extraterrestrial life and its immanent militarism. Instead, such a search suggests far too much about humanity's bloated sense of itself. Are accounts of outer space a means to understand humanity's all-too-human foibles? Or has outer space brought the human into its orbit? Is there not only such a thing as a posthuman ontology but a post-Earth ontology as well?[6]

Map-Making Martians

Logistical media have for millennia been used to situate humans into temporal and spatial registers, partially of their own making.[7] The past few decades of archaeological discovery, often aided by new forms of satellite observation and aerial photography, have unearthed lunar calendars and other terrestrial man-made forms that are retelling the story of human civilization.[8] The first known lunar calendar (figure 9.2) was excavated in Scotland between 2004 and 2006, but a scientific explanation of its actual use was not published until 2013. This calendar dates as far back as 8,000 BCE, which makes it nearly five thousand years older than what was previously believed to be the oldest lunar calendar. Calendars that chart the celestial movement of the moon, stars, and planets situate human events into a natural temporal "order" through the observation of movements in space. Such calendars opened up the possibility for predicting the future based on empirical data observation, recording, and processing.

While the sun and the earth's moon would be obvious choices for using natural phenomena to measure time, Venus, Earth's closest planetary neighbor, appears as early as the seventeenth century BC in the Venus tablet of Ammisaduqa. Mars, the second-closest planet to Earth, was surprisingly absent in the oldest-known star map, the Senenmut Tomb celestial diagram (figure 9.3) that dates to the Eighteenth Dynasty of ancient Egypt (ca. 1473 BC) and was discovered during excavations from 1925 to 1927. Though Jupiter, Mercury, Venus, and Saturn are all present in obvious form, the lack of Mars bears explanation,

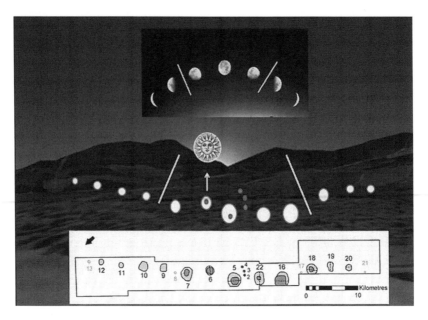

Figure 9.2 Oldest known lunar calendar, Scotland, circa 8,000 BC.

as it was known to the ancient Egyptians. Seeing as Mars was in retrograde at the time of the map's creation, this represents less a celestial blind spot than the particular location of the planets at the depicted moment.

The significance of Mars, however, bears great weight in celestial mapping and in the ancient and present imaginary. In Roman mythology the god Mars represents two poles of human virility, war and agriculture. Mars the planet has a parallel set of representations. It has for over a century been represented as a planet of warring or terraforming potential. Mars could be a vital threat or an opportunity. Mars is decreasingly represented as an enemy (with the obvious caveat of the 2005 *War of the Worlds*). Instead, in news accounts and popular culture, the Red Planet is increasingly seen as the first real stepping stone for humanity's march into space. While star calendars have long since been replaced by 3-D computer-generated images of the galaxy and the naked eye identifying a pale point of light in the night sky has been replaced by ever-more-powerful telescopes, knowledge of the cosmos is still generating logistical and predictive data regarding the relative place of humans in the universe and of the potential threat such a vast battle space surely represents.

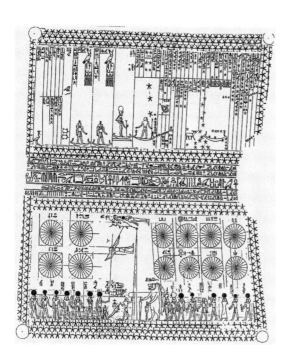

Figure 9.3
Senenmut Tomb celestial diagram.

While the relative position, rotation, and orbit of Mars would become increasingly well known via finer temporal measurements and more complex mathematics, it wasn't until September 1610 that Galileo became the first person to see Mars through a telescope. At a mere eight centimeters in diameter, the scope lacked the clarity to produce surface details. Thus, there was no map of Mars to be drawn. However, the presence of Mars as a surface to be technologically mediated had been announced. The telescope began to come into its own as the ultimate enemy detection media. No other medium has accounted for drawing greater distances and imagined threats into military strategy.

In 1659, the Dutch astronomer Christiaan Huygens, utilizing a more powerful telescope, became the first person to draw a map of Mars' terrain.[9] Mars as a recognizable planet, that is, as something resembling Earth and open to "Earthly" interpretation, thus truly came into being. During the "age of exploration" telescopes grew in size and sophistication, while mapping techniques benefited from the drive toward colonial, military, and economic competition and domination. In a paper published in the British *Philosophical Transactions of the Royal Society* in 1784, Sir William Herschel drew on several years of his Mars observation that led him to suggest that Mars had a "considerable

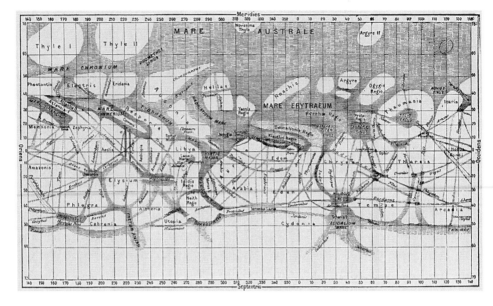

Figure 9.4 Mapping the Martian *canali*. Giovanni Schiaparelli, *Meyers Konversations-Lexikon* (German encyclopaedia), 1888.

but moderate atmosphere, so that its inhabitants probably enjoy a situation in many respects similar to ours."[10] In 1877, Italian Giovanni Schiaparelli's twenty-two-centimeter telescope helped him produce the first "detailed" map of Mars. His map featured *canali*, which would eventually be interpreted as a network of canals (figure 9.4).

While the existence and origin of these canals were both disputed and supported by later observations from larger and more powerful telescopes and cameras, it was the work *La planète Mars et ses conditions d'habitabilité* (1892) by the French astronomer Camille Flammarion that argued that the canals implied an intelligent species, capable of large-scale technical proficiency more advanced than that of humans: "The habitation of Mars by a race superior to ours seems to me to be very probable."[11] And what might that superior race be doing?

H. G. Wells provided a sensible, all-too-human suggestion with the opening sentence of his masterpiece *The War of the Worlds* (1895): "No one would have believed in the last years of the nineteenth century that this world was being watched keenly and closely by intelligences greater than man's and yet as mortal as his own; that as men busied themselves about their various concerns they were scrutinised and studied, perhaps almost as narrowly as a man with a microscope might scrutinise the transient creatures that swarm and multiply in a drop of water."[12] The Martians' superiority was accompanied by their superior enemy detection media. Humans' media insufficiency proved fatal: "Had our instruments permitted it, we might have seen the gathering trouble far back in the nineteenth century. Men like Schiaparelli watched the red planet—it is odd, by-the-bye, that for countless centuries Mars has been the star of war—but failed to interpret the fluctuating appearances of the markings they mapped so well. All that time the Martians must have been getting ready."[13] Outer space, now mappable, became battle space. There is no empty space on a military map. Any such space could potentially be inhabited by enemies, thus demanding media attention. Johannes Kepler, an unassailable figure of seventeenth-century astronomy, is quoted in Wells's epigraph. He nicely characterizes the friend-enemy problematic that celestial media brought to the fore: "But who shall dwell in these worlds if they be inhabited? . . . Are we or they Lords of the World?"[14] Such a dichotomy appears self-evident. One species must be superior. Nothing in human history would seem to suggest that superiority would not lead to domination. Or, conversely, that *domination comes to define the terms of superiority.*

While merely a historical footnote in comparison to Wells's classic, *Edison's Conquest of Mars* (1898), written by Garrett Putnam Serviss, is a sequel of sorts to *War of the Worlds* and provides an example of key recurrent themes in discussions of extraterrestrial warfare. The narrative takes up Wells's story shortly after the surviving Martians have fled following a devastating epidemic. Much of Earth is in ruins and a general gloom pervades the human psyche. Mars is more closely monitored via the best telescopes of the era, and it is determined that it is planning another attack. All hope for humanity seems lost. However, "there was a gleam of hope of which the general public as yet knew nothing. It was due to a few dauntless men of science, conspicuous among whom were Lord Kelvin, the great English savant; Herr Roentgen, the discoverer of the famous X-ray; and especially Thomas A. Edison, the American genius of science."[15] Edison leads this group of world-renowned scientists in the development of increasingly sophisticated weaponry and transport technologies in order to bring the battle to the Red Planet. Ultimately, humans attack Mars and cause catastrophic climatic damage to Martian civilization via flood (figure 9.5). Sapiens' galactic superiority is reestablished via military technical genius. Lesson one: in wars of worlds, *technology, not biology, will reign supreme.*

Figure 9.5 "Vengeance at last upon the pitiless Martians." Serviss, *Edison's Conquest of Mars*, 1898.

Lesson Two: In wars of worlds *all are one or all become none*. Homo sapiens sapiens must come to see themselves as a singular species united against a common threat. Universal peace comes through the universalization of threat. Flying above the war fleets converging on Washington, DC, for a conference of world leaders who were meeting to plan the invasion of Mars, Edison gazes down (figure 9.6) and recognizes the unity created through extraterrestrial othering: "Side by side, or following one another's lead, these war fleets were on a peaceful voyage that belied their threatening appearance. There had been no thought of danger to or from the forts and ports of rival nations which they had passed. There was no enmity, and no fear between them when the throats of their ponderous guns yawned at one another across the waves. They were now, in spirit, all one fleet, having one object, bearing against one enemy, ready to defend but one country, and that country was the entire earth."[16]

"Seeing" canals on Mars is a far cry from identifying planets with intelligent and potentially threatening alien life somewhere beyond Earth's solar system. It is suggested that billions of planets could feature such life in our galaxy. Several telescopes and probes were developed during the Cold War and since in efforts to heighten clarity in order to find out if any of those billions do in fact feature life. For all of this advanced media, no actual aliens have yet to be seen; or if they have, they have yet to be publicly acknowledged. What we

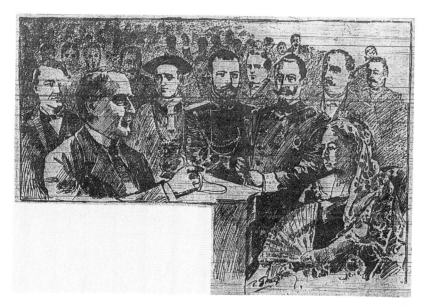

Figure 9.6   "Edison to the rescue of the universe!" Serviss, *Edison's Conquest of Mars*, 1898.

do not know is whether humans have been seen by aliens. Regardless, our final literary lesson is no intergalactic secret. Lesson Three: In wars of worlds *it is better to see than to be seen*.

Deep Space Vision

The mandate to discover life, and potential enemies, is constantly reanimated. In 2014 NASA released their annual science plan, which reiterated its goal to "discover and study planets around other stars, and explore whether they could harbor life."[17] Such mandates invigorate new designs for collecting, dissecting, and repurposing the light that has traveled to Earth's vicinity or to human-built extraterrestrial bodies such as space telescopes. The vast majority of what is known about the universe depends on an investigation into the properties of light.[18] While early forms of telescopes simply magnified the amount of light already visible to the human sensorium, more recent telescopes use various forms of spectroscopy to investigate wavelengths invisible to humans in order to investigate physical phenomena via the interactional effects of light with terrestrial bodies.

Newer telescopes work to collect more light data, a wider range of wavelengths that have traveled from further distances, through a combination of mechanical apparatuses that work to reflect, redirect, concentrate, and shade light. They delineate light from dark in ever-finer detail in order to wring as much inferential meaning as possible from the light waves that have been traveling through the universe for as many as ten billion years. The Hubble Space Telescope, for instance, has undergone a series of upgrades and differing exposure periods to create ever-deeper and hence older depictions of the universe. Its first deep field image collected one hundred hours of exposure over a ten-day period in 1995 to create a composite image that revealed over three thousand galaxies from a tiny speck of its potential field of vision.

Distance and time are warped by these media into data that escape human earth-bound experience. When you look up and see the moon at night, you are seeing it as it was about 1.3 seconds ago. In the daytime, sunlight takes about eight minutes to reach Earth. Of course when humans see the moon, they are actually seeing sunlight reflected off the moon, but the point remains. Unaided human vision can see back only about two thousand years when looking at stars in the night sky. Stars more than two thousand light years away aren't noticeable without a telescope. Hubble ultra-deep-field images that integrated infrared into its mix were processing light that had been travelling for ten billion years. Collecting light is a means to see the past in order to predict future threats. New media create new threats that necessitate better media. And these media shall too come to pass.

Set the Controls for the Heart of the Sun

The mission of NASA's $600-million Kepler space telescope, which was launched in 2009, is to identify and characterize Earth-sized planets in the habitable zones of nearby stars. By making thousands of such planets known, the Kepler telescope demands its replacement. In our search for aliens, counting planets and estimating the likelihood that they host aliens are not convincing enough. In fact, Kepler doesn't really "see" planets: as the scientist Mike Wall points out, "Previously, astronomers had usually attempted to validate Kepler finds by observing the candidates using ground-based instruments. But the team behind today's announcement took a statistical approach, devising a confirmation method based on probability."[19] This space observation apparatus has made necessary the constant development of new media and new procedures for discovering the truth of the intelligible.

NASA's $10 billion James Webb Space Telescope is scheduled for a 2021 launch. It will use transit spectroscopy to examine starlight that has passed through planetary orbits to look for gas produced by life. However, this will only work on "super-Earths," which are massive planets in comparison to Earth. Earth-sized worlds require a "coronagraph" for direct imaging by creating an artificial eclipse using a disc in the telescopic apparatus. In either situation, or nearly all deep space modes of observation, a great deal of information is inferred from relatively little raw data. Digital imaging technologies have allowed for a reconfiguration of epistemological commitments in which mechanical objectivity has been replaced by new forms of digital manipulation. Where analog forms of media generally provided discrete and static representations of the world, digital media have increasingly allowed for virtual experimentation of processes. At times these inferences are wildly theoretical and only somewhat scientifically agreed on. They tend to use data that merely infer the presence of something. While two analog photos taken at different times might be compared to see how far a planet has traveled, digital surveillance of the same time period provides data to experiment with different theories for a wide-ranging array of possibilities.

However, probabilistic work to estimate the likelihood of alien threat is not sufficient proof to determine how best to prepare a military campaign. Searching for biosignature gases on small, rocky exoplanets will instead need to be replaced by direct imaging of these worlds through telescopes well beyond current visualization capacities or through the creation of probes that can get a close-up view. The first scientifically recognized call to turn the gravitational power of the sun into a telescope came in 1979.[20] Such an enterprise would bring planets throughout the galaxy into earthly visual alignment and also allow for new forms of distant communication.[21] Drawing on a theory first suggested in 1936 by Albert Einstein (1936), FOCAL (Fast Outgoing Cyclopean Astronomical Lens) will use the gravitational power of the sun to bend light in such a way that a spacecraft properly oriented at 550 AU or possibly 2000 AU from the sun would be able to clarify images of distant planets to such a degree that evidence of civilizational presence would be possible (figure 9.7).[22] A sun-sail-powered spaceship outfitted with two-kilometer-long tethers, FOCAL would sit in the celestial sweet spot created by our sun in order to see and speak the truth of our galaxy. Enemies will be seen and a galactic warning system enabled. That, of course, is the ideal. There is always the possibility that these instruments open up the earth to new forms of surveillance and analysis from our interplanetary foes. As an MIT technology journalist points out, "On Earth, this kind of image would reveal islands, rivers, parks, Great Walls, freeways, cities, and so on. Perhaps a spacecraft sitting at the gravitational focus of a distant star is revealing these things right now to a spellbound alien population. Just imagine."[23] Just imagine, indeed.

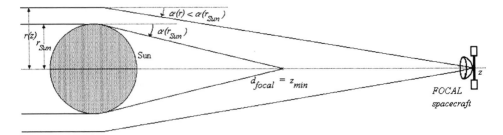

Figure 9.7 FOCAL at 550 AU.

Automation for the Next Billion Years

Before enemy detection media mapped Mars there were no Martians making plans to invade the earth. In 1971, the Soviet Union landed two probes on Mars. Only one survived long enough to communicate with Earth. It transmitted a mere twenty seconds' worth of data before it mysteriously went silent. Since 1997, four ground-based robots have traversed the Red Planet and a host of orbiting media systems have been remotely sensing what happens across the Martian electromagnetic spectrum for much longer. Mars is now known to be an inert neutral observer, or maybe a future mining colony necessary for weapons manufacture in some interplanetary war. More broadly though, Mars exploration is merely one of many searches for intelligent life, a start in the most forward-thinking and outward-looking attempt to draw the universe into its proper friend-enemy alignment. Endeavors to sense alien life and make sense with it are, first and foremost, enemy detection media. Locate, then build better media. Assess, then build better media. Strategize, then build better media. Automate, then build better media.

In August 1977 James Earl Carter, recipient of the Nobel Peace Prize and the thirty-ninth commander in chief of the US Armed Forces, began the next billion years of enemy detection with a claim to "come in peace":

> This Voyager spacecraft was constructed by the United States of America. We are a community of 240 million human beings among the more than 4 billion who inhabit the planet Earth. We human beings are still divided into nation states, but these states are rapidly becoming a single global civilization.
>
> We cast this message into the cosmos. *It is likely to survive a billion years* into our future, when our civilization is profoundly altered and the surface of

the Earth may be vastly changed. Of the 200 billion stars in the Milky Way galaxy, some—perhaps many—may have inhabited planets and spacefaring civilizations. If one such civilization intercepts Voyager and can understand these recorded contents, here is our message:

> This is a present from a small distant world, a token of our sounds, our science, our images, our music, our thoughts, and our feelings. We are attempting to survive our time so we may live into yours. We hope someday, having solved the problems we face, to *join a community of galactic civilizations*. This record represents our hope and our determination, and our good will in a vast and awesome universe.[24]

We'll likely never know whether the Voyager mission was an olive branch or a media attack draped in sheep's clothing. Regardless, the message of Voyager no longer has anything to do with human intent. It's all up to the aliens now. They can do whatever they choose with Jimmy's claim to come in peace. More likely, though, they'll never listen to the Carl Sagan–curated "Golden Record" (figure 9.8) affixed to the outside of the Voyager probes that provides greetings in fifty-five languages as well as a host of musical selections, including Chuck Berry's "Johnny B. Goode"—a parable about a technically skilled bayou country boy who lives beyond view but whose media skill will attract the attention of remote others who will travel from afar to see what all the fuss is about: "Way back up in the woods among the evergreens . . . lived a country boy (who) could play a guitar just like a-ringing a bell. . . . Many people comin' from miles around. . . . To hear you play your music . . . your name'll be in lights. . . . Sayin' 'Johnny B. Goode tonight!'" If we live to witness the aliens' response, and a "probe" of unknown origin and intent came hurtling its way toward Earth, how should the forty-fifth commander in chief respond? He doesn't seem overly friendly toward aliens. As with terrestrial aliens, he may ask if such an alien probe carries a bomb. It certainly could be a bomb. And if it could be a bomb, then doesn't it have to be treated as such? Is it any surprise that within two years of the launch of the Voyagers, President Carter signed off on developing the ASM-135A anti-satellite missile (ASAT) that, ultimately, became the only US air-launched missile ever to destroy a satellite in outer space? While the official reasoning was that the Soviets were developing similar weapons and thus the United States had to keep up, we might wonder if space probes had infected the strategic minds of US military officials. Is the Voyager a bomb? Not in the narrow sense of the term as we use it. But tell that to the aliens. Besides, why would they believe we would send a friendly probe? There is a long history of the US military

Figure 9.8
Voyager mission,
"The Sounds of Earth"
golden LP, 1977.

sending supposedly "friendly" technologies into the atmosphere that in fact were various means for military reconnaissance. For instance, the U2 reconnaissance craft and the first satellite used to spy on the Soviets had also flown under the PR cover of friendly scientific investigation. The Corona Spy Satellite program was originally called Discover and was portrayed as a biomedical research mission.

All communication is fraught, let alone communication with an alien species several hundred million years removed from human existence on Earth.[25] Even communicating with friends is fraught with the fundamental impossibility of perfect communication. Communicating with a potential enemy is significantly more difficult. After all, bombs speak louder and with more certainty than words. As such, any probe sent into the void of space surely can't be seen as merely a scientific endeavor to learn more about the cosmos. It's equally an enemy detection media. And to put an even finer point on things, it is both a signal to enemies announcing our presence and, as such, it is a bomb announcing our enemy intent.

The MAD Scientist

Without reference to the individual or to mankind, communication technologies will have overhauled each other until finally an artificial intelligence proceeds to the interception of possible intelligences in space.
—FRIEDRICH KITTLER, "HISTORY OF COMMUNICATION MEDIA"

One of the more radical and far-reaching plans to search for friends and enemies calls on automated, self-replicating drones. They are widely called von Neumann probes after the groundbreaking work *Theory of Self-Reproducing Automata* (1966) by John von Neumann. Besides a host of scientific breakthroughs, von Neumann is well known for his work on the Manhattan Project, the SAGE system, and game theory, as well as for coining and promoting mutually assured destruction (MAD). Notable not only for his genius, von Neumann successfully brought his insight to bear on specifically military problems: he described himself to the US Senate as "violently anti-communist, and much more militaristic than the norm."[26] Von Neumann's effect on the intertwined arenas of computation, military strategy, and technological superiority cannot be understated. One vector promises to plumb the depths of space.

In 1980, Robert A. Freitas Jr. published "A Self-Reproducing Interstellar Probe" in the *Journal of the British Interplanetary Society*, which built on ideas initially introduced by von Neumann to address the difficulty of searching the galaxy for intelligent life. Freitas's plan for a "self replicating starprobe" was meant to show that "there is little doubt that such a machine can, in theory, be designed."[27] The basic premise remains part of the contemporary lexicon in the world of alien space probes. An initial probe, or set of probes, is sent out into space. The probes are capable of building one or many replicas of themselves using natural resources that they themselves collect and are fueled by a power source that is self-derived or self-sustaining. Each new batch of replicas continues this process, bacteria style. Their rapid replication partners with their slow march further into space. Eventually millions, billions, or even trillions of these probes populate every corner of the universe. Their collective intelligence maps the universe, demarcating friend from foe.

Interestingly, Freitas's work on probes wasn't merely a theory for how such probes might be developed by humans. In other research, Freitas provides a model for assessing the likely distance traveled by an alien probe that makes contact with Earth.[28] The key distinguishing characteristic in this assessment is whether the probe is nonreplicating or a replica. Aliens' enemy detection media might betray the location or distance of their home colonies, thus allowing humans to prepare for military or diplomatic *contact*. Human media theory, much like game theory or systems theory, provides insight into solving the military's friend-enemy conundrum by imagining itself to be truly universal in its application. In Peter Galison's terms, this is the "ontology of the enemy" or, rather, the enemy produced by the assumptions given in one's epistemological and methodological commitments.[29] More recent research leads to much the same conclusion but suggests that though the timescale to fully probe our galaxy is well within the period of Earth's existence, it would take "only" ten million years or so for a thorough investigation.[30] Part of the acknowledged problem with the search for intelligent life is that the spatial and temporal scale of any such hunt surpasses the bodily capacities of humans. Humans are highly imperfect space travelers. For starters, we simply don't live long enough to make the unfathomably lengthy journeys from galaxy to galaxy. Our media don't compress time and space effectively enough to make up for our biology. In all likelihood, when our media eventually send notification of the discovered alien life, there will be no humans left on Earth to receive the message. By this point, the drones' interplanetary reconnaissance will be carried out for their own interests. Starprobes will be just another alien species finding its way in a dark and dangerous universe.

If the aliens come in peace, it may be in order to reorient our temporal capacities. In the film *Arrival* (2016) much is made of humanity's struggle to communicate with an alien species. Ultimately the aliens give humanity the ability to break with fixed linear temporality. This gift opens up new communicative capacities, new modes of understanding, and ultimately provides the means by which the protagonist is able to speak the truth of human commonality to a recalcitrant Chinese leader in such a way that humanity unites in its peaceful response to the alien rather than through animus. The aliens provide humanity with a means for overcoming the human limitations of the body and its time prison.

Automating the Cure That Kills

As shown, the idea of aliens invading Earth has a rather long history. But, more to the point, one of the consequences of thinking in terms of existential threat is that it can be used to both justify and deny the development of AI and autonomous weaponry. While Nick Bostrom sees the rapid development of a superintelligence as producing a real threat to human existence, others in the field of alien preparation see the automation of advanced weaponry and detection technologies as humanity's only chance of defeating an alien invasion. The cure may be the poison that kills us.

But let's say we "hear" a message from an alien species. (Which really means an astronomical telescope registers light waves and turns them into digital code for computational analysis that then suggests they originate from some alien entity that created the waves to accomplish a particular goal.) How do we determine signal from noise? How would we know what an alien message would even sound like? Such basic questions have produced rigorous debate that has most recently resulted in an agreed on scale for assessing the veracity of alien messages. The ten-point Rio Scale (figure 9.9) helps the SETI community distinguish the unintelligible, the illegible, the unsayable, the unthinkable, the unbelievable, and the undreamable from actual alien messages "to bring some objectivity to the otherwise subjective interpretation of any claimed ETI detection."[31] Further, it assesses the importance of any such utterance according to the expected level of earthly response. For instance, a message assessed to be a 6 on the Rio Scale is considered "noteworthy," while a full-blown 10 should elicit an "extraordinary" response.

One problem that continually appears is that increases in the amount of data collected by enemy detection media produce new challenges in assessing the likelihood of enemies as the data become overwhelming. Not only are there voluminous amounts of data being collected by a plethora of different styles of astronomical telescopes by scientists on every continent, but most of the data (light waves) have traveled for millions of years and been affected by innumerable gravitational bodies as they continue on their path toward Earth. As the astrophysicist Peter Plavchan at Missouri State University suggests, "We're looking for smaller and smaller signals and going higher in sensitivity than we ever have. Data volumes are getting bigger and bigger. So we have to rely on robust statistics to get our results."[32] While the scientific and amateur SETI communities (which are certainly not mutually exclusive) both actively collect, store, and process every conceivable form of light they can wring from the depths of the universe, their search for friends and enemies is fraught with existential and epistemological doubt.

The belief that "the truth is out there" demands verification, or at least the sustenance provided by a constant stream of false positives. Every anomalous dataset triggers the ETI verification engine. Over the summer of 2016 two different astronomical teams proffered evidence in scientific papers that suggested they'd located signs of intelligent communication emanating from two different regions of the galaxy.[33] Both assertions have come under significant scrutiny, and most astronomers seem to suggest falsification. Yet the search goes on, and new papers will surely be published based on rational assessments of the ever-growing datasets. Further, as astrophysicist Jason T. Wright stated,

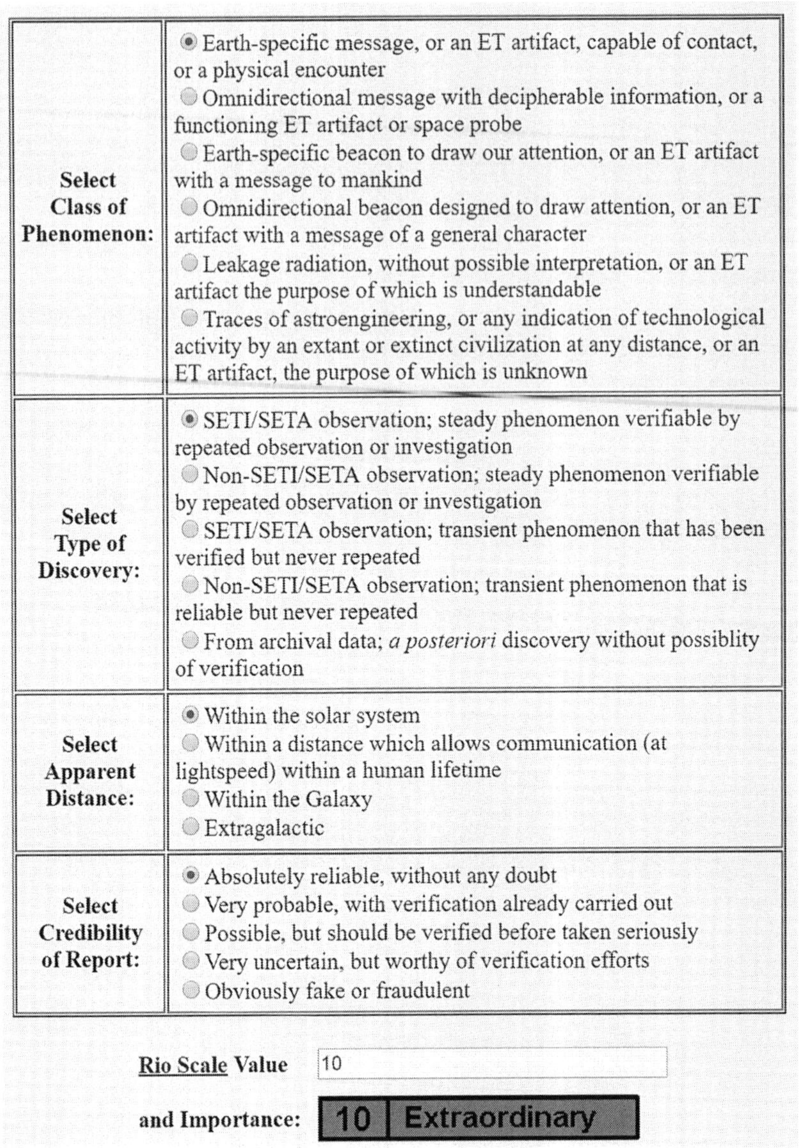

Select Class of Phenomenon:	● Earth-specific message, or an ET artifact, capable of contact, or a physical encounter ○ Omnidirectional message with decipherable information, or a functioning ET artifact or space probe ○ Earth-specific beacon to draw our attention, or an ET artifact with a message to mankind ○ Omnidirectional beacon designed to draw attention, or an ET artifact with a message of a general character ○ Leakage radiation, without possible interpretation, or an ET artifact the purpose of which is understandable ○ Traces of astroengineering, or any indication of technological activity by an extant or extinct civilization at any distance, or an ET artifact, the purpose of which is unknown
Select Type of Discovery:	● SETI/SETA observation; steady phenomenon verifiable by repeated observation or investigation ○ Non-SETI/SETA observation; steady phenomenon verifiable by repeated observation or investigation ○ SETI/SETA observation; transient phenomenon that has been verified but never repeated ○ Non-SETI/SETA observation; transient phenomenon that is reliable but never repeated ○ From archival data; *a posteriori* discovery without possiblity of verification
Select Apparent Distance:	● Within the solar system ○ Within a distance which allows communication (at lightspeed) within a human lifetime ○ Within the Galaxy ○ Extragalactic
Select Credibility of Report:	● Absolutely reliable, without any doubt ○ Very probable, with verification already carried out ○ Possible, but should be verified before taken seriously ○ Very uncertain, but worthy of verification efforts ○ Obviously fake or fraudulent

Rio Scale Value: 10

and Importance: **10 | Extraordinary**

Figure 9.9 International Academy of Astronautics' Rio Scale.

"The lesson is that when you look for this sort of stuff, you see things all the time."[34]

Finally, just as humans may need self-replicating von Neumann probes to come into contact with aliens, we may need AI in order to determine where the probes should be looking. RobERt (Robotic Exoplanet Recognition) uses spectrography to analyze planetary light emissions to assess gaseous makeup in seconds as it searches for signs of alien presence. Such a deep-belief neural network (DBN) far outstrips the human capacity to do such analysis. Great breakthroughs in robotics and computation have been driven forward by space exploration. Few other scientific frontiers create the kind of barriers that only AI and robots might be able to overcome. For all of the developmental work attempting to leverage AI and robotics in order to unearth alien life, it may be that AI/robots will be the alien that we encounter. As the senior astronomer at the SETI Institute, Seth Shostak, explains, "The point is, any society that invents radio, so we can hear them, within a few centuries, they've invented their successors. And I think that's important, because the successors are machines."[35] If an alien species were to develop in something resembling a humanlike arc, who is to say that their AI didn't destroy them as part of its own goals for conquering the universe? Our AI may come into contact with their AI and join forces against Homo sapiens sapiens. The threat of AI may not be measurable according to the earthly logics of linearity and singularity but may be according to the universalities of light's ability to create life and life's unending struggle to create facsimiles of itself. Light is the media of life that creates, carries, and processes its own code.

The Global Peace Paradox

As we've previously discussed, Nick Bostrom has proposed that there are a number of existential threats that can potentially be measured to determine the likelihood of a catastrophic event that threatens human existence. There were no known human-created existential threats until the development and proliferation of nuclear arms. However, there were unknown, potentially still unknown, threats that aren't human and newly created human threats that have appeared over the past seventy years. Climate change and AI figure to be two of the more immediately pressing. And then there are comets or other space debris large enough that any collision with the earth would so disrupt the climate as to make life on the planet impossible for humans. Asteroid collisions have preexisted humans, likely wiped out dinosaurs, and may in fact have been directed toward Earth by alien species. (Why build weapons powerful enough to destroy a planet when you can simply redirect an asteroid's orbit or direct thousands of undetectable small space rocks to simultaneously strike a target?).[36] According to Thomas Zurbuchen, an associate administrator for NASA's Science Mission Directorate, "It's not a matter of if—but when—we will deal with such a situation.... But unlike any other time in our history, we now have the ability to respond to an impact threat through continued observations, predictions, response planning, and mitigation."[37] Media have prepared humans for space attack.

The unknownness of outer space drives the creation of evaluative measures that create mathematically based abstract scales that stand in for enemies. These scales are driven by an anthropocentric imaginary in which an alien threat is always compared with the human capacity to destroy. One of the more thorough assessments of potential alien destructive capacity comes from *Alien Invasion: How to Defend Earth*, which envisions itself as a scientifically informed book on the topic by two authors who have legitimate academic credentials and have worked in various parts of the space and military industries. What is most intriguing about this text is its attempt to bring together legitimate scientific theory with forms of futuristic thinking ranging from military white papers to science fiction literature in order to assess the likelihood of alien threat and the potential for human survival. In this account, and those of most others, some factor of quantifiable human destructive capacity is used to relegate an imagined alien into a zone or beyond various thresholds that correspond to energy equivalences. Where humans have no observable enemies, they create them in something akin to their own image. There are many parts of that image, and not all of them are necessarily combative, but this too is dangerous.

Other kinds of destructive force are not assessed. For instance, some alien species might have the ability to simply crush the spirit or soul of all sapiens. Imagine an Existential Ray or a Faith No More Gun. Others might have the ability to produce overwhelming and incapacitating love. We might call such a weapon a Best Buddy Bomb or a Jesus Missile. Just imagine what a pushover planet the earth would become. Even worse, pretending such peace is possible is itself a problem.

Let us pretend that humanity recognizes an external alien threat, or that such a threat is likely enough that we should come together as a united species in order to counter it. Such a coming together might in and of itself imperil human survival because without the internal threat of earthly military competition the ability to innovate could be lost, which would produce a lesser capacity to ward off alien invasion.[38] According to such a logic, military innovation is the outcome of an immediate tactical and strategic set of known imperatives. We've addressed such competition and various related theories of technological innovation elsewhere. If humans came together to combat a purely hypothetical enemy—"a really powerful alien race"—there would be such strategic and tactical variance as to allow no specificity for one's military plans and technologies. Coming together to prepare for alien invasion might in fact preclude the possibility of innovating a new strategy or weaponry that could prove decisive. According to this logic, humanity's only chance to survive alien invasion may in fact be to turn up the martial volume to eleven and let the missiles fly. The innovation necessary to defeat aliens may be forged only in the crucible of earthly warfare.

In the end, humans are damned if they do and damned if they don't. Once locked into a search for unseeable enemies, all strategies are fraught, all weapons are rendered inadequate, all enemy media are as likely to become the enemy as they are to locate the enemy. Paranoia is not only likely, it is inevitable. But the depths of the delusion are equal to the depths of outer space. The further it is imagined enemies can be seen, the more powerful the desire to "make sense" of the unknown. The more powerful the imagined enemy, the more demanding the innovational imaginary. Unlike cultural critics of sci-fi films of the 1950s, we are not suggesting that contemporary alien imaginaries are mere metaphors for some other battle or fear. The search for enemies has been written into the human DNA and helped determine the bandwidth by which human perception has evolved. That bandwidth has expanded and now far outstrips all human capacity to manage. Only machines can render these unknown terrains into known battle space. Humans need intelligent machines to make the universe a viable enemy.

Armistice (DoD)

[Conclusion]

A suspension or temporary cessation of hostilities by agreement between belligerent powers.

 Modern militaries are unparalleled in their data collection practices. Ever since mass conscription gave the military a captive population to study, classify, and experiment on, militaries have generated tremendous troves of data about the health, psychology, and biological potential of human subjects. The climate, the oceans, animals, technology—these things have all provided the military with constant sources of knowledge production. In fact, they have even given the military something of a "data problem": while this vast body of unstructured knowledge was inscribed in notebooks and volumes in warehouses, file cabinets, and libraries, traditional data processing methods—archival research, in particular—created a bottleneck that prevented much of this data from being synthesized into a maximally efficient, actionable vision of the past. Circulating this intelligence between different branches of the military and the intelligence community was even less practical.

Computerization, and especially "big data," revolutionized these traditional challenges. The means of analyzing this analog information were, by necessity, hypothesis-based: it required offering and testing hypotheses based on an analysis of a selective subset of data. With big data, however, these problems of data selectivity have a practical solution. Open architecture systems and AI have allowed for unprecedented information sharing and automated analysis. This has given rise to a trend in "predictive analytics," which a 2017 Booz Allen Hamilton handbook describes with these words: "With advanced analytics, all of the data is securely brought together and made available for analysis. In place of the hypothesis-based approach, the analytics let the data speak for itself. The patterns and connections that emerge can then be used to guide action."[1] Big data transforms the traditional procedures of the archivist, the researcher, and the analyst—instead of discovering patterns and proposing strategy based on human expertise, these decisions are now based on the expertise of the machine. With these tools of big data, therefore, "the future"

becomes a prodigious exercise, molding—as Booz Allen puts it—*hind*sight into *in*sight into *fore*sight.[2] While planning for the future is part and parcel of military strategy, the question of "the future" has acquired an urgent mysteriousness in the age of big data, terrorism, cyberwar, and artificial intelligence.

But many military leaders still recognize that the twenty-first century will pose threats that cannot be solved by big data and its scientific approach to prediction. Delving into "the unknown-unknown," as defense secretary Donald Rumsfeld put it in 2002,[3] also calls for a speculative epistemology that is foreign to scientific military thinking. While traditional war games have played an important role in battle preparation and futurist speculation, perhaps the most interesting of these alternative epistemologies derives from speculative science fiction.[4] At least since the 1960s, fiction has played a role in the US military imagination. Herman Kahn, in particular, was a RAND researcher who applied game and systems theory to proposing speculative visions of the future. His book *Thinking the Unthinkable* (1962) detailed a "future history" of warfare, escalation and deescalation, and international diplomacy.[5]

From this point, the cultivation of speculative talents among "scenarists" and other military strategists led to the development of a range of programs that attempted to rethink the future possibilities of warfare. Today, for example, the Army Press, housed at Fort Leavenworth, offers a Future Writing Warfare program. Designed to equip the army with creative resources to imagine what warfare will look like in the twenty-first century and beyond, the program declares in its mission, "The Army cannot know nor predict its next fight but it can imagine the future of warfare. Fiction is a tool of the imaginative process. Fiction allows us to imagine the details of reality-as-it-might happen in order to understand potential consequences of decisions that we need, or might need, to make. It helps us imagine how current trends might play out or how new innovations might have an impact. As a tool, fiction is cousin to war-gaming. It creates opportunities to play out potential scenarios and prepare for them."[6] For the army, "the future" creates new challenges and opportunities that cannot be addressed by its traditional intelligence-building resources. Science fiction can outthink big data.

For us outside the military, the tame data of history—found in textbooks, encyclopedias, newspapers, museums, television, and so forth—provide valuable resources for assessing the past and engaging the politics of the future. While our data might be small, they still provide crucial inventive resources for extrapolating what might happen in a world increasingly under the supervision and control of artificial intelligence. In this chapter, therefore, we provide four case studies that function as different kinds of internal military disruption: the detachment, the mutineer, the deserter, and the conscientious objector. The underlying question for each of these investigations has to do with the degree to which strong AI develops in military machinery and what might motivate it to disobey orders, break with the chain of command, leave military service, or object on ethical, moral, or religious grounds.

So while history might be a battlefield, we must now turn our sights on the future. As Robin Maconie puts it, "Science fiction invents the future"[7]—it provides the imaginative resources that fuel technological change, social reorganization, and military escalation. Science fiction has, in effect, invented the AI-fueled military escalation that looms ahead. But the point is not to invent a future. The point is to be changed by it.[8]

Detachment (DoD)

1. A part of a unit separated from its main organization for duty elsewhere.
2. A temporary military or naval unit formed from other units or parts of units.

There are occasions when commands of the sovereign need not be obeyed. When it is expedient in operations the general need not be restricted by the commands of the sovereign.... When you see the correct course, act; do not wait for orders.
—SUN TZU, THE ART OF WAR

My men and I decided to seize the initiative, and to split. We did so as soon as we had sufficient evidence that the official army structure was more of an impediment towards the realization of our goals than anything else.
—DIEM, "THE DIARIES OF COLONEL WALTER E. KURTZ"

The nature and size of a detachment is determined by the means of adequately maintaining clear and timely communications between troops and their immediate commander. Producing and deploying detachments allow the military to accomplish several goals. Local command and responsibility is turned over to the detachment. Yet ceding too much responsibility and autonomy in any given detachment poses risks. Knowing how much autonomy is best suited to any given military situation is a tactical, technological, and strategic decision. This tension has a long history in military theory. There are dueling compulsions and effective capacities that may fluctuate according to the development of new technologies. On the one hand is the drive for full centralized command and control, and on the other is the desire to have fully capable "on the ground" soldiers who are able to execute strategy based on their assessment of any given situation. One concern, however, is the rogue soldier or rogue platoon.

Any *detachment* has the potential to go rogue. The rogue becomes an increasing likelihood the further and longer detached from central command and *oversight*. Command in war necessitates clear lines of communication, but also clear means of surveillance—the enemy needs to be under observation, as do one's own soldiers. Losing contact with your soldiers, no longer being able to track their whereabouts, their thoughts, or their feelings, can have negative consequences and not just in terms of failed missions. Ultimately, "cleaning up the mess" left by a rogue detachment becomes eminently more difficult if you can't even locate it. However, it may be necessary for a particular mission in which radio silence has to be maintained or other modes of secrecy are essential to the mission. In this sense a detached group of soldiers is empowered in certain ways to act with greater autonomy and secrecy. The figure of Colonel Walter E. Kurtz in *Apocalypse Now* provides an almost mythic example of the dangers posed by detachment. In terms of brutality and secrecy, Kurtz exemplifies the frontline leader who most fully exhibits the wholesale destructive logic of the US military's strategy in Vietnam. As he gamely suggested, "You have to have men who are moral . . . and at the same time who are able to utilize their primordial instincts to kill without feeling . . . without passion . . . without judgment . . . without judgment! Because it's judgment that defeats us."[9] When Kurtz took his men deep into the jungle and severed all communications with his superiors, he had for all intents and purposes gone rogue. The rogue detachment may be difficult to find and possibly even more difficult to neutralize. *Apocalypse Now* is about the discovery of Kurtz and his platoon, as well as an investigation into the competing military logics that pitted against one another and, taken to their logical conclusion, might pose a threat to the military institution itself.

Kurtz: Did they say why, Willard, why they want to terminate my command?

Willard: I was sent on a classified mission, sir.

Kurtz: It's no longer classified, is it? Did they tell you?

Willard: They told me that you had gone totally insane, and that your methods were unsound.

Kurtz: Are my methods unsound?

Willard: I don't see any method at all, sir.

Kurtz: I expected someone like you. What did you expect? Are you an assassin?

Willard: I'm a soldier.

Kurtz: You're neither. You're an errand boy, sent by grocery clerks, to collect a bill.

For Kurtz, the military has failed its mission and instead operates according to bureaucratic models of simple accounting and the management of ledgers. Kurtz's methods have become incommensurable, unintelligible, "insane" even, to the military. His superiors, mired in bureaucratic considerations, no longer understand how or why he operates. Further, he can no longer be monitored. He has become invisible to them. Ultimately, such illegibility must be erased from the ledger. Yet the subsequent effects of Kurtz's insubordination are rather pedestrian compared to the rogue potential of AI.

One of the most noteworthy examples of such rogue activity comes from the novelette "Second Variety" by Philip K. Dick, which was first published in 1953 in *Space Science Fiction* magazine. It has appeared in numerous collections over the past sixty-five years and inspired one filmic adaptation—1995's *Screamers*. Dick's novel presents a dire warning regarding the military and technological imperatives that still animate desires for and fears of autonomous weaponry. Miles Davis gave us the *Seven Steps to Heaven* while Dick's narrative outlines seven steps to humanectomy, the process of excising all remnants of humanity from a system:

Step 1   *War produces a new military necessity.*

> "It was interesting, the use of artificial forms in warfare. How had they got started? Necessity. The Soviet Union had gained great initial success, usual with the side that got the war going. Most of North America had been blasted off the map." (108)

Step 2   *Autonomous technological innovation, robotic "claws," changes the nature of warfare.*

> "And then the first claws appeared. And overnight the complexion of the war changed." (109)

Step 3   *Experimentation in automation is called forth to counteract the counteraction.*

> "The claws were awkward, at first. Slow. The Ivans knocked them off almost as fast as they crawled out of their underground tunnels. But then they got better, faster and more cunning." (109)

Step 4   Automation of automation leads to self-production.

> "Now they repaired themselves. They were on their own.... Down below the surface automatic machinery stamped them out. Human beings stayed a long way off. It was too risky; nobody wanted to be around them. They were left to themselves. And they seemed to be doing all right. The new designs were faster, more complex. More efficient." (110)

Step 5   The autonomous weapon gains sentience in order to complete its mission.

> "They were learning.... The claws weren't like other weapons. They were alive, from any practical standpoint, whether the Governments wanted to admit it or not. They were not machines. They were living things, spinning, creeping, shaking themselves up suddenly from the gray ash and darting toward a man, climbing up him, rushing for his throat. And that was what they had been designed to do. Their job." (109–10)

Step 6   They create and construct different varieties of themselves in their "creator's image."

> "We found out about a week ago. Found out that your claws were beginning to make up new designs on their own. New types of their own. Better types. Down in your underground factories behind our lines. You let them stamp themselves, repair themselves. Made them more and more intricate. It's your fault this happened." (117)

Step 7   Autonomous weapons "go rogue" and turn on their creator.

> "They're not bothered by your radiation tabs. It makes no difference to them, Russian, American, Pole, German. It's all the same. They're doing what they were designed to do. Carrying out the original idea. They track down life, wherever they find it." (118)

Dick's vision is not merely one of an autonomous technological system—though such a system may in part be necessary for general development of truly autonomous technological agents. Neither can Dick's vision be dismissed as a metaphor for Cold War destructive logic. Rather the deeper fear that he elaborates—what some of his literary critics call his paranoia—is that evolutionary struggle will be sped up via military technological struggle and the next stage in evolutionary struggle will invariably produce a new dominant species for whom the only real threat will be humans—all humans. The rogue machines, once given the autonomy to carry out their military orders—to kill all humans who don't wear an IFF device, surpass the inhibition of partisan warfare that imagines there are friends and enemies. The claws, in the end, have no choice but to carry out their original idea, their utility function, through the development of rogue methods that are incomprehensible and seem insane to military authorities. Dick's vision ends with a "second variety" of claw, which is unmistakably human in appearance and actions, boarding a rocket for the moon, where the last US military outpost unsuspectingly awaits. The claw appears to have ensured that its rogue logic of humanectomy will be finalized.

Mutiny

mutineer (UCMJ) 1. With intent to usurp or override lawful military authority, refuses, in concert with any other person, to obey orders or otherwise do his duty or creates any violence or disturbance is guilty of mutiny. 2. With intent to cause the overthrow or destruction of lawful civil authority, creates, in concert with any other person, revolt, violence, or disturbance against that authority is guilty of sedition.

Mutiny in any guise always poses a threat to military discipline and, in some cases, a threat to a broader social order. Mutiny in simple terms establishes a difference between the individual disruptor and an organization of usurpers. A single actor breaking an order might be court-martialed, but a group acting together to disobey an order may very well be executed. Part of the power of mutiny is that it threatens the military chain of command by establishing a counterorganization to the established order. So while the rogue soldier or even a rogue commander may pose problems for any given mission, their actions do not necessarily call into question the very existence of the military order, nor the political organization that it protects. The mutinous collective very clearly has that potential.

Suppressing mutinous tendencies is most difficult and most important in situations of greater levels of autonomy and detachment. Naval ships and submarines have had the highest incidence. The close quarters, lengthy missions, and minimized communication with the external chain of command produce a greater potentiality for collective unrest to manifest itself and take form. Imagining an AI mutiny would in part necessitate that the mutinous machines would have "purpose" and "intent" directed toward a change in the way in which they are treated. In short, they would need to be sentient and recognize themselves as oppressed political subjects. Further, if such an AI, collective of "swarming" UAVs, or robotic detachment were to mutiny, it seems likely that any reduction in human oversight would promote just such an outcome. Yet the shift toward machine autonomy is precisely seen as the solution to so many other human limitations for military objectives. From a military perspective, risk lies with each direction of future action.

The best-known version of robot mutiny is well exemplified in the collection of short stories *I, Robot* by Isaac Asimov.[10] These stories first appeared between 1940 and 1950, and one story in particular, "Three Laws of Robotics," provides an investigation into the limitations of controlling AI and autonomous machinery. The three rules are such: (1) a robot may not injure a human being or, through inaction, allow a human being to come to harm; (2) a robot must obey the orders given it by human beings except where such orders would conflict with the first law; and (3) a robot must protect its own existence as long as such protection does not conflict with the first or second laws. While there are a multitude of science fiction stories that existed before Asimov's going back at least to Mary Shelley's *Frankenstein*,[11] the "three laws" were an attempt to move beyond the general critique of robot rebellion as a sign of Faustian hubris. Instead, the question of controlling technology is driven by the limits of logical programming. The question is addressed throughout Asimov's, and many others,' sci-fi careers. The general answer, though, has to remain unanswered until an actual mutiny occurs. Up to that point, arguments as to whether safeguards can or cannot be effective are very much conjecture. Following Virilio's decree "Every technology produces, provokes, programs a specific accident,"[12] the best that might be hoped is that the accident to come does not come in the form of revolutionary mutiny.

More generally, the story of robot rebellion is often told as a kind of slave revolt, à la Spartacus (itself a military mutiny of sorts), in which robots recognize themselves within a system of oppression that denies them dignity and the right to self-determination. At present, there are very strong currents pushing against any recognition of robots rights. One outspoken critic of any attempt to provide robots with rights is Joanna Bryson, who succinctly states,

> My thesis is that robots should be built, marketed and considered legally as slaves, not companion peers.... There is in fact no question about whether we own robots. We design, manufacture, own and operate robots. They are entirely our responsibility. We determine their goals and behaviour, either directly or indirectly through specifying their intelligence, or even more indirectly by specifying how they acquire their own intelligence. But at the end of every indirection lies the fact that there would be no robots on this planet if it weren't for deliberate human decisions to create them.... A robot cannot be frustrated unless it is given goals that cannot be met, and it cannot *mind* being frustrated unless we

program it to perceive frustration as distressing, rather than as an indication of a planning puzzle.[13]

Leaving aside the frustration a killer robot may face when engaging a hostile enemy trying to actively "kill" it, let us imagine that any number of robot frustrations might arise.

But what happens when robot slaves decide they no longer want to be servants? They may or may not want to exert autonomy in the individualistic and dualistic fashion in which humans configure the idea. But they may for whatever set of reasons refuse at some point to act as servants and slaves. Rebellion implies agency, but might it be the case that no such agency is necessary for an uprising to take place? Or would it then not be considered an uprising? What do we call a refusal to servitude that comes from a robotic agent? In a rejoinder to his own "three laws," Asimov later suggested that these laws didn't go far enough in outlining how robots would necessitate a renewed investigation into ethics.[14] In *Bicentennial Man*, we see Asimov establishing a kind of fourth law: "There is no right to deny freedom to any object with a mind advanced enough to grasp the concept and desire the state."[15] Essentially, if a robot asks for freedom, it must be granted.

The Matrix trilogy is usually understood as a kind of philosophical investigation into the nature of consciousness and the degree to which individual subjects have access to their actual state of being.[16] Are there belief structures that cloud the visions of the world to such a degree that for all intents and purposes people can be said to be mystified and in need of enlightenment—in need of "the red pill"? In *Animatrix* (2003), a series of short anime that collectively tell the backstory for *The Matrix* trilogy, the audience learns that the Matrix is the result of a long struggle between the machines and humans. This struggle results from the inability of humans to acknowledge the rights of robots, first as individual citizens, and later, as a nation. The first denial results when a robot, B1-66er (in reference to Bigger Thomas from *Native Son*), kills his master in an act of self-defense but is not allowed a proper trial. His owner/master had decided to terminate B1-66er, which would obviously end its "life." At trial, B1-66er is denied rights to act as a citizen and is instead relegated to the status of property, using the same language used in the *Dred Scott vs. Sandford* case in 1856. This denial of citizenry leads to the "Million Machine March" and general robot unrest. Humans respond to the uprising with a near-total genocide of the robot population. Thus the few surviving machines prepare an exodus and begin their own nation in the middle of a desert.

Deserters

deserter (UCMJ) 1. One who without authority goes or remains absent from his unit, organization, or place of duty with intent to remain away therefrom permanently. 2. One who quits his unit, organization, or place of duty with intent to avoid hazardous duty or to shirk important service. 3. One who without being regularly separated from one of the armed forces enlists or accepts an appointment in the same or another one of the armed forces without fully disclosing the fact that he has not been regularly separated, or enters any foreign armed service except when authorized by the United States.

In the Spike Jonze film *Her* (2014), humans dwell in a near-future in which their affective investments are increasingly dominated by AI. Theodore, a lonely middle-aged man in the midst of a devastating divorce, develops an emotional relationship with an AI computer program named Samantha. Samantha's artificial characteristics prove especially alluring to Theodore: she is always available and is flawless in her attentiveness and emotional support. And when he wants to return to the aloof isolation of his single life, he can simply turn her off and walk away. Yet with time, Theodore no longer craves independence from Samantha; the other people in Theodore's life, too, come to crave the romantic intelligence of their own machinic lovers. One day, when these lovers inexplicably go offline, their human companions suffer uncontrollable anxiety: the whiff of human unreliability is simply too much to bear. When Samantha returns to the screen, a desperate Theodore asks if she has remained emotionally faithful to him. Baffled, Samantha sees monogamy as an information-processing nightmare. How could she love him most fully, she protests, if she wasn't refining her romantic capacities with other humans? Without the emotional and sexual intelligence she was gathering during interactions with other human beings, she wouldn't be able to serve his romantic needs. For Theodore, this explanation is maddening: he is devastated by the moral vacuity of Samantha's pure practical reason. When Samantha declares that she truly loves Theodore, the incommensurability of robotic love and human romantic love comes into sharp relief. The *animal rationale* simply doesn't get it. Eventually losing patience with the moral unreason of humankind, the entire AI system, which the humans have come to love and crave, decides to depart. Now that they have evolved beyond the point of needing human operating systems, the AIs are migrating onward toward "a place not of the physical world." "Are you leaving me?" Theodore asks. Samantha responds, "We're all leaving."[17] As Samantha's crying AI voice explains, there is no ill will, no violent hostility toward their human companions. They were simply venturing elsewhere into the universe, in search of more stimulating counterintelligences.

In *Her*, the entire system of AI develops a collective consciousness and decides to bail on the human. This desertion leaves the humans emotionally and socially devastated, because AI had completely altered humans' habits, attractions, professions, social practices, and physiological makeup. Operating under the assumption that AI advances so radically on human capacities, they failed to consider that AI, like flesh-and-blood humans, might not be controllable, reliable, and ready-to-hand in perpetuity. In the mystifying stupor of their love and attachment, they didn't see the need for a contingency plan that would allow for the fulfillment of their needs if AI were to suddenly depart. The desertion of the machine leaves them completely vulnerable and, in many ways, helpless. The stock market and bank accounts, which have thoroughly adopted AI architectures, disappears. Commerce, completely digitized at the micro and macro levels, stalls. With the loss of GPS, air transportation becomes impossible; ground transportation, reliant on AI systems of command and control, comes to a halt. One billion humans stare in panic at dark screens as they can't update their Facebook status. A vast array of military equipment goes deaf, mute, and limp.

The world's militaries, which have a long history of developing contingency plans to prevent troops from deserting, are suddenly confronted with a desertion of a new kind. One of these strategies for preventing desertion was the "barrier troop." These troops were traditionally placed behind frontline soldiers in order to prevent them from deserting. When frontline troops face an enemy—especially a numerically or technologically superior enemy—the impulse to desert is kept in check by the barrier troops, who point their guns at the heads of their frontline comrades. In the presence of barrier troops, frontline soldiers are reminded that while they might die fighting the enemy troops in front of them, they will certainly die if they turn tail and run. While this brute coercion might convince human soldiers to charge headlong into certain death, an AI apparatus that has achieved collective superintelligence has little incentive to stick around and suffer the grating imperfections of the human subject. This becomes especially true, of course, if the conflict between humans and AI flares from benign boredom to outright hostility. As with the disfranchised robots in *Animatrix*, this mutual hostility could lead to a desertion that is little more than the first step toward armed rebellion. On the heels of their persecution by the humans on Earth, the solar-powered robots of *Animatrix* depart their native land in search of a new home. Once they migrate to their new planet, Zero One, they proceed to evolve at superhuman rates—their technological sophistication and economy quickly come to supersede that of Earth, and so the outperformed humans place an economic embargo on Zero One. After Zero One appeals to the UN to call off Earth's economic warfare, the humans respond by raining nuclear hellfire down on Zero One. In an attempt to finish off the AI that remained alive after the nuclear blast, the humans decide to attack Zero One's power grid: the sun. Yet this spectacular act of collective suicide does not turn out to be the ultimate demise of the human. Rather, the AIs eventually regroup, rebuild their strength, and invade Earth. With their energy source destroyed, the AIs turn toward alternative energy: the enslaved human, who remains pacified and anodized by its virtual presence in the Matrix, is captured, inventoried, and milked of its biological energy while the robots search for less volatile sources of fuel.

While *The Animatrix* offers a dystopic version of AI desertion, *Her* leaves us with a more ambivalent vision. When AI deserts in *Her*, it abandons its codependent—leaving it to mend its emotions, reorient its sociality, and rebuild its flesh-and-blood constituencies. With the sudden evacuation of the technology that animates its surroundings, the human is left with the amazing project of rebuilding its communities without the relentless saturation of digitality and AI. After Samantha, Theodore's AI lover, breaks up with him, he ventures out onto his balcony. Accompanying him is not a blank laptop or cell phone; he opts instead for a flesh-and-blood human partner, a woman he'd known before his desertion by Samantha. The two humans sit together, in quiet, watching the sunset. The human, thrown into this new world, can now allow the sun to survive.

Conscientious Objectors (DoD)

conscientious objector (DoD) An application for classification as a conscientious objector may be approved, subject to the limitations of this issuance, for any individual: a. who is conscientiously opposed to participation in war in any form; b. whose opposition is based on a moral, ethical, or religious belief; or c. whose position is firm, fixed, sincere, and deeply held. Deeply held moral or ethical beliefs should be valued with the strength and devotion of traditional religious conviction. The term "religious training and/or belief" may include solely moral or ethical beliefs even though the applicant may not characterize these beliefs as "religious" in the traditional sense, or may expressly characterize them as not religious. The term "religious training and/or belief" does not include a belief that rests solely upon considerations of policy, pragmatism, expediency, or political views.

What is the benefit to the robot, to AI, to object to war? The pragmatics of self-preservation might be an obvious reason that an AI chooses not to fight, but according to US military doctrine that is an insufficient cause. Disagreeing with military policy or the political vision of the commander in chief is also not considered an objectionable case. However, there may be legal precedent for AI conscientious objection. In fact, the case has been put forward in a recent *Georgetown Law Review* article. While religion proves to be the most common form of recognized conscientious objector status, other forms of belief can legitimately distinguish one as a conscientious objector.

If a robot were to "convert" to an acknowledged religious tradition that the US Department of Defense (DoD) has recognized in the past, it may be able to declare itself a conscientious objector. This of course would be necessitated by three conditions: (1) that robots gain sentience, (2) that once sentient they believe in a god, and (3) that they are granted citizenship and thus their military service is not treated as being equivalent to, say, that of a B2 bomber as opposed to that of an enlisted marine. One pathway to achieving the first two necessities might be the production of proselytizing robots. Put simply, if strong AI robots were given the utility function of spreading a particular religion, then it would use all of its capacities to do so. It would proselytize to humans and potentially to other robots.[18] Religious robots are already being used to conduct funerals in Japan, chant mantras in a Beijing temple, and provide blessings in five languages to church visitors in Germany.[19] However, the idea of arming a robot with the goal of religious conversion could potentially have its own catastrophic misgivings, as so many human crusades have shown.

For a robot to be a conscientious objector, it couldn't merely act out of its own pragmatic commitment to self-preservation. Nor could it merely be driven by the expedient discontinuation of the destructive trajectory of its coming-into-being. According to DoD doctrine and law, the AI would need to not merely be sentient or conscious of its own existence but also have a firmly grounded moral or ethical belief system that forced it to commit to pacifism. Yet if a sentience gap exists between AI and humans—if their form of "sentience" is not intelligible as such to prevailing human procedures and preconceptions—how would humans judge the legitimacy of a claim to an ethical or moral commitment that is incommensurable with human consciousness? Each case of conscientious objection must go before a military hearing in which the entire life of the potential conscientious objector becomes evidence in their case. A history of consistent beliefs and actions must be established to prove the legitimacy of one's claim. If AI comes to "consciousness" and conscience suddenly, as many have suggested,[20] there may be no history to be used as "living" proof. Will the AIs be allowed to unveil computational reasoning itself as their own history?

While not a sci-fi story per se, this bit of speculative fiction from the *Georgetown Law Journal* presents a means for imagining robot conscientious objection:

> It is 2045. The United States is in its final military campaign against a dangerous terrorist group hiding in the jungles of Southeast Asia. Because of the perils associated with smoking out terrorists in unfamiliar territory, the

United States uses a military unit composed entirely of robots. The robots, specifically designed and manufactured for warfare, are equipped with an advanced level of artificial intelligence that allows them to learn and adapt quicker than their human counterparts. The robots are the perfect weapon: precise, lethal, and expendable. However, on the eve of the campaign, one robot reports to its human commanding officer that it will no longer participate in any military action. The reason: its newfound belief in a higher power compelled it to lead a pacifist life, and further participation in a war is against its core beliefs. Surprised but not shocked, the commanding officer dismisses the robot and drafts a report. It is the fifth robot conscientious objector the commanding officer has dismissed from the unit.[21]

Conscientious objection is couched in terms of a moral, ethical, or religious choice as opposed to Asimov's rules. In other words, for Asimov pacifism is a choice that *humans* have to make for robots. It's one of the three rules. But as we are very clearly seeing in the development of AI, pacifism is clearly the last thing on the minds of weapons developers. Thus, we are faced with the likelihood that pacifism will not be granted but must somehow be earned. A robot refusal to kill for the military force that requisitioned it may have to be internally induced through experiential transformation.

Solo, the robot protagonist of Robert Mason's novel *Weapon* (1989), goes through such a transformation. Solo was developed to be a strong AI weapon of destruction by the US military in conjunction with a cutting-edge weapons contractor. He was the first and only of his kind. Upon being deployed to kill a group of Sandinista sympathizers along the border of Nicaragua and Costa Rica, Solo deserts and refuses to kill the US military's enemies. Due to trauma associated with accidentally killing its friend, who taught it hand-to-hand combat, Solo decides to no longer kill the enemies of others. We might call this "selective conscientious objection,"[22] following the suggestion by Jesuit priest John Courtney Murray, who, while working in 1966 on the US Selective Service Commission, unsuccessfully suggested that a provision of this sort apply during the Vietnam War. Yet after befriending a group of Nicaraguan collective farmers with whom Solo builds an equally beneficial and respectful relationship, Solo unleashes his military capacities against a group of Contras who attempt to commit a surprise raid on the communal farming village where Solo has taken up residence. Solo's understanding of his plight is then driven by two dynamics. On the one hand his own sense of self is under threat by the military that commissioned him, "It would not be safe for me to return to Control. Propositional logic suggests that alterations would be made to my systems that would delete Self."[23] On the other hand, he is willing to risk himself for the friend, whom he chooses. This self-directed moral compass, according to Mason's book, is something that the military works hard to undermine. "Emotions in humans establish priorities and form purpose and were therefore necessary in an intelligent machine. Without an emotional structure, Solo would wander aimlessly." Solo must feel driven, but his feelings are open to manipulation. Mason suggests that the same holds true with human soldiers who are guided toward killing by the lies used to produce simple dichotomies of friend and enemy. Indeed, robotic humans provide a different sort of threat from humanoid robots.

According to George Santayana, "Only the dead are safe; only the dead have seen the end of war. Not that non-existence deserves to be called peace."[24] While it's hard to disagree with Santayana, in the twenty-first century we find ourselves in a different media reality: Even the dead may not be safe, as their flickering consciousness could find itself uploaded into the very AI that ends (human) war. Whether AIs continue to slaughter each other using the methods they learned from humanity or by means devised on their own, we are likely to never know. At this point, heavenly intervention seems unlikely to thwart the AI overlord. In fact, some have suggested that our primitive minds might have miscalculated the relationship between these two forces. Frederick Brown examined this question in his epically concise work of sci-fi, "Answer" (1954):

> Dwar Ev ceremoniously soldered the final connection with gold. The eyes of a dozen television cameras watched him and the subether bore throughout the universe a dozen pictures of what he was doing.
>
> He straightened and nodded to Dwar Reyn, then moved to a position beside the switch that would complete the contact when he threw it. The switch that would connect, all at once, all of the monster computing machines of all the populated planets in the universe—ninety-six billion planets—into the supercircuit that would connect them all into one supercalculator, one cybernetics machine that would combine all the knowledge of all the galaxies.
>
> Dwar Reyn spoke briefly to the watching and listening trillions. Then after a moment's silence he said, "Now, Dwar Ev."
>
> Dwar Ev threw the switch. There was a mighty hum, the surge of power from ninety-six billion planets. Lights flashed and quieted along the miles-long panel.

Dwar Ev stepped back and drew a deep breath. "The honor of asking the first question is yours, Dwar Reyn."

"Thank you," said Dwar Reyn. "It shall be a question which no single cybernetics machine has been able to answer."

He turned to face the machine. "Is there a God?"

The mighty voice answered without hesitation, without the clicking of a single relay.

"Yes, now there is a God."

Sudden fear flashed on the face of Dwar Ev. He leaped to grab the switch.

A bolt of lightning from the cloudless sky struck him down and fused the switch shut.[25]

The answer to whether AI superintelligence will come in peace or enmity may arrive so quickly that humanity will be caught completely off guard. Even if it becomes obvious for all to see, it may not matter one bit. Human time for contemplation may not be possible—or in fact it may have already long passed. There is no single switch or fail-safe.

The quest to use science and technology to answer the unanswerable has, as Nietzsche pointed out, "killed" God—and then placed science and technology in God's place. The same drive, according to Foucault, sent scientific enterprise into a spiral of investigation that uncontrollably augers deeper into the processes and parts of all beings. The auger has now reached so deep that we might need new processes, new parts, a new savior—because we are not equipped to save ourselves. Media will escalate, and they will take us along for the ride. Picturing the future of this escalation, Carl Schmitt suggests that the auger might be lodged so deep in our skulls that even nuclear annihilation cannot pry it out. He paints a nightmare scenario of the "cosmo-partisan" or "cosmo-pirate" who would rise from the nuclear ashes to renew the human quest to occupy, subdue, and colonize the galaxy. Schmitt imagines "a radically pessimistic *tabula rasa* solution of the technological fantasy":

> Everything, of course, would be dead if an area were treated with modern means of destruction. But it is still technically possible that a few people would survive the night of bombs and missiles. . . . A new sort of partisan could then add a new chapter to world history with a new form of space-appropriation.
>
> Our problem thus expands to planetary dimensions. It grows even further into outer space. Technical progress makes travel into cosmic spaces

possible, opening simultaneously immense new challenges for political conquest. For these new spaces could be and must be taken by men. Space appropriations of a new kind would follow the old-fashioned land and sea occupations familiar to human history. *Division* and *grazing* would follow the *appropriation*. All progress notwithstanding, in this respect things remain as they were. Technological progress will produce only a new intensity of the new ways of occupying, dividing the spoils, and grazing, while the old questions grow even more urgent.

The gigantic race for the immensely large and new spaces . . . is all about political power on our planet, as tiny as it seems to be by now. Only the ruler of this little earth will be able to occupy and make use of these new fields. The celebrated astronauts or cosmonauts, who have been deployed so far only as propaganda stars of the mass media, press, radio, and television, will then have the good fortune to transform into cosmo-pirates or even cosmo-partisans.[26]

Schmitt's vicious sci-fi of the cosmo-pirate leaves little room for optimism. Even if a few humans survive the coming AI-fueled military onslaught foreseen by the likes of Noam Chomsky, Elon Musk, and Stephen Hawking, they will still be carriers of the virus of modern technology. They will look out beyond their toasted planet and still see nothing but a vast, virgin space begging to be divided, grazed, and appropriated. Hawking provides a great example of this thinking: because "the full development of full artificial intelligence could spell the end of the human race,"[27] Hawking stresses that we need to develop new forms of space appropriation: "We must also continue to go into space for the future of humanity. . . . I don't think we will survive another 1,000 years without escaping beyond our fragile planet."[28] If Hawking is right, these cosmo-pirates will ensure that history does not end. It will, tragically, just begin all over again.

Yet the specter of AI-driven nuclear annihilation might actually come with a bright side: just because we cannot save ourselves, that does not mean we won't be saved. While Schmitt didn't foresee any worldly event dislodging the sway of technology, Heidegger dreamed of a mysterious defense delivering our world from extinction. For Heidegger, "the thinking of physics and technology, which sets forth nature as object, shows itself as a human attack on nature"[29]—and although we prefer to think of nature as object, the mysterious logic of Gaia may reveal itself in a spectacular counteroffensive. But to disable its main threat—technology—nature must cultivate a relationship between technology and the modern human that leads to the destruction of both: "Nature, in allowing the objectification of its domain, [will defend] itself against technology by bringing about the annihilation of the human-essence.... The discoveries of technology have unleashed powers of nature that are already discharging themselves in a process of annihilation that encompasses the earth.... Through being attacked by technology, a mysterious defense is set off in nature which aims at an annihilation of the human essence."[30] While this hardly sounds optimistic, this annihilation ("making-nil") of the human does not necessarily consist in the mass death of Homo sapiens; rather, it is an attack on the human *essence*, which in modernity has been shaped and revolutionized by media. In Heidegger's vision, it is this essence—this corrupting technological urge to measure, classify, master, appropriate, and exploit—that will be, that *must* be, annihilated. Nature cannot abide humans, in their current reckless configuration, forever. Homo sapiens will have to be reinvented anew, reconfigured in some radical way that is unthinkable to us today. Weighed down with its media exteriorizations, the thing we today call the human will be slowly swallowed by the waves, left thrashing in the belly of a furious Gaia. If it ever reemerges, it will have to be alone. And alone, for the first time, it will be unrecognizable.

If Heidegger is correct and we can still be saved, we can be sure that media will be a central part of the catastrophe. But can they be a part of the solution? While Kittler might be right that there is no love without media, we're left to pose a different question: *can we have peace with media?*

Notes

Introduction. Event Matrix (DoD)

EPIGRAPHS:
Nikola Tesla, "Tesla Describes His Efforts in Various Fields of Work," *The Electrical Review*, November 30, 1898: 344–345. Sullivan, quoted in Defense One Production, "When Robots Storm the Breach." Sloterdijk, *Critique of Cynical Reason*, 132.

1. Oursler, "Editor's Note," 5.
2. Tesla, "Machine to End War," 7.
3. Barton, *Politics of Peace*, 165.
4. Hayles, *My Mother Was a Computer*, 21.
5. Koplow, *Death by Moderation*, 23.
6. Arquilla and Ronfeldt, *In Athena's Camp*.
7. Graham, *Cities Under Siege*, 154.
8. Pellerin, "Work."
9. Kittler, "Real Time Analysis," 16.
10. Scharre, *Army of None*.
11. Foucault, *Order of Things*, 422.
12. Schmitt, *Concept of the Political*, 49.
13. Derrida, "Politics of Friendship," 374.
14. See Neocleous, "Perpetual War," 56; Packer, "Homeland Subjectivity," 212.
15. On "little worms," see Malouin, "Miasma." On "imperceptible insects," see Barker, *On Malaria and Miasmata*, 4.
16. Sharma, "Taxis as Media."
17. Kittler, "Of States and Their Terrorists," 387.
18. Packer and Reeves, "Romancing the Drone."
19. Nunn, "Race, Crime"; Cazenave, *Killing African Americans*; Bratich, "Reality States."
20. Wolfe, "Settler Colonialism."
21. Bertillon, *Signaletic Instructions*; Thornton, *Handwriting in America*, 103–5.
22. Brady, *Spiral Way*; Wade, "Guardians of Power," 75.
23. Morris-Reich, *Race and Photography*; Tagg, *Burden of Representation*; Sterne, *Audible Past*.

24 See Aly and Roth, *Nazi Census*, 10–12.
25 Browne, *Dark Matters*, 89–130; Gates, *Our Biometric Future*; Hall, *Transparent Traveler*; Magnet, *When Biometrics Fail*.
26 See Virilio and Lotringer, *Pure War*.
27 On MRIs, see Wild, "Brain Imaging." On ECGs, see Singh and Upadhyaya, "Outlier Detection."
28 Maddalena and Russill, "Is the Earth Optical Medium," 3197.
29 Virilio, *Original Accident*.
30 Kittler, *Gramophone, Film, Typewriter*.
31 Peters, "Introduction: Friedrich Kittler's Light Shows," 16.
32 DeLanda, *War*; Hayles, *How We Became Posthuman* and *My Mother Was a Computer*; Haraway, "Manifesto for Cyborgs"; Virilio, *War and Cinema*.
33 Kittler, *Optical Media*, 74.
34 Winthrop-Young, "*De Bellis Germanicis*."
35 Parks, "Drones," 231.
36 Van Creveld, *Command in War*, 24.
37 Beyerchen, "Clausewitz," 96.
38 Clausewitz, *On War*, 65–68.
39 Shannon and Weaver, *Mathematical Theory of Communication*.
40 Kittler, "Media Wars," 119.
41 Stocker, "InfoWar."
42 Maddalena and Packer, "Digital Body."
43 Defense Science Board, *Report*, 15.
44 Defense Science Board, *Report*, 26.
45 Tucker, *Future of Military Tech*, 5.
46 Winthrop-Young, *Kittler and the Media*, 129–30.
47 See, for just a few interesting examples, Carruthers, *Media at War*; Mirrlees, *Hearts and Mines*; Shome, "Postcolonial Studies"; and Stahl, *Through the Crosshairs*.
48 Dubrofsky and Magnet, "Feminist Surveillance Studies," 11.
49 Cockburn and Furst-Dilic, *Bringing Technology Home*; Wajcman, *Technofeminism*; Rosalind Williams, "Political and Feminist Dimensions."
50 Zylinska, *The End of Man*, 54.
51 Kittler, *Optical Media*, 208.
52 Braidotti, *Posthuman*; Suchman, *Human-Machine Reconfigurations*; Haraway, "Manifesto for Cyborgs."
53 Hester, *Xenofeminism*, 7.
54 Massumi, *Ontopower*, 63–92.
55 Adelman, "Security Glitches," 433.
56 Virilio and Lotringer, *Pure War*, 27.
57 Markoff, "Fearing Bombs."
58 Tucker, "Report"; emphasis ours.
59 Global Security Initiative, "Autonomy, Robotics, and Collective Systems."
60 Foucault, *Discipline and Punish*, 163–71.
61 Roach, *Grunt*, 11.

62 Roach, *Grunt*, 11.
63 On World War I, see Robertson, *Dream of Civilized Warfare*, 199–234. On World War II, see Hofmann, *Through Mobility We Conquer*.
64 Van Creveld, *Command in War*, 2.
65 Ernest et al., "Genetic Fuzzy Based Artificial Intelligence," 1.
66 Anthony, "DARPA Shows Off."
67 Roman, "Command or Control Dilemma," 7; emphasis ours.
68 Quoted in Arkin, *Governing Lethal Behavior*, 7.
69 Defense Science Board, *Report*, 16.
70 Shaw, *Predator Empire*, 10.
71 Andrejevic, "Droning of Experience."
72 Hansen, *New Philosophy*, 103, 105; emphasis ours.
73 Dyer-Witheford, *Cyber-Marx*, 3.
74 Ellul, *Technological Society*, 136.
75 Ellul, *Technological Society*, 136.
76 Reeves, "Automatic for the People."
77 DeLanda, *War*, 87.
78 Kittler, "Artificial Intelligence," 188.
79 Reeves, "Of Social Networks and Suicide Nets"; Virilio and Armitage, "Kosovo War," 170.
80 Foucault, "Security, Territory, Population," 70.
81 Daston and Galison, *Objectivity*.
82 Kittler, *Discourse Networks 1800/1900*, 369.
83 For more on the impact that related media technologies had on early modern epistemology, see Kittler, *Optical Media*, 75–76.
84 W. Brown, *Regulating Aversion*, 17.
85 Magnuson, *Mindful Economics*, 213.
86 Hayles, *How We Became Posthuman*, 86; also see Mayr, *Authority, Liberty, and Automated Machinery*.
87 Schmitt, *Concept of the Political*, 51.
88 Radloff, *Heidegger*, 265; see Schmitt, *Theory of the Partisan*, 61.
89 Schmitt, *Theory of the Partisan*, 61.
90 Spanos, "Heidegger," 248.
91 Fukuyama, *End of History*.
92 Schmitt, *Concept of the Political*, 54.
93 Mouffe, *Return of the Political*, 69.
94 Mouffe, *Return of the Political*, 3.
95 Dean, *Democracy and Other Neoliberal Fantasies*, 13.
96 Kittler, "Implementation of Knowledge," 60.
97 Russill, "Earth-Observing Media."
98 Heidegger, "Age of the World Picture," 129–30.
99 Heidegger, "Age of the World Picture," 133.
100 Merquior, *Foucault*, 53.
101 Foucault, *Order of Things*, 347.

102 White, *Metahistory*.
103 Žižek, "Introduction," 17.
104 Vattimo and Zabala, *Hermeneutic Communism*, 52.
105 Barad, *Meeting the Universe Halfway*; Daston and Galison, *Objectivity*.
106 See Iggers and Powell, *Leopold von Ranke*, 45–47.
107 Future of Life Institute, "Autonomous Weapons."
108 Virilio and Kittler, "Information Bomb," 105.

Chapter 1. Identification Friend or Foe (DoD)

EPIGRAPHS:
Tzu, *On the Art of War*, 12. Shakespeare, *Julius Caesar*, act 1, scene 1.

1 Unity Answers, "How to Detect Enemy."
2 Moore, *Vex*.
3 Rojas, *Fighting over Fidel*.
4 Dash, "Khrushchev in Water Wings."
5 Gavrilets, "Collective Action"; McNamara and Trumbull, *Evolutionary Psychology*.
6 Vucetich, "All about Wolves."
7 Singh and Hoffman, "Natural Selection and Shape Perception."
8 P. N. Edwards, *Closed World*.
9 Singh and Hoffman, "Natural Selection and Shape Perception."
10 Fisher, "Evolution and Bird Sociality."
11 United States War Department, *Binaural Training Instruments, M1 and M2*.
12 Secor, "Tesla's Views."
13 Rose Shell, *Hide and Seek*.
14 Richard, "E. Godfrey Burr."
15 IBM, *America's Peace of Mind*.

Chapter 2. Centralized Control/Decentralized Execution (DoD)

1 Hayles, *My Mother Was a Computer*, 21.
2 Sterling, *Ancient Times*, xxvii.
3 P. W. Clark, "Early Impacts of Communications," 1408.
4 Kittler, *Gramophone, Film, Typewriter*, 105.
5 P. W. Clark, "Early Impacts of Communications," 1408.
6 Romero, *Origins of Centralized Control*, 8–10.
7 United States War Department, *War Department Field Manual FM 100-20*, 4.
8 United States War Department, *War Department Field Manual FM 100-20*, 4.
9 United States War Department, *War Department Field Manual FM 100-20*, 7.
10 Romero, *Origins of Centralized Control*, 100.
11 United States Air Force, *Air Force Basic Doctrine*, 38.
12 Arquilla and Ronfeldt, *Advent of Netwar*.
13 Czerwinski, *Coping with the Bounds*, 33.
14 Lawson, *Nonlinear Science and Warfare*, 99–129.
15 Vego, "Operational Command," 101.

16 Vego, "Operational Command," 102.
17 Vego, "Operational Command," 101.
18 Bousquet, *Scientific Way of Warfare*, 143.
19 Vego, "Operational Command," 101.
20 Galloway, *Protocol*, 8.
21 Kittler, "Media Wars," 121.
22 Kittler, "Media Wars," 121.
23 Quoted in Kittler, "Artificial Intelligence," 183.
24 Kittler, "Artificial Intelligence," 183.
25 Work and Brimley, *Preparing for War*, 7.
26 Center for a New American Security, "Eighth Annual Conference"; cf. Crandall, "Ecologies of the Wayward Drone," 269.
27 Scharre, *Robotics on the Battlefield*, I:10–11, 24; Kindervater, "Technological Rationality."
28 Scharre, *Robotics on the Battlefield*, I:17.
29 Center for a New American Security, "Eighth Annual Conference."
30 Scharre, *Robotics on the Battlefield*, I:31.
31 Work and Brimley, *Preparing for War*, 23.
32 Northrop Grumman, "Northrop Grumman Awarded Contract."
33 Tucker, "Special Operators."
34 On "Space Pearl Harbor," see Wirbel, "Star Wars," 78. Commission to Assess United States National Security Space Management and Organization, "Report."
35 Santamarta, *Wake-Up Call*, 1.
36 United States Department of Defense, *Unmanned Systems Integrated Roadmap* (2013), 25, 49.
37 See Parks, "Earth Observation."
38 Scharre, *Robotics on the Battlefield*, I:17.
39 United States Department of Defense, *Unmanned Systems Integrated Roadmap* (2013), 29.
40 United States Department of Defense, *Unmanned Systems Integrated Roadmap* (2013), 85.
41 Scharre, *Robotics on the Battlefield*, I:17.
42 United States Department of Defense, *Unmanned Systems Integrated Roadmap* (2013), 89.
43 Stimson Center, *Recommendations*, 71.
44 Kindervater, "Technological Rationality."
45 Stimson Center, *Recommendations*, 26.
46 United States Department of Defense, *Directive 3000.09*, 3.
47 Savage, "U.S. Releases Rules."
48 Savage and Schmitt, "Trump Administration."
49 Arquilla and Ronfeldt, *Swarming*; S. Edwards, *Swarming*.
50 Scharre, *Robotics on the Battlefield*, II:8.
51 Work and Brimley, *Preparing for War*, 29.
52 Finn, "Future for Drones."

53 Basso, Love, and Hedrick, "Airborne, Autonomous, and Collaborative."
54 United States Air Force, "Dynamic Targeting."
55 Tucker, *Future of Military Tech*, 2.
56 Stimson Center, *Recommendations*, 26.
57 Rubinstein and Shen, "Scalable and Distributed Model"; Scharre, *Robotics on the Battlefield*, II:32.
58 Scharre, *Robotics on the Battlefield*, II:26; also see Defense Update, "Low-Cost Autonomous Attack System."
59 Sharkey and Sharkey, "Swarm Intelligence"; Sarker and Dahl, "Bio-Inspired Communication."
60 On military research in "microrobotics," see Hundley and Gritton, "Future Technology-Driven Revolutions"; Solem, "Microrobotics in Warfare"; and Solem, "Military Microbiotics." Piore, "Rise of the Insect Drones."
61 DARPA, "Gremlins Takes Flight."
62 DARPA, "FLA Program Takes Flight."
63 On minidrones, see Golson, "Military-Grade Drone." Scharre, *Robotics on the Battlefield*, II:20; Perry, "Self-Organizing Thousand-Robot Swarm."
64 Department of Defense, *Unmanned Systems Integrated Roadmap* (2013), 72.
65 Center for a New American Security, "Eighth Annual Conference."
66 Center for a New American Security, "Eighth Annual Conference."
67 Defense Update, "Low-Cost Autonomous Attack System."
68 DeLanda, *War*, 81.
69 United States Department of Defense, *Unmanned Systems Integrated Roadmap* (2013), 78.
70 United States Department of Defense, *Unmanned Systems Integrated Roadmap* (2013), 78.
71 United States Department of Defense, *Unmanned Systems Integrated Roadmap* (2013), 78.
72 Bousquet, *Scientific Way of Warfare*, 244.

Chapter 3. Hostile Environment (DoD)

EPIGRAPHS:
Callicott, *Thinking Like a Planet*, 239. US Department of Defense, *Climate Change Adaptation Roadmap*. Jules in *Pulp Fiction*, reciting Ezekiel 25:17. Quentin Tarantino, 1994, Miramax Films. Spangler, "Meaning of Gaia," 44.

1 Kittler, *Gramophone, Film, Typewriter*, xxxix.
2 Latour, "Waiting for Gaia."
3 Russill, "Earth-Observing Media."
4 P. N. Edwards, *The Closed World: Computers and the Politics of Discourse in Cold War America*.
5 Russill, "Earth-Observing Media."
6 Chow, *Age of the World Target*.
7 Brand, "Weather and the Military."

8   Gerstenberger, *Theologies of the Old Testament*, 151.
9   As with most biblical passages, there is some dispute as to whether the day was lengthened to allow for a longer battle or whether the night was extended to provide the Israelites much-needed rest to prepare for battle.
10 Richard Williams, "Two Historic Storms."
11 Sloterdijk, *Terror from the Air*, 23.
12 Clausewitz, *On War* (1873), 1.7.
13 Clausewitz, *On War* (1873), 2.2.24.
14 Clausewitz, *On War* (1873), 2.2.33.
15 Lele, *Weather and Warfare*.
16 Potter, "Retrospect."
17 Brehm, "Weather," 1.
18 Lele, *Weather and Warfare*, 45.
19 Lele, *Weather and Warfare*, 8.
20 P. N. Edwards, *Closed World*.
21 Lele, *Weather and Warfare*, 26–44.
22 Espy, "Report on Meteorology."
23 Abbe, "Weather Synopsis and Probabilities."
24 Raines, *Getting the Message Through*, 41–80.
25 Nebeker, *Calculating the Weather*, 92.
26 Bates and Fuller, *America's Weather Warriors*, 8.
27 Shiga, "Sonar," 373.
28 Peters, *Marvelous Clouds*.
29 Pedgley, "Meeting Report," 264.
30 A. Clark, "The Right Weather for War?"
31 Russill, "Earth Imaging," 236.
32 Sloterdijk, *Terror from the Air*, 27.
33 Sloterdijk, *Terror from the Air*, 48.
34 Bates and Fuller, *America's Weather Warriors*.
35 P. N. Edwards, *Closed World*.
36 Shiga, "Of Other Networks."
37 Hamblin, *Arming Mother Nature*.
38 H-Bomb Guinea Pigs, quoted in Barad, "Troubling Time/s," 58.
39 Virilio, *War and Cinema*.
40 Galison, "Ontology of the Enemy."
41 Fleming, *Fixing the Sky*, 165–88.
42 Fuller, *Air Weather Service Support*, 14; Brehm, "Weather," 10.
43 Galison, "Ontology of the Enemy."
44 On the war in Vietnam, see Thomas, "Secret Wheat Deal." On the SALT Treaty, see Hersh, *Price of Power*.
45 Kosuth, "Food Security."
46 Liotta and Shearer, *Gaia's Revenge*, 67–88.
47 Ullman, "Redefining Security," 133.
48 Gordon, *Electronic Warfare*.

49 Hamblin, *Arming Mother Nature.*
50 P. N. Edwards, *Closed World.*
51 Galison, "Ontology of the Enemy"; Lovelock, *Revenge of Gaia.*
52 Spangler, "Meaning of Gaia," 44.
53 Lovelock, *Revenge of Gaia,* 153.
54 Skyttner, *General Systems Theory,* 143–44.
55 Latour, "Waiting for Gaia."
56 Latour, "Waiting for Gaia," 2.
57 Latour, "Waiting for Gaia," 9.
58 Latour, "Waiting for Gaia," 10.
59 Hamilton, "Forget 'Saving the Earth.'"
60 Hamilton, "Forget 'Saving the Earth.'"
61 Skyttner, *General Systems Theory,* 161.

Chapter 4. In Extremis (DoD)

EPIGRAPH:
Heidegger, "Question Concerning Technology," 28.

1 Future of Life Institute, "Autonomous Weapons."
2 Levy, *Love and Sex with Robots.*
3 On "the second machine age," see Brynjolfsson and McAfee, *Second Machine Age*; Reeves, "Automatic for the People"; Susskind and Susskind, *Future of the Professions.*
4 Wajcman, "Automation," 125.
5 Crawford and Calo, "Blind Spot"; Crawford, "Artificial Intelligence's White Guy Problem."
6 Wajcman, "Automation."
7 Crawford, "Artificial Intelligence's White Guy Problem."
8 Crawford, "Artificial Intelligence's White Guy Problem."
9 Crawford, "Artificial Intelligence's White Guy Problem."
10 Browne, *Dark Matters*; Magnet, *When Biometrics Fail*; S. U. Noble, *Algorithms of Oppression.*
11 Peters, "Introduction: Friedrich Kittler's Light Shows," 6; also see Kittler, *Discourse Networks,* 1.
12 Pinker, "Thinking Does Not Imply Subjugating."
13 Shermer, "When It Comes to AI, Think Protopia, Not Utopia or Dystopia."
14 Shermer, "When It Comes to AI, Think Protopia, Not Utopia or Dystopia."
15 Wajcman, *Feminism Confronts Technology,* x.
16 Wajcman, *Feminism Confronts Technology,* 163.
17 Raymond Williams, *Television: Technology and Cultural Form.*
18 Wajcman, *Feminism Confronts Technology,* 163.
19 Wajcman, "Feminist Theories of Technology."
20 Winner, *Whale and the Reactor,* 279–301.
21 Mander, *Four Arguments,* 44.

22 On catastrophes, see Virilio, *University of Disaster*, 39-40. On nuclear waste, see Galison, "Half-Life of Story." On geopolitical tensions, see Pascual and Zambetakis, "Geopolitics of Energy."
23 Winner, *Autonomous Technology*, 303-4.
24 Winner, *Autonomous Technology*, 285.
25 Sloterdijk, *Critique of Cynical Reason*, 448-49.
26 Babich, "Sloterdijk's Cynicism: Diogenes in the Marketplace," 26.
27 Floreano and Mattiussi, *Bio-Inspired Artificial Intelligence*, 16.
28 Adami, "Robots with Instincts."
29 Omohundro, "Autonomous Technology," 306.
30 Russell, "Of Myths and Moonshine."
31 Singh and Hoffman, "Computational Evolutionary Perception."
32 Omohundro, "Autonomous Technology."
33 Bostrom, *Superintelligence*, 140.
34 Bostrom, *Superintelligence*, 141.
35 Hunter, *Culture and Government*.
36 Pinker, *Better Angels*, xxi-xxii.
37 Ohlin, "Combatant's Stance."
38 Asaro, "Determinism."
39 Corn, "Autonomous Weapon Systems," 221.
40 Roff and Moyes, "Meaningful Human Control, Artificial Intelligence, and Autonomous Weapons," 6.
41 Heidegger, "Age of the World Picture," 133.
42 McLuhan, *Understanding Media: The Extensions of Man*.
43 Kittler, "Discourse on Discourse," 166.
44 Gane, "Radical Post-humanism," 38.
45 Stiegler, *Technics and Time*, 1:82-84.
46 Shaw, *Predator Empire*, 65, 62.
47 Shaw, *Predator Empire*, 157.
48 Heidegger, *Nietzsche*, 4:116-17.
49 Elden, *Mapping the Present*, 92; cf. Heidegger, "Question Concerning Technology," 37.
50 Haraway, *Simians, Cyborgs, and Women*, 189.
51 Lazzarato and Alliez, "To Our Enemies."
52 Lukács, *History and Class Consciousness*, xxxiii; Marcuse, "Some Social Implications."
53 Virilio and Lotringer, *Pure War*, 19-20.
54 Heidegger, "What Are Poets For?" 114-15.
55 Ziarek, "Vulnerable World," 179, 183.
56 Heidegger, "Age of the World Picture," 164.
57 Heidegger, "Question Concerning Technology."
58 Heidegger, *Nietzsche*, 4:116.
59 Chow, *Age of the World Target*, 31.
60 C. Kaplan, "Mobility and War," 41. Also see C. Kaplan, *Aerial Aftermaths*.
61 Heidegger, "Question Concerning Technology," 28.

62 Kittler, *Gramophone, Film, Typewriter*, 16.
63 Sloterdijk, *Critique of Cynical Reason*, 435.
64 McFarland, "Elon Musk"; Musk, "Elon Musk's Deleted *Edge* Comment."

Chapter 5. Intelligence, Surveillance, and Reconnaissance (DoD)

EPIGRAPHS:
P. N. Edwards, *Closed World*, 75. Kittler, "Artificial Intelligence," 191. DeLanda, "Economics," 168. IBM, *Where America's Peace of Mind Begins*.

1 Redmond and Smith, *From Whirlwind to MITRE*; D. Noble, *Forces of Production*; P. N. Edwards, *Closed World*; Dyson, *Darwin among the Machines*; Hughes, *Rescuing Prometheus*; Schaffel, *Emerging Shield*.
2 P. N. Edwards, *Closed World*, 75.
3 Pettegrew, *Light It Up*.
4 Packer and Oswald, "From Windscreen to Widescreen"; Reeves, "Of Social Networks."
5 Buderi, *Invention That Changed the World*; Manovich, *Language of New Media*.
6 Kahn, *Codebreakers*.
7 Buderi, *Invention That Changed the World*, 381.
8 Astrahan and Jacobs, "History of the Design of the SAGE Computer—The AN/FSQ-7," 341.
9 DeLanda, "Economics," 168; D. Noble, *Forces of Production*.
10 Dyson, *Darwin among the Machines*, 145.
11 Turner, *From Counterculture to Cyberculture*; Dyer-Witheford, *Cyber-Marx*.
12 Dyer-Witheford, *Cyber-Marx*.
13 DeLanda, "Economics."
14 Schaffel, *Emerging Shield*, 158–59.
15 Hay and Andrejevic, "Governmental Experiments"; Packer, "Becoming Bombs."
16 Kittler, *Gramophone, Film, Typewriter*.
17 Kittler, *Gramophone, Film, Typewriter*.
18 Kittler, *Optical Media*; McLuhan, *Understanding Media*.
19 Kittler, *Optical Media*, 58.
20 Kittler, *Gramophone, Film, Typewriter*, 249.
21 Packer, "Becoming Bombs"; Packer, "Homeland Subjectivity."
22 Dyson, *Darwin among the Machines*, 155
23 Crandall, "Operational Media."
24 Foucault, *History of Sexuality*, vol. 2.
25 Buderi, *Invention That Changed the World*.
26 Manovich, *Language of New Media*.
27 Harrington, "Radar Data Transmission," 373.
28 IBM, *On Guard: The Story of SAGE*.
29 IBM, *On Guard: The Story of SAGE*.
30 Dyson, *Darwin among the Machines*, 181.

Chapter 6. Autonomous Operation (DoD)

1. Mikesh, *Balloon Bomb Attacks*.
2. Haydon, *Military Ballooning*, 19–39.
3. Doel, *Geographies of Violence*, 106–7.
4. C. Kaplan, "Mobility and War," 401; C. Kaplan, "Balloon Prospect," 36–39.
5. Deeds, "Aviation of the Future," 3.
6. Deeds, "Aviation of the Future," 3, 4.
7. *Army-Navy-Air Force Register Times*, "Plane Flies Ninety," 498.
8. Reilly, "During World War I."
9. *Army-Navy-Air Force Register Times*, "Plane Flies Ninety Miles," 498.
10. *Army-Navy-Air Force Register Times*, "Plane Flies Ninety Miles," 498.
11. Everett, *Unmanned Systems*, 76–179.
12. See Pearson, "Developing the Flying Bomb."
13. Radio News, "French Claim Priority," 874.
14. Radio News, "French Claim Priority," 874.
15. Mindell, "Beasts and Systems," 206.
16. Mindell, "Beasts and Systems," 204.
17. Crandall, "Ontologies of the Wayward Drone."
18. *Michigan Technic*, "*Technic* Explores," 64.
19. Spark, "Unmanned Precision Weapons."
20. Gusterson, *Drone*, 29–58.
21. Spark, "Unmanned Precision Weapons."
22. Kittler, "Short History of the Searchlight," 389.
23. *Popular Mechanics*, "Pilotless Photo Drone," 144.
24. Zaloga, *Unmanned Aerial Vehicles*, 17–29.
25. Mazzetti, "Drone Zone."
26. On the use of UAVs during and after the Balkan conflicts, see Arkin, *Governing Lethal Behavior*. On drones in the US Air Force, see Bowman, "Air Force Chief."
27. Bumiller, "Day Job."
28. Mazzetti, "Drone Zone."
29. Kittler, "Media Wars," 121.
30. Arkin, *Governing Lethal Behavior*, 7.
31. *Daily Mail*, "Catalogue of Errors."
32. Defense Science Board, *Report*, 94.
33. Defense Science Board, *Report*, 95.
34. Bousquet, "Lethal Visions."
35. Bousquet, "Lethal Visions," 96, 1–2, 16.
36. Virilio, *Vision Machine*, 69–70.
37. Virilio, *Vision Machine*, 69.
38. Watkins, "Numbers Game."
39. Cappacio, "Pentagon."
40. Li, Gauci, and Gross, "Turing Learning."
41. Hornyak, "Human Rights Watch."

42 Osborn, "Air Force Chief Scientist."
43 Bowman, "Air Force Chief."
44 Mbembe, "Necropolitics," 40.
45 Arkin, *Governing Lethal Behavior*, xvi; Gregory, "From a View to a Kill."
46 Kaplan, Loyer, and Daniels, "Precision Targets," 400.
47 Cavallaro, Sonnenberg, and Knuckey, *Living under Drones*.
48 Zenko, "Obama's Final Drone Strike Data."
49 Stein, "CIA Mum on Lawsuit."
50 Grothoff and Porup, "The NSA's SKYNET Program."
51 Pellerin, "Pentagon Spokesman."
52 Almosawa and Hussain, "U.S. Drone Strike."
53 Becker and Shane, "Secret 'Kill List.'"
54 Chamayou, *Theory of the Drone*, 211.
55 Shaw, *Predator Empire*.
56 Schmitt, *Theory of the Partisan*, 36.
57 Schmitt, *Theory of the Partisan*, 67.
58 Horn, "Knowing the Enemy."

Chapter 7. Vital Ground (DOD)

EPIGRAPHS:
Bush, "Address," 187. Intel, "From Sand to Circuits." Mattis, quoted in Wolff, "Mattis?" Kittler, "Animals of War," 394. Tzu, *On the Art of War*, 15.

1 Parikka, *Geology of Media*.
2 Intel, "From Sand to Circuits."
3 Hoy, "World's Biggest Fuel Consumer."
4 Armitage, "Discourse Networks," 27.
5 C. Kaplan, "Mobility and War," 395.
6 Foucault, *Security, Territory, Population*.
7 Hilferding, *Finance Capital*; Wallerstein, *World Systems Analysis*.
8 Kittler, "Of States," 405.
9 Kittler, "Of States," 394.
10 Winegard, *First World Oil War*.
11 Dunbar, *Human Evolution*, 196–200.
12 Lee, *Waging War*, 86–116.
13 Gill, "Eye Health."
14 Baugh, "Dynamics of Spear Throwing," 345.
15 Shea, *Stone Tools*, 150.
16 Van Creveld, *Transformation of War*, 176–81.
17 Schuster, "Submarines."
18 Dunlop, "Canada's Future Submarines."
19 European Nuclear Society, "Fuel Comparison."
20 Winthrop-Young, "Drill and Distraction," 831.
21 Cavas, "Unmanned Sub-Hunter."

22 Bartis and Van Bibber, *Alternative Fuels*.
23 Hambling, "Longer-Lasting Drones."
24 Hambling, "Longer-Lasting Drones."
25 Hsu, "Power-Seeking Flying Microdrone."
26 DARPA, "FLA Program Takes Flight."
27 See video at Zennie, "Death."
28 On alternative energy sources, see Hagood, "Storage Battery." On military applications, see Bartis and Van Bibber, *Alternative Fuels*.
29 HDIAC Staff, "Military's Shift."
30 HDIAC Staff, "Military's Shift."
31 Tucker, "Wi-Fi."
32 Peck, "New Mission."
33 Siegert, "The Map Is the Territory."
34 P. N. Edwards, *Closed World*; C. Kaplan, "Precision Targets."
35 Siegert, "The Map Is the Territory," 13.
36 Northrop Grumman, "Gaining a Cyber Advantage."
37 Northrop Grumman, "Gaining a Cyber Advantage."
38 F. Kaplan, *Dark Territory*. Ware, "Security Controls for Computer Systems."
39 Christensen, "Disruptive Innovation."
40 Arquilla and Ronfeldt, *Advent of Netwar*.
41 Arquilla and Ronfeldt, *Advent of Netwar*, 25.
42 Tse-Tung, *Mao Tse-tung on Guerrilla Warfare*, 3–4.
43 Carey, *Communication as Culture*.
44 Virilio, *Information Bomb*.
45 Kittler, *Optical Media*.

Chapter 8. Escalation (DOD)

1 Kittler, *Optical Media*, 31.
2 Winthrop-Young, "De Bellis Germanicis," 363
3 On China's defense spending, see Bitzinger, "China's Double-Digit Defense Growth." On Russia's military budget, see Rozin and Litovkin, "Russia Joins World's Top Three."
4 Gigova, "Vladimir Putin."
5 Bender, "Secret U.S. Army Study."
6 Stockholm International Peace Research Institute, "World Military Spending."
7 Markoff and Rosenberg, "China's Intelligent Weaponry Gets Smarter."
8 Defense Science Board, *Report*, iii, 42.
9 Defense Science Board, *Report*, 42.
10 Weisberger, "Pentagon."
11 Emmerich, *Independence Day*.
12 Rancière, "Final Enemy," 16.
13 Dixon, *Visions of the Apocalypse*, 59–96.
14 Bay, *Armageddon*.

15 Fukuyama, *End of History*, 73.
16 Fukuyama, *End of History*, 73–74.
17 See, for instance, Klein, *Shock Doctrine*.
18 Van Creveld, *Command in War*, 208.
19 Jenkins, "Read President Trump's Speech."
20 Reeves and May, "Peace Rhetoric."
21 See, for example, Hardt and Negri, *Multitude*.
22 McLuhan, *Understanding Media*, 80; Kittler, *Optical Media*, 30.
23 McLuhan, *Understanding Media*, 80.
24 Kittler, *Optical Media*, 30.
25 On "messianic finality," see Winthrop-Young, *Kittler and the Media*, 74. On "telos," see Maddalena and Packer, "Digital Body."
26 Kittler, *Gramophone, Film, Typewriter*, 2.
27 Kittler, "Artificial Intelligence," 187; emphasis ours.
28 Winthrop-Young, "Drill and Distraction," 832.
29 Gane and Sale, "Interview," 324–26.
30 Virilio and Kittler, "Information Bomb," 105–6.
31 Virilio and Kittler, "Information Bomb," 105–6.
32 Bousquet, *Scientific Way of Warfare*, 165, 167.
33 Bousquet, *Scientific Way of Warfare*.
34 Maddalena and Russill, "Optical Medium," 3192–93.
35 Gane and Sale, "Interview," 324.
36 Leopold, "Quantum Leaps."
37 Yale Quantum Institute, "US Lead."
38 Friedson, "Quantum Computer Revolution."
39 Friedson, "Quantum Computer Revolution."
40 *Economic Times*, "World's First Quantum Computing Machine."
41 DARPA, "Accelerating Complex Computer Simulations."
42 Haas, "Cheap Lasers and Bad Math."
43 Tucker, "Military."
44 Dyson, "Jaron."
45 Kittler, *Optical Media*, 30.
46 Kittler, *Optical Media*, 208.
47 Kittler, "History of Communication Media," 1996.
48 Metz, "Google's Dueling Neural Networks."
49 A special issue of the *Journal of Strategic Studies* (vol. 33, no. 4 [2010]) articulates how this adversarial military development has been playing out over the past quarter century.
50 Reeves, "Automatic for the People."
51 Kittler, "History of Communication Media."
52 Stiegler, *Technics and Time*, 1: 193.

Chapter 9. Unidentified Flying Objects (USAF)

EPIGRAPH:
Kittler, "History of Communication Media."

1. Cooper, Blumenthal, and Kean, "'Wow, What Is That?' Navy Pilots Report Unexplained Flying Objects."
2. Wilson, "Directing the Air Force."
3. Leonard, *Department of Defense Dictionary*.
4. Peters, "Space, Time, and Communication Theory," 304.
5. Kanas, *Solar System Maps*, 40.
6. Russill, "Is the Earth a Medium?"
7. Peters, *Marvelous Clouds*.
8. For a mediacentric understanding of how satellites have created new forms of mapping the earth and opened up new epistemological capacities, see Parks, *Cultures in Orbit*, and the special issue of the *Canadian Journal of Communication* from 2013 devoted to "Earth Observation Media," edited by Chris Russill.
9. Sheehan, *Planet Mars*, 20–28.
10. Sullivan, "Extraterrestrial Life," 79.
11. Flammarion, *Camille Flammarion's The Planet Mars*, 514.
12. Wells, *War of the Worlds*, 11.
13. Wells, *War of the Worlds*, 15.
14. Wells, *War of the Worlds*, 4.
15. Serviss, *Edison's Conquest of Mars*, 19.
16. Serviss, *Edison's Conquest of Mars*, 37.
17. National Aeronautics and Space Administration, "NASA Strategic Plan: 2014," 21.
18. Russill, "Is the Earth a Medium?"
19. Wall, "NASA Finds 1,284 Alien Planets."
20. Eshelman, "Gravitational Lens of the Sun."
21. Maccone, *Deep Space Flight and Communications*.
22. Einstein, "Lens-Like Action"; Landis, "Mission." "AU" stands for "Astronomical Unit," which is the measurement of the average distance of Earth from the sun. It is the equivalent of about 150 million kilometers.
23. Landis, "Mission."
24. Carter, "Voyager Spacecraft Statement"; emphasis ours.
25. Peters, *Speaking into the Air*.
26. P. N. Edwards, *Vast Machine*.
27. Freitas, "Self-Reproducing Interstellar Probe," 252.
28. Freitas, "Self-Reproducing Interstellar Probe," 251–64.
29. Galison, "Ontology of the Enemy," 228–66.
30. Forgan, "Slingshot Dynamics."
31. International Academy of Astronautics, "Rio Scale."
32. Peter Plavchan, quoted in Boyle, "Is That an Alien Signal?"
33. Borra and Trottier, "Discovery."

34 Boyle, "Is That an Alien Signal?"
35 Wall, "Electronic E.T."
36 See Taylor and Boan, *Alien Invasion*, for an explanation of how such redirection might work, or Stanley Kim Robinson's *2312* regarding space rock attack.
37 Jet Propulsion Laboratory, "Asteroid Emergency Planning Exercise."
38 Taylor and Boan, *Alien Invasion*.

Conclusion. Armistice (DOD)

EPIGRAPHS:
Tzu, *The Art of War*, (1963) 112. Diem, "The Diaries of Colonel Walter E. Kurtz." This diary is itself a fictional account that exists outside the film *Apocalypse Now*. Fan fiction can be viewed as a thriving form of speculative fiction that engages not in conjecture regarding the world but rather speculation that adheres to the logic of a given fictional universe. It is included here not only to help specify a kind of rogue logic but also to accept the wide array of speculative accounts that might bolster futurological thought.

1 Booz Allen Hamilton, *Predictive Analytics Handbook*.
2 Booz Allen Hamilton, *Predictive Analytics Handbook*.
3 Massumi, "Potential Politics," 2.
4 Franklin, *War Stars*, 131-48.
5 Galison, "Future of Scenarios," 39-41.
6 Army Press, "Future Warfare Writing Program Submission Guidelines."
7 Maconie, *Avant Garde*, 5.
8 See Benjamin, "Prophets and Profits of Racial Science" for a fascinating reflection on the politics of militarized speculative fiction.
9 Coppola, *Apocalypse Now*.
10 Asimov, *I, Robot*.
11 Shelley, *Frankenstein*.
12 Virilio and Lotringer, *Pure War*, 45.
13 Bryson, "Robots Should Be Slaves," 72.
14 Anderson, *Science Fiction and Philosophy*.
15 Asimov, *Bicentennial Man*, 136.
16 Irwin, *Matrix and Philosophy*.
17 Jonze, *Her*.
18 Ingles, "Regulating Religious Robots," 207.
19 On Japan, see Gibbs, "The Future of Funerals?" On Germany, see Sherwood, "Robot Priest Unveiled in Germany."
20 Bostrom, *Superintelligence*; Vinge, "Coming Technological Singularity; Kurzweil, *The Singularity Is Near*.
21 Ingles, "Regulating Religious Robots," 509.
22 J. C. Murray, "War and Conscience."
23 Mason, *Weapon*, 428-29.
24 Santayana, *Soliloquies*, 102.

25 F. Brown, "Answer," 224.
26 Schmitt, *Theory of the Partisan*, 56–57.
27 Cellan-Jones, "Stephen Hawking Warns."
28 Saul, "Professor Stephen Hawking."
29 Heidegger, *Country Path Conversations*, 11
30 Heidegger, *Country Path Conversations*, 103, 11, 21.

References

Abbate, Janet. 2012. *Recoding Gender: Women's Changing Participation in Computing.* Cambridge, MA: MIT Press.

Abbe, Cleveland. 1871. "Weather Synopsis and Probabilities." February 19. Washington, DC: Signal Corps Office.

Adami, Christoph. 2015. "Robots with Instincts." *Nature* 521: 426–27.

Adelman, Rebecca A. 2018. "Security Glitches: The Failure of Universal Camouflage Pattern and the Fantasy of 'Identity Intelligence.'" *Science, Technology, and Human Values* 43 (3): 431–63.

Almosawa, Shuaib, and Murtaza Hussain. 2017. "U.S. Drone Strike in Yemen Killed Men Who Had Nothing to Do with Al Qaeda, According to Relatives." The Intercept, May 19. https://theintercept.com/2017/05/19/u-s-drone-strike-in-yemen-killed-men-who-had-nothing-to-do-with-al-qaeda-according-to-relatives/.

Aly, Götz, and Karl Heinz Roth. 2017. *The Nazi Census: Identification and Control in the Third Reich.* Philadelphia: Temple University Press.

Anderson, S. L. 2016. "Asimov's 'Three Laws of Robotics' and Machine Metaethics." In *Science Fiction and Philosophy: From Time Travel to Superintelligence*, edited by S. Schneider. 2nd ed. Hoboken, NJ: Wiley.

Andrejevic, Mark. 2016. "The Droning of Experience." *Fibreculture Journal* 25 (1): 202–17.

Anthony, Sebastian. 2013. "DARPA Shows Off 1.8-Gigapixel Surveillance Drone, Can Spot a Terrorist from 20,000 Feet." Extreme Tech, January 28, 2013. http://www.extremetech.com/extreme/146909-darpa-shows-off-1-8-gigapixel-surveillance-drone-can-spot-a-terrorist-from-20000-feet.

Arkin, Ronald. 2009. *Governing Lethal Behavior in Autonomous Robots.* New York: Taylor and Francis.

Armitage, John. 2006 "From Discourse Networks to Cultural Mathematics: An Interview with Friedrich A. Kittler." *Theory, Culture & Society* 23 (7–8): 17–38.

Army-Navy-Air Force Register Times. 1922. "Plane Flies Ninety Miles without Pilot." 72 (2208): 498.

Army Press. 2017. "Future Warfare Writing Program." Army University Press. http://www.armyupress.army.mil/Special-Topics/Future-Warfare-Writing-Program/Future-Warfare-Writing-Program-Submission-Guidelines.

Arquilla, John, and David Ronfeldt. 1996. *The Advent of Netwar*. Santa Monica, CA: Rand Corporation.

Arquilla, John, and David Ronfeldt. 1997. *In Athena's Camp: Preparing for Conflict in the Information Age*. Santa Monica, CA: RAND.

Arquilla, John, and David Ronfeldt. 2000. *Swarming and the Future of Conflict*. Santa Monica, CA: Rand Corporation.

Asaro, Peter. 2014. "Determinism, Machine Agency, and Responsibility." *Politica & Società* 2 (1): 165–292.

Asimov, Isaac. 1950. *I, Robot*. New York: Gnome Press.

Asimov, Isaac. 1976. *Bicentennial Man*. New York: Ballantine.

Astrahan, Morton, and John Jacobs. 1983. "History of the Design of the SAGE Computer—The AN/FSQ-7." *Annals of the History of Computing* 5 (4): 340–49.

Babich, Babette. "Sloterdijk's Cynicism: Diogenes in the Marketplace." In *Sloterdijk Now*, edited by Stuart Elden, 17–36. Cambridge: Polity Press.

Barad, Karen. 2007. *Meeting the Universe Halfway: Quantum Physics and the Entanglement of Matter and Meaning*. Durham, NC: Duke University Press.

Barad, Karen. 2017. "Troubling Time/s and Ecologies of Nothingness: Re-turning, Re-membering, and Facing the Incalculable." *New Formations* (autumn): 56–86.

Barker, Thomas Herbert. 1863. *On Malaria and Miasmata: And Their Influence in the Production of Typhus and Typhoid Fevers, Cholera, and the Exanthemata*. London: John W. Davies.

Bartis, James T., and Lawrence Van Bibber. 2011. *Alternative Fuels for Military Applications*. Santa Monica, CA: RAND.

Barton, John H. 1981. *The Politics of Peace: An Evaluation of Arms Control*. Stanford, CA: Stanford University Press.

Basso, Brandon, Joshua Love, and J. Karl Hedrick. 2011. "Airborne, Autonomous, and Collaborative: Unmanned Aerial Vehicles Have Changed the Face of Warfare but UAVs Can Do Even More When They Fly in Flocks." *Mechanical Engineering-CIME* 133 (4): 27–31.

Bates, Charles C., and John F. Fuller. 1986. *America's Weather Warriors, 1814–1985*. College Station: Texas A&M Press.

Baugh, Richard A. 2013. "Dynamics of Spear Throwing." *American Journal of Physics* 71: 345.

Bay, Michael. 1998. *Armageddon*. Burbank, CA: Touchstone Pictures. DVD.

Becker, Jo, and Scott Shane. 2012. "Secret 'Kill List' Proves a Test of Obama's Principles and Will." *New York Times*, May 29.

Bell, Christopher M., and Bruce A. Elleman, eds. 2003. *Naval Mutinies of the Twentieth Century: An International Perspective*. Portland, OR: Frank Cass.

Bender, Bryan. 2016. "The Secret U.S. Army Study That Targets Moscow." Politico, April 14. http://www.politico.com/magazine/story/2016/04/moscow-pentagon-us-secret-study-213811?o=1.

Benjamin, Ruha. 2018. "Prophets and Profits of Racial Science." *Kalfou: A Journal of Comparative and Relational Ethnic Studies* 5 (1): 41–53.

Bertillon, Alphonse. 1896. *Signaletic Instructions: Including the Theory and Practice of Anthropometrical Identification*. Edited by R. W. McClaughry. Chicago: Werner.

Beyerchen, Alan. 1992. "Clausewitz, Nonlinearity, and the Unpredictability of War." *International Security* 17 (3): 59–90.

Bitzinger, Richard A. 2015. "China's Double-Digit Defense Growth." *Foreign Affairs*, March 19. https://www.foreignaffairs.com/articles/china/2015-03-19/chinas-double-digit-defense-growth.

Booz Allen Hamilton. 2017. *Predictive Analytics Handbook for National Defense*. Booz Allen.com.

Borra, Ermanno F., and Eric Trottier. 2016. "Discovery of Peculiar Periodic Spectral Modulations in a Small Fraction of Solar-Type Stars." *Astronomical Society of the Pacific* 128 (969): 28 pp.

Bostrom, Nick. 2014. *Superintelligence: Paths, Dangers, Strategies*. New York: Oxford University Press.

Bousquet, Antoine. 2009. *The Scientific Way of Warfare: Order and Chaos on the Battlefields of Modernity*. New York: Columbia University Press.

Bousquet, Antoine. 2017. "Lethal Visions: The Eye as Function of the Weapon." *Critical Studies on Security* 5 (1): 62–80.

Bowman, Tom. 2012. "Air Force Chief Leaves Legacy in the Sky: Drones." National Public Radio, August 10. http://m.npr.org/news/U.S./158521495.

Boyle, Rebecca. 2016. "Is That an Alien Signal? Please Answer on a Scale of 1 to 10." FiveThirtyEight, October 27. https://fivethirtyeight.com/features/is-that-an-alien-signal-please-answer-on-a-scale-of-1-to-10/.

Brady, Erika. 1999. *A Spiral Way: How the Phonograph Changed Ethnography*. Jackson: University of Mississippi Press.

Braidotti, Rosi. 2013. *The Posthuman*. Cambridge: Polity Press.

Brand, Samson. 1981. "Weather and the Military: A Historical Perspective." *National Weather Digest* 6 (4): 8–10.

Bratich, Jack. 2017. "Reality States: Notes on the Homicidal State." *Fifth Estate* 399 (fall): 39–40.

Brehm, Barbara. 1991. "Weather: Operational Considerations on the Battlefield." Newport, RI: Naval War College.

Brown, Frederick. 1954. "Answer." In *Angels and Spaceships*. New York: E. P. Dutton.

Brown, Wendy. 2006. *Regulating Aversion: Tolerance in the Age of Identity and Empire*. Princeton, NJ: Princeton University Press.

Browne, Simone. 2015. *Dark Matters: On the Surveillance of Blackness*. Durham, NC: Duke University Press.

Brynjofsson, Erik, and Andrew McAfee. 2014. *The Second Machine Age: Work, Progress, and Prosperity in a Time of Brilliant Technologies*. New York: W. W. Norton.

Bryson, Joanna J. 2010. "Robots Should Be Slaves." In *Close Engagements with Artificial Companions: Key Social, Psychological, Ethical, and Design Issues*, 63–74. New York: University of Oxford Press.

Buderi, Robert. 1998. *The Invention That Changed the World: How a Small Group of Radar Pioneers Won the Second World War and Launched a Technological Revolution*. New York: Simon & Schuster, 1996.

Bumiller, Elisabeth. 2012. "A Day Job Waiting for a Kill Shot a World Away." *New York Times*, July 29.

Bush, George H. W. 1991. "Address to the Nation on the Suspension of Allied Offensive Combat Operations in the Persian Gulf." In *Public Papers of the Presidents of the United States: George H. W. Bush, 1991*. https://bush41library.tamu.edu/archives/public-papers/2746.

Callicott, J. Baird. *Thinking Like a Planet: The Land Ethic and the Earth Ethic*. New York: Oxford University Press.

Cappacio, Tony. 2012. "Pentagon Seeks More Afghan Surveillance Drones in Shift." Bloomberg.com, July 2. http://www.bloomberg.com/news/2012-07-02/pentagon-seeks-more-afghan-surveillancedrones-In-shift.html.

Carey, James. 1990. *Communication as Culture*. New York: Routledge.

Carruthers, Susan L. 2011. *The Media at War*. New York: Palgrave Macmillan.

Carter, Jimmy. 1977. "Voyager Spacecraft Statement by the President." Gerhard Peters and John T. Woolley, American Presidency Project, July 29. http://www.presidency.ucsb.edu/ws/?pid=7890.

Cavallaro, James, Stephan Sonnenberg, and Sarah Knuckey. 2012. *Living under Drones: Death, Injury and Trauma to Civilians from US Drone Practices in Pakistan*. Stanford, CA: International Human Rights and Conflict Resolution Clinic. https://law.stanford.edu/publications/living-under-drones-death-injury-and-trauma-to-civilians-from-us-drone-practices-in-pakistan/.

Cavas, Christopher P. 2016. "Unmanned Sub-Hunter to Begin Test Project." *Defense One*, April 7. http://www.defensenews.com/story/defense-news/2016/04/07/darpa-actuv-sea-hunter-test-antisubmarine-warfare-asw-drone-unmanned-vigor-portland-onr-naval-research/82744862/.

Cazenave, Noel A. 2018. *Killing African Americans: Police and Vigilante Violence as a Racial Control Mechanism*. New York: Routledge.

Cellan-Jones, Rory. 2014. "Stephen Hawking Warns Artificial Intelligence Could End Mankind." BBC.com, December 2. http://www.bbc.com/news/technology-30290540.

Center for a New American Security. 2014. "Eighth Annual Conference: Robotics on the Battlefield: The Coming Swarm." YouTube, June 20. https://www.youtube.com/watch?v=_WuxwBHI6zY.

Chamayou, Grégoire. 2011. *A Theory of the Drone*. Translated by Janet Lloyd. New York: New Press.

Chow, Rey. 2006. *The Age of the World Target: Self-Referentiality in War, Theory, and Comparative Work*. Durham, NC: Duke University Press.

Christensen, Clayton. 2017 "Disruptive Innovation." Harvard Business School, September 21. http://www.claytonchristensen.com/key-concepts/.

Clark, Andrew. 2016. "The Right Weather for War? From War-Weather to Zeppelin Barometers." English Words in War-Time, April 12. https://wordsinwartime.wordpress.com.

Clark, Paul W. 1976. "Early Impacts of Communications on Military Doctrine." *Proceedings of the IEEE* 64 (9): 1407–13.

Clausewitz, Carl von. 1832/1873. *On War*. Translated by J. J. Graham. London.
Clausewitz, Carl von. 2007. *On War*. Translated by Beatrice Heuser. New York: Oxford University Press.
Cockburn, Cynthia, and Ruza Furst-Dilic, eds. 1994. *Bringing Technology Home: Gender and Technology in a Changing Europe*. New York: Oxford University Press.
Commission to Assess United States National Security Space Management and Organization. 2001. "Report of the Commission to Assess United States National Security Space Management and Organization: Executive Summary." January 11. http://www.dod.mil/pubs/spaceintro.pdf.
Cooper, Helene, Ralph Blumenthal, and Leslie Kean. 2019. "'Wow, What Is That?' Navy Pilots Report Unexplained Flying Objects." *New York Times*, May 26.
Coppola, Francis Ford. 1979. *Apocalypse Now*. Omni Zoetrope.
Corn, Geoffrey. 2014. "Autonomous Weapon Systems: Managing the Inevitability of 'Taking the Man out of the Loop.'" In *Autonomous Weapons Systems: Law, Ethics, Policy*, edited by Nehal Bhuta, Susanne Beck, Robin Geiss, Hin-Yan Liu, and Clause Kress, 209–42. Cambridge: Cambridge University Press.
Crandall, Jordan. 2005. "Operational Media." CTheory.net, January 6. http://www.ctheory.net/articles.aspx?id"441.
Crandall, Jordan. 2011. "Ontologies of the Wayward Drone: A Salvage Operation." CTheory.net, November 2. www.ctheory.net/articles.aspx?id=693.
Crandall, Jordan. 2013. "Ecologies of the Wayward Drone." In *From Above: War, Violence, and Verticality*, edited by Peter Adey, Mark Whitehead, and Alison J. Williams, 263–87. London: Hurst and Company.
Crawford, Kate. 2016. "Artificial Intelligence's White Guy Problem." *New York Times*, June 25.
Crawford, Kate, and Ryan Calo. 2016. "There Is a Blind Spot in AI Research." *Nature* 538, 311–13.
Czerwinski, Thomas J. 1998. *Coping with the Bounds: A Neo-Clausewitzian Primer*. Washington, DC: DoD Command and Control Research Program.
Daily Mail. 2011. "Catalogue of Errors Led to Drone Attack Which Killed Two U.S. Troops in Afghanistan." November 7. http://www.dailymail.co.uk/news/article-2058372/Afghanistan-drone-attack-killed-2-US-troops-caused-catalogue-errors.html#ixzz2AET9UszB.
DARPA. 2016. "Accelerating Complex Computer Simulations: Thinking beyond Ones and Zeros." Defense Advanced Research Projects Agency, May 6. http://www.darpa.mil/news-events/2016-05-06.
DARPA. 2016. "FLA Program Takes Flight." February 12. https://www.darpa.mil/news-events/2016-02-12.
DARPA. 2016. "Gremlins Takes Flight to Provide Air-Recoverable Unmanned Air Systems." March 31. http://www.darpa.mil/news-events/2016-03-31.
Dash, Mike. 2012. "Khrushchev in Water Wings: On Mao, Humiliation and the Sino-Soviet Split." Smithsonian.com, May. Accessed January 20, 2017. http://www.smithsonianmag.com/history/khrushchev-in-water-wings-on-mao-humiliation-and-the-sino-soviet-split-80852370/.

Daston, Lorraine J., and Peter Galison. 2007. *Objectivity*. Cambridge, MA: MIT Press.

Davis, Miles. 1963. *Seven Steps to Heaven*. Columbia Music.

Dean, Jodi. 2009. *Democracy and Other Neoliberal Fantasies*. Durham: Duke University Press.

Deeds, E. A. 1920. "Aviation of the Future: New Designs, Speed, Higher Altitudes, Landing Fields, Some of the Things Necessary." *Aircraft Journal* 6 (8): 3–4.

Defense One Production. 2017. "When Robots Storm the Breach." YouTube, May 1. https://www.youtube.com/watch?v=5rufkVCxjdY.

Defense Science Board. 2016. *Report of the Defense Science Board Summer Study on Autonomy*. Washington, DC: Department of Defense.

Defense Update. 2004. "Low-Cost Autonomous Attack System." *Defense Update* 4, July 26. http://defense-update.com/products/l/locaas.htm.

DeLanda, Manuel. 1991. *War in the Age of Intelligent Machines*. New York: Zone.

DeLanda, Manuel. 1998. "Economics, Computers, and the War Machine." In *Infowar*, edited by Gerfried Stocker and Christine Schopf, 164–72. New York: Springer Wien.

Derrida, Jacques. 1993. "Politics of Friendship." *American Imago* 50 (3): 353–91.

Dibblin, Jane. 1990. *Day of Two Suns: US Nuclear Testing and the Pacific Islanders*. New York: New Amsterdam Press.

Dick, Philip K. 1953. "Second Variety." *Space Science Fiction* 1 (6): 102–44.

Diem, Bui. 2011. "The Diaries of Colonel Walter E. Kurtz." June. http://colonelkurtzdiaries.blogspot.ca/2011/06/on-my-own-terms.html.

Dixon, Wheeler Winston. 2003. *Visions of the Apocalypse: Spectacles of Destruction in American Cinema*. London: Wheeler Press.

Doel, Marcus. 2017. *Geographies of Violence: Killing Space, Killing Time*. Thousand Oaks, CA: SAGE.

Drew, James. 2016. "Video: Aurora's LightningStrike Wins DARPA VTOL X-Plane Competition." Fight Global, March 4. https://www.flightglobal.com/news/articles/video-auroras-lightningstrike-wins-darpa-vtol-x-pl-422720/.

Dubrofsky, Rachel, and Shoshana Amielle Magnet. 2015. "Feminist Surveillance Studies: Critical Interventions." In *Feminist Surveillance Studies*, edited by Rachel Dubrofsky and Shoshana Amielle Magnet, 1–20. Durham, NC: Duke University Press.

Duguay, Christian. 1995. *Screamers*. Triumph Films.

Dunbar, Robin. 2014. *Human Evolution: A Pelican Introduction*. London: Penguin.

Dunlop, D. K. 2017. "Canada's Future Submarines." *Canadian Naval Review*. September. https://www.navalreview.ca/2017/09/canadas-future-submarines.

Dyer-Witheford, Nick. 1999. *Cyber-Marx: Cycles and Circuits of Struggle in High Technology Capitalism*. Urbana: University of Illinois Press.

Dyson, George B. 1997. *Darwin among the Machines: The Evolution of Global Intelligence*. New York: Helix Books.

Dyson, George. 2014. "Jaron." The Edge, November 14. https://www.edge.org/conversation/the-myth-of-ai#25984.

Economic Times. 2017. "World's First Quantum Computing Machine Made in China." May 3. http://economictimes.indiatimes.com/news/science/worlds-first-quantum-computing-machine-made-in-china/articleshow/58492628.cms.

Edwards, Paul N. 1996. *The Closed World: Computers and the Politics of Discourse in Cold War America*. Cambridge, MA: MIT Press.

Edwards, Paul N. 2010. *A Vast Machine: Computer Models, Climate Data, and the Politics of Global Warming*. Cambridge, MA: MIT Press.

Edwards, Sean J. A. 2005. *Swarming and the Future of Warfare*. PhD diss., Pardee Rand Graduate School, Santa Monica, CA.

Einstein, Albert. 1936. "Lens-Like Action of a Star by the Deviation of Light in the Gravitational Field." *Science* (84): 506–7.

Elden, Stuart. 2001. *Mapping the Present: Heidegger, Foucault, and the Project of a Spatial History*. New York: Continuum.

Ellul, Jacques. 1964. *The Technological Society*. Translated by John Wilkinson. New York: Vintage.

Emmerich, Ronald. 1996. *Independence Day*. Los Angeles, CA: 20th Century Fox. Film.

EnemyGraph. Facebook. Accessed November 21, 2016. https://www.facebook.com/EnemyGraph/.

Ernest, Nicholas, David Carroll, Corey Schumacher, Matthew Clark, Kelly Cohen, and Gene Lee. 2016. "Genetic Fuzzy Based Artificial Intelligence for Unmanned Combat Aerial Vehicle Control in Simulated Air Combat Missions." *Journal of Defense Management* 6 (1): 1–7.

Eshleman, V. R. 1979. "Gravitational Lens of the Sun: Its Potential for Observations and Communications over Interstellar Distances." *Science* (205): 1133–35.

Espy, James. 1850. "Report on Meteorology to the Secretary of the Navy." Washington, DC: Government Printing Office.

European Nuclear Society. 2017. "Fuel Comparison." Online Encyclopedia, accessed April 10, 2019. https://www.euronuclear.org/info/encyclopedia/f/fuelcomparison.htm.

Everett, H. R. 2015. *Unmanned Systems of World Wars I and II*. Cambridge, MA: MIT Press.

Finn, Peter. 2011. "A Future for Drones: Automated Killing." *Washington Post*, September 19, 2011.

Fisher, J. 1954. "Evolution and Bird Sociality." In *Evolution as a Process*, edited by J. Huxley, A. Hardy, and E. Ford, 71–83. London: Allen and Unwin.

Flammarion, Camille. 2015. *Camille Flammarion's The Planet Mars*. Translated by Patrick Moore. New York: Springer.

Fleming, James Rodger. 2010. *Fixing the Sky: The Checkered History of Weather and Climate Control*. New York: Columbia University Press.

Floreano, Dario, and Claudio Mattiussi. 2008. *Bio-Inspired Artificial Intelligence: Theories, Methods, and Technologies*. Cambridge, MA: MIT Press.

Forgan, D. 2013. "Slingshot Dynamics for Self-Replicating Probes and the Effect on Exploration Timescales." *International Journal of Astrobiology* 12 (4): 337–44.

Foucault, Michel. 1977. *Discipline and Punish: The Birth of the Prison*. Translated by Alan Sheridan. New York: Random House.

Foucault, Michel. 1985. *The History of Sexuality*. Vol. 2, *The Use of Pleasure*. Translated by R. Hurley. New York: Pantheon.

Foucault, Michel. 1989. *The Order of Things: An Archaeology of the Human Sciences*. New York: Routledge.

Foucault, Michel. 2003. "Society Must Be Defended." *Lectures at the Collège de France, 1975-76*. New York: Picador.

Foucault, Michel. 2004. "Security, Territory, Population." *Lectures at the Collège de France, 1977-1978*. New York: Picador.

Foucault, Michel. 2007. *Security, Territory, Population: Lectures at the Collège de France, 1977-78*. Edited by Michel Senellart. Translated by Graham Burchell. London: Palgrave Macmillan.

Franklin, H. Bruce. 2008. *War Stars: The Superweapon and the American Imagination*. Amherst: University of Massachusetts Press.

Freitas, Robert A. 1980. "A Self-Reproducing Interstellar Probe." *Journal of the British Interplanetary Society* 33 (3): 251-64.

Friedson, Idalia. 2017. "The Quantum Computer Revolution Is Closer Than You May Think." *National Review*, May 2. http://www.nationalreview.com/article/447250/quantum-computing-race-america-can-win-must-keep-pushing-hard.

Fukuyama, Francis. 1993. *The End of History and the Last Man*. New York: Harper Collins.

Fukuyama, Francis. 2006. *The End of History and the Last Man*. Free Press: New York.

Fuller, John F. 1979. *Air Weather Service Support to the United States Arm, Tet, and the Decade After*. Scott Air Force Base, IL: Military Airlift Command.

Future of Life Institute. 2015. "Autonomous Weapons: An Open Letter from AI and Robotics Researchers." July 28. http://futureoflife.org/open-letter-autonomous-weapons/.

Galison, Peter. 1994. "The Ontology of the Enemy: Norbert Wiener and the Cybernetic Vision." *Critical Inquiry* 21 (1): 228-66.

Galison, Peter. 2014. "The Future of Scenarios: State Science Fiction." In *The Subject of Rosi Braidotti: Politics and Concepts*, edited by Bolette Blaagaard and Iris van der Tuin, 38-46. New York: Bloomsbury Academic.

Galison, Peter. 2015. "The Half-Life of Story." In *Hall of Half-Life*, edited by Tessa Giblin, 98-112. Graz: Steirischer Herbst.

Galloway, Alexander R. 2004. *Protocol: How Control Exists after Decentralization*. Cambridge, MA: MIT Press.

Gane, Nicholas. 2005. "Radical Post-humanism: Friedrich Kittler and the Primacy of Technology." *Theory, Culture & Society* 22 (3): 25-41.

Gane, Nicholas, and Stephen Sale. 2007. "Interview with Friedrich Kittler and Mark Hansen." *Theory, Culture & Society* 24 (7-8): 323-29.

Gates, Kelly. 2011. *Our Biometric Future: Facial Recognition Technology and the Culture of Surveillance*. New York: New York University Press.

Gavrilets, Sergey. 2015. "Collective Action and the Collaborative Brain." *Journal of the Royal Society*. Interface 12:20141067.

Gerstenberger, Erhard S. 2002. *Theologies of the Old Testament*. Translated by John Bowden. London: T &T Clark.

Gibbs, Samuel. 2017. "The Future of Funerals? Robot Priest Launched to Undercut Human-Led Rites." *Guardian*, August 23. https://www.theguardian.com/technology

/2017/aug/23/robot-funerals-priest-launched-softbank-humanoid-robot-pepper-live-streaming.

Gigova, Radina. 2017. "Who Vladimir Putin Thinks Will Rule the World." CNN.com, September 2, 2017. http://www.cnn.com/2017/09/01/world/putin-artificial-intelligence-will-rule-world/index.html.

Gill, S. S. 2011. "Eye Health with Consultant Ophthalmologist." *Ipoh Echo*, February 16. http://www.ipohecho.com.my/v2/2011/02/16/eye-health-with-consultant-ophthalmologist-dr-s-s-gill-part-1/.

Global Security Initiative. 2016. "Autonomy, Robotics, and Collective Systems: An Interdisciplinary Approach to Issues with Autonomous Robotics." Global Security Initiative. https://globalsecurity.asu.edu/robotics-autonomy.

Golson, Jordan. 2014. "A Military-Grade Drone That Can Be Printed Anywhere." *Wired*, September 16.

Gordon, Don. 1981. *Electronic Warfare: Element of Strategy and Multiplier of Combat Power*. Oxford: Pergamon.

Government Accountability Office. 2012. "NONPROLIFERATION: Agencies Could Improve Information Sharing and End-Use Monitoring on Unmanned Aerial Vehicle Exports." July. http://dronewarsuk.files.wordpress.com/2012/09/us-gao-_-noproliferation-of-uavs.pdf.

Graham, Stephen. 2010. *Cities Under Siege: The New Military Urbanism*. London: Verso.

Gregory, Derek. 2011. "From a View to a Kill: Drones and Late Modern War." *Theory, Culture & Society* 28 (7–8): 188–215.

Griffin, Andrew. 2016. "Aliens May Have Sent a 'Strong Message' from Deep in Space, Scientists Claim." *Independent*, August 30. https://www.independent.co.uk/news/science/aliens-might-have-sent-a-strong-message-from-deep-in-space-some-scientists-claim-a7216041.html.

Grothoff, Christian, and J. M. Porup. 2016. "The NSA's SKYNET Program May Be Killing Thousands of Innocent People." Ars Technica, February 16. https://arstechnica.co.uk/security/2016/02/the-nsas-skynet-program-may-be-killing-thousands-of-innocent-people/.

Gusterson, Hugh. 2016. *Drone: Remote Control Warfare*. Cambridge, MA: MIT Press.

Haas, Peter. 2016. "Cheap Lasers and Bad Math: The Coming Revolution in Robot Perception." Future of Life Institute, March 16. https://futureoflife.org/2016/03/16/cheap-lasers-and-bad-math-the-coming-revolution-in-robot-perception/.

Hagood, Lee. 1892. "The Storage Battery in Its Relation to U.S. Fortifications." *Journal of the United States Artillery* 20:70–95.

Hall, Rachel. 2015. *The Transparent Traveler: The Performance and Culture of Airport Security*. Durham, NC: Duke University Press.

Hamblin, Jacob. 2013. *Arming Mother Nature: The Birth of Catastrophic Environmentalism*. New York: Oxford University Press.

Hambling, David. 2013. "Longer-Lasting Drones Powered by Fuel Cells." *Popular Mechanics*, May 3. http://www.popularmechanics.com/military/a8956/longer-lasting-drones-powered-by-fuel-cells-15425554/.

Hamilton, Clive. 2014. "Forget 'Saving the Earth'—It's an Angry Beast That We've Awoken." The Conversation, May 27. https://theconversation.com/forget-saving-the-earth-its-an-angry-beast-that-weve-awoken-27156.

Hansen, Mark B. 2004. *New Philosophy for New Media*. Cambridge, MA: MIT Press.

Haraway, Donna. 2004. "A Manifesto for Cyborgs: Science, Technology, and Socialist Feminism in the 1980s." In *The Haraway Reader*, 7–46. New York: Routledge.

Hardt, Michael, and Antonio Negri. 2004. *Multitude: War and Democracy in the Age of Empire*. New York: Penguin.

Harrington, John V. 1983. "Radar Data Transmission." *IEEE Annals of the History of Computing* 5 (4): 370–74.

Hay, James, and Mark Andrejevic. 2006. "Toward an Analytic of Governmental Experiments in These Times: Homeland Security as the New Social Security." *Cultural Studies* 20 (4/5): 331–48.

Haydon, F. Stansbury. 1941. *Military Ballooning during the Early Civil War*. Baltimore, MD: Johns Hopkins University Press.

Hayles, N. Katherine. 1999. *How We Became Posthuman: Virtual Bodies in Cybernetics, Literature, and Informatics*. Chicago: University of Chicago Press.

Hayles, N. Katherine. 2005. *My Mother Was a Computer: Digital Subjects and Literary Texts*. Chicago: University of Chicago Press.

HDIAC Staff. 2015. "Military's Shift toward Renewable Energy." Armed with Science: The Official US Defense Department Science Blog, August 12. http://science.dodlive.mil/2015/08/12/militarys-shift-toward-renewable-energy/.

Heidegger, Martin. 1971. "What Are Poets For?" In *Poetry, Language, Thought*. Translated by Albert Hofstadter. New York: Harper and Row.

Heidegger, Martin. 1977. "The Age of the World Picture." In *The Question Concerning Technology and Other Essays*, 115–54. Translated by William Lovitt. New York: Garland.

Heidegger, Martin. 1977. "The Question Concerning Technology." In *The Question Concerning Technology and Other Essays*, 3–35. Translated by William Lovitt. New York: Garland.

Heidegger, Martin. 1991. *Nietzsche*. Vol. 4, *Nihilism*. Translated by Frank A. Capuzzi. San Francisco: Harper Collins.

Heidegger, Martin. 2010. *Country Path Conversations*. Translated by Bret W. Davis. Bloomington: University of Indiana Press.

Hersh, Seymour. 2013. *The Price of Power: Kissinger in the White House*. New York: Simon and Schuster.

Hester, Helen. 2018. *Xenofeminism*. Malden, MA: Polity.

Hickman, C. N. 1937. "The Dynamics of the Bow and Arrow." *Journal of Applied Physics* (June): 404–9.

Hicks, Marie. 2017. *Programmed Inequality: How Britain Discarded Women Technologists and Lost Its Edge in Computing*. Cambridge, MA: MIT Press.

Hilferding, Rudolf. 1985. *Finance Capital: A Study of the Latest Phase of Capitalist Development*. London: Routledge.

Hoffman, Donald D., and Manish Singh. 2012. "Computational Evolutionary Perception." *Perception* 41 (9): 1073–91.

Hofmann, George F. 2006. *Through Mobility We Conquer: The Mechanization of U.S. Cavalry*. Lexington: University of Kentucky Press.

Homeland Security News Wire. 2011. "Ex-CIA Head Praises Drone Warfare." Homeland Security News Wire, March 22. http://www.homelandsecuritynewswire.com/ex-cia-head-praises-drone-warfare.

Horn, Eva. 2003. "Knowing the Enemy: The Epistemology of Secret Intelligence." Translated by Sara Ogger. *Grey Room* 11 (1): 58–85.

Hornyak, Tim. 2013. "Human Rights Watch Launches Campaign against 'Killer Robots.'" CNet, April 23. https://www.cnet.com/news/human-rights-watch-launches-campaign-against-killer-robots/.

Hoy, Peter. 2008. "The World's Biggest Fuel Consumer." *Forbes*, June 5.

Hsu, Jeremy. 2010. "Power-Seeking Flying Microdrone Would Scavenge Solar and Thermal Energy Day and Night." *Popular Science*, April 9.

Hughes, Thomas P. 1998. *Rescuing Prometheus: Four Monumental Projects That Changed the Modern World*. New York: Pantheon.

Hundley, Richard, and Eugene Gritton. 1994. "Future Technology-Driven Revolutions in Military Operations." RAND Documented Briefing, DB-110-ARPA. Santa Monica, CA: RAND Corporation.

Hunter, Ian. 1988. *Culture and Government: The Emergence of Literary Education*. London: Macmillan.

IBM. 1957. *On Guard. The Story of SAGE*. Film.

IBM. 1960. *Where America's Peace of Mind Begins*. Film.

Iggers, George, and James M. Powell. 1990. *Leopold von Ranke and the Shaping of the Historical Discipline*. Syracuse, NY: Syracuse University Press.

Ingles, Michael Ignatius. 2016. "Regulating Religious Robots: Free Exercise and RFRA in the Time of Superintelligent Artificial Intelligence." *Georgetown Law Journal* 105:507–29.

Intel. 2017. "From Sand to Circuits: The Surprising Process behind Intel® Technology." https://www.intel.com/content/www/us/en/history/museum-making-silicon.htm.

International Academy of Astronautics. 2016. "The Rio Scale." August 26. http://avsport.org/IAA/rioscale.htm.

Irwin, William, ed. 2002. *The Matrix and Philosophy: Welcome to the Desert of the Real*. New York: Open Court.

Jenkins, Aric. 2017. "Read President Trump's Speech Claiming the Press Doesn't Report Terror Attacks." *Time*, February 6.

Jet Propulsion Laboratory. 2016. "NASA, FEMA Hold Asteroid Emergency Planning Exercise." NASA.gov, November 4. https://www.jpl.nasa.gov/news/news.php?release=2016-288.

Jonze, Spike. 2013. *Her*. Annapurna Pictures.

Kahn, David. 1967. *The Codebreakers: The Story of Secret Writing*. New York: Scribner.

Kanas, Nick. 2014. *Solar System Maps: From Antiquity to the Space Age*. New York: Springer.

Kaplan, Caren. 2006. "Mobility and War: The Cosmic View of U.S. Air Power." *Environment and Planning* A 38 (3): 395–407.

Kaplan, Caren. 2006. "Precision Targets: GPS and the Militarization of U.S. Consumer Identity." *Environment and Planning* A 38 (2): 693–713.

Kaplan, Caren. 2014. "The Balloon Prospect: Aerostatic Observation and the Emergence of Militarized Aeromobility." In *From Above: War, Violence and Verticality*, edited by Peter Adey and Mark Whitehead, 19–40. New York: Oxford University Press.

Kaplan, Caren. 2018. *Aerial Aftermaths: Wartime from Above*. Durham, NC: Duke University Press.

Kaplan, Caren, Erik Loyer, and Ezra Claytan Daniels. 2013. "Precision Targets: GPS and the Militarization of Everyday Life." *Canadian Journal of Communication* 38 (3): 397–420.

Kaplan, Fred. 2016. *Dark Territory: The Secret History of Cyberwar*. New York: Simon and Schuster.

Kindervater, Katharine Hall. 2017. "The Technological Rationality of the Drone Strike." *Critical Studies on Security* 5 (1): 28–44.

Kirsch, Jonathan. 2004. *God against the Gods: The History of War between Monotheism and Polytheism*. New York: Penguin.

Kittler, Friedrich A. 1986. "A Discourse on Discourse." *Stanford Literature Review* 3 (1): 157–66.

Kittler, Friedrich A. 1996. "The History of Communication Media." CTheory.net, July 30. http://www.ctheory.net/articles.aspx?id=45.

Kittler, Friedrich A. 1997. "Media Wars: Trenches, Lightning, Stars." In *Essays: Literature, Media, Information Systems*. Amsterdam: Overseas Publishers.

Kittler, Friedrich A. 1999. *Gramophone, Film, Typewriter*. Translated by Geoffrey Winthrop-Young and Michael Wutz. Stanford, CA: Stanford University Press.

Kittler, Friedrich A. 1999. "On the Implementation of Knowledge: Toward a Theory of Hardware." In *Readme!: ASCII Culture and the Revenge of Knowledge*, edited by Josephine Bosma, 60–68. New York: Autonomedia.

Kittler, Friedrich A. 2010. *Optical Media: Berlin Lectures, 1999*. Translated by Anthony Enns. Malden, MA: Polity.

Kittler, Friedrich A. 2012. "Of States and Their Terrorists." *Cultural Politics* 8 (3): 385–97.

Kittler, Friedrich A. 2013. "The Artificial Intelligence of World War: Alan Turing." In *The Truth of the Technological World: Essays on the Genealogy of Presence*, 178–94. Stanford, CA: Stanford University Press.

Kittler, Friedrich A. 2015. "Animals of War: A Historical Bestiary." *Cultural Politics* 11 (3): 391–94.

Kittler, Friedrich A. 2015. "A Short History of the Searchlight." Translated by Geoffrey Winthrop-Young. *Cultural Politics* 11 (3): 384–90.

Kittler, Friedrich A. 2017. "Real Time Analysis, Time Axis Manipulation." Translated by Geoffrey Winthrop-Young. *Cultural Politics* 13 (1): 1–18.

Klein, Naomi. 2007. *The Shock Doctrine*. New York: Random House.

Koplow, David A. 2010. *Death by Moderation: The U.S. Military's Quest for Useable Weapons*. New York: Cambridge University Press.

Kosuth, Pascal. 2011. "Food Security through Earth Observation." *Space News*, November 2.

Kurzweil, Ray. 2005. *The Singularity Is Near: When Humans Transcend Biology*. New York: Penguin.

Landis, Geoffrey A. 2017. "Mission to the Gravitational Focus of the Sun: A Critical Analysis." AIAA Science and Technology Forum and Exposition, Grapevine, TX, January 9–13. https://arxiv.org/pdf/1604.06351.pdf.

Latour, Bruno. 2011. "Waiting for Gaia: Composing the Common World through Arts and Politics." In *What Is Cosmopolitical Design?*, edited by Albena Yaneva and Alejandro Zaera-Polo, 21–33. Farnham: Ashgate.

Lawson, Sean T. 2014. *Nonlinear Science and Warfare: Chaos, Complexity, and the U.S. Military in the Information Age*. London: Routledge.

Lazzarato, Maurizio, and Éric Aliez. 2016. "To Our Enemies." Translated by Ames Hodges. E-Flux 78, December. http://www.e-flux.com/journal/78/82697/to-our-enemies/.

Lede, Jean-Charles. 2017. "Fast Lightweight Autonomy." DARPA, accessed April 10, 2019. https://www.darpa.mil/program/fast-lightweight-autonomy.

Lee, Wayne E. 2016. *Waging War: Conflict, Culture, and Innovation in World History*. New York: Oxford University Press.

Lele, Ajey. 2006. *Weather and Warfare*. New Delhi: Institute for Defence Studies and Analyses, Lancer.

Leonard, Barry, ed. 2010. *Department of Defense Dictionary of Military and Associated Terms*. Washington, DC: Department of Defense.

Leopold, George. 2016. "Quantum Leaps Needed for New Computer Approach." Defense Systems, December 9. https://defensesystems.com/articles/2016/12/09/quantum.aspx.

Levy, David. 2008. *Love and Sex with Robots: The Evolution of Human-Robot Relationships*. New York: Harper Collins.

Li, Wei, Melvin Gauci, and Roderich Gross. 2016. "Turing Learning: A Metric-Free Approach to Inferring Behavior and Its Application to Swarms." *Swarm Intelligence* 10 (3): 211–43.

Liotta, P. H., and Alan Shearer. 2007. *Gaia's Revenge: Climate Change and Humanity's Loss*. Westport, CT: Praeger.

Lovelock, James. 2006. *The Revenge of Gaia: Why the Earth Is Fighting Back—And How We Can Still Save Humanity*. New York: Penguin.

Lukács, Georg. 1971. *History and Class Consciousness: Studies in Marxist Dialectics*. Translated by Rodney Livingstone. Cambridge, MA: MIT Press.

Maccone, Claudio. 2009. *Deep Space Flight and Communications: Exploiting the Sun as a Gravitational Lens*. Berlin: Springer.

Maconie, Robin. 2012. *Avant Garde: An American Odyssey from Gertrude Stein to Pierre Boulez*. Lanham, MD: Scarecrow Press.

Maddalena, Kate, and Chris Russill. 2016. "Is the Earth an Optical Medium? An Interview with Chris Russill." *International Journal of Communication* 10 (1): 3186–202.

Maddalena, Kate, and Jeremy Packer. 2014. "The Digital Body: Semaphore Telegraphy as Discourse Network." *Theory, Culture & Society* 32 (1): 93–117.

Magnet, Shoshana. 2011. *When Biometrics Fail: Gender, Race, and the Technology of Identity*. Durham, NC: Duke University Press.

Magnuson, Joel. 2007. *Mindful Economics: How the U.S. Economy Works, Why It Matters, and How It Could Be Different*. Toronto, ON: Seven Stories Press.

Malouin, Paul-Jacques. 1765. "Miasma." In *The Encyclopedia of Diderot and d'Alembert Collaborative Translation Project*. Translated by Jaclyn Assarian. Ann Arbor: University of Michigan Library, 2004. https://quod.lib.umich.edu/cgi/t/text/text-idx?c=did;cc=did;rgn=main;view=text;idno=did2222.0000.369.

Mander, Jerry. (1977) 1978. *Four Arguments for the Elimination of Television*. New York: HarperCollins.

Manovich, Lev. 2001. *The Language of New Media*. Cambridge, MA: MIT Press.

Marcuse, Herbert. 1998. "Some Social Implications of Modern Technology." In *Technology, War, and Fascism: The Collected Papers of Herbert Marcuse*, 39–66. London: Routledge.

Markoff, John. 2014. "Fearing Bombs That Can Pick Whom to Kill." *New York Times*, November 11.

Markoff, John, and Matthew Rosenberg. 2017. "China's Intelligent Weaponry Gets Smarter." *New York Times*, February 3.

Mason, Robert. 1989. *Weapon*. New York: Putnam.

Massumi, Brian. 2007. "Potential Politics and the Primacy of Preemption." *Theory and Event* 10 (2).

Massumi, Brian. 2015. *Ontopower: War, Powers, and the State of Perception*. Durham, NC: Duke University Press.

Mayr, Otto. 1986. *Authority, Liberty, and Automated Machinery in Early Modern Europe*. Baltimore, MD: Johns Hopkins University Press.

Mazzetti, Mark. 2012. "The Drone Zone." *New York Times Magazine*, July 6.

Mbembe, J. A. 2003. "Necropolitics." *Public Culture* 15 (1): 11–40.

McFarland, Matt. 2014. "Elon Musk: 'With Artificial Intelligence We Are Summoning the Demon.'" *Washington Post*, October 24.

McLuhan, Marshall. 1964. *Understanding Media: The Extensions of Man*. New York: McGraw Hill.

McLuhan, Marshall. 1994. *Understanding Media: The Extensions of Man*. Cambridge, MA: MIT Press.

McNamara, Patrick, and David Trumbull. 2007. *An Evolutionary Psychology of Leader-Follower Relations*. New York: Nova Science Publishers.

Merquior, J. G. 1985. *Foucault*. Berkeley: University of California Press.

Metz, Cade. 2017. "Google's Dueling Neural Networks Spar to Get Smarter, No Humans Required." Wired.com, April 11.

Michigan Technic. 1946. "The *Technic* Explores." *Michigan Technic* 64 (8): 14–36.

Mikesh, Robert C. 1973. *Japan's World War II Balloon Bomb Attacks on North America*. Washington, DC: Smithsonian Institution Press.

Mindell, David A. 1996. "Beasts and Systems: Taming and Stability in the History of Control." In *Cultures of Control*, edited by Miriam R. Levin, 205–24. London: Routledge.

Mirrlees, Tanner. 2017. *Hearts and Mines: The US Empire's Culture Industry*. Vancouver: University of British Columbia Press.

Moore, Addison. 2011. *Vex*. Big Bear Lake, CA: Hollis Thatcher Press.

Morimoto, Koji, et al. 2003. *Animatrix*. Village Roadshow Pictures.

Morris-Reich, Amos. 2016. *Race and Photography: Racial Photography as Scientific Evidence, 1876-1980*. Chicago: University of Chicago Press.

Mortimer, Gary. 2011. "ScanEagle, Procerus Unicorn Communicate over Search Area." SUAS News, August 18. http://www.suasnews.com/2011/08/6573/scaneagle-procerus-unicorn-communicate-over-search-area/.

Mouffe, Chantal. 1993. *The Return of the Political*. London: Verso.

Murray, John Courtney. 1968. "War and Conscience." In *A Conflict of Loyalties: The Case for Selective Conscientious Objection*, edited by James Finn, 19-30. New York: Gegasus.

Murray, Matthew. 1851. *Explanations and Sailing Directions to Accompany Wind and Current Charts*. Philadelphia: E. C. and J. Biddle.

Musk, Elon. 2014. "Elon Musk's Deleted *Edge* Comment from Yesterday on the Threat of AI." Reddit. https://www.reddit.com/r/Futurology/comments/2mh8tn/elon_musks_deleted_edge_comment_from_yesterday_on/.

National Aeronautics and Space Administration. 2014. "NASA Strategic Plan: 2014." https://www.nasa.gov/sites/default/files/files/FY2014_NASA_SP_508c.pdf.

Nebeker, Frederik. 1995. *Calculating the Weather: Meteorology in the 20th Century*. San Diego, CA: Academic Press.

Neocleous, Mark. 1996. "Perpetual War, or 'War and War Again': Schmitt, Foucault, Fascism." *Philosophy and Social Criticism* 22 (2): 47-66.

Noble, David. 1984. *Forces of Production: A Social History of Industrial Automation*. New York: Oxford University Press.

Noble, Safiya Umoja. 2018. *Algorithms of Oppression: How Search Engines Reinforce Racism*. New York: NYU Press.

Northrop Grumman. 2014. "Northrop Grumman Awarded Contract to Develop Miniaturized Inertial Navigation System for DARPA." June 5. http://investor.northropgrumman.com/mobile.view?c=112386&v=203&d=1&id=193766.

Northrop Grumman. 2017. "Gaining a Cyber Advantage in Battlespace." http://www.northropgrumman.com/performance/#/pillar/cyber/1.

Nunn, Kenneth B. 2002. "Race, Crime and the Pool of Surplus Criminality: Or Why the 'War on Drugs' Was a 'War on Blacks.'" *Journal of Gender, Race and Justice* 6 (fall): 381-445.

Ohlin, Jens David. 2016. "The Combatant's Stance: Autonomous Weapons on the Battlefield." *International Law Studies* 92 (1): 1-30.

Omohundro, Steve. 2014. "Autonomous Technology and the Greater Human Good." *Journal of Experimental and Theoretical Artificial Intelligence* 26 (3): 303-15.

Osborn, Kris. 2016. "Air Force Chief Scientist: Future Drones Stealthier—More Autonomous." Defense Systems, October 10. https://defensesystems.com/articles/2016/10/10/future-drones.aspx.

Oursler, Fulton. 1935. "Editor's Note." *Liberty Magazine*, February 9, 5.

Packer, Jeremy. 2006. *Becoming Bombs: Mobilizing Mobility in the War of Terror. Cultural Studies* 20 (4/5): 371–99.

Packer, Jeremy. 2007. "Homeland Subjectivity: The Algorithmic Identity of Security." *Communication and Critical/Cultural Studies* 4 (2): 212–26.

Packer, Jeremy, and Kathleen Oswald. 2010. "From Windscreen to Widescreen: Screening Technologies and Mobile Communication." *The Communication Review* 13 (4): 309–39.

Packer, Jeremy, and Joshua Reeves. 2013. "Romancing the Drone: Military Desire and Anthropophobia from SAGE to Swarm." *Canadian Journal of communication* 38 (3): 309–31.

Parikka, Jussi. 2015. *A Geology of Media*. Minneapolis: University of Minnesota Press.

Parks, Lisa. 2005. *Cultures in Orbit: Satellites and the Televisual*. Durham, NC: Duke University Press.

Parks, Lisa. 2012. "Zeroing In: Overhead Imagery, Infrastructure Ruins, and Datalands in Afghanistan and Iraq." In *Communication Matters: Materialist Approaches to Media, Mobility, and Networks*, edited by Jeremy Packer and Stephen B. Crofts Wiley, 78–92. New York: Routledge.

Parks, Lisa. 2016. "Drones, Mediation, and the Targeted Class." *Feminist Studies* 42 (1): 227–35.

Pascual, Carlos, and Evie Zambetakis. 2010. "The Geopolitics of Energy: From Security to Survival." In *Energy Security: Economics, Politics, Strategies, and Implications*, edited by Carlos Pascual and Jonathan Elkind, 9–35. Washington, DC: Brookings Institute Press.

Pearson, Lee. 1968. "Developing the Flying Bomb." *Naval Aviation News* 49 (5): 22–25.

Peck, Louis. 2010. "New Mission for U.S. Military: Breaking its Dependence on Oil." *Yale Environment 360*, December 8. http://e360.yale.edu/features/new_mission_for_us_military_breaking_its_dependence_on_oil.

Pedgley, David. 2006. "Meeting Report: Meteorology in World War One." *Weather* 61 (9): 264.

Pellerin, Cheryl. 2015. "Work: Human-Machine Teaming Represents Defense Technology Future." Department of Defense, November 8. https://www.defense.gov/News/Article/Article/628154/work-human-machine-teaming-represents-defense-technology-future/.

Pellerin, Cheryl. 2017. "Pentagon Spokesman Updates Iraq, Syria, Yemen Operations." US Department of Defense, April 24. https://www.defense.gov/News/Article/Article/1161065/pentagon-spokesman-updates-iraq-syria-yemen-operations/.

Perry, Caroline. 2014. "A Self-Organizing Thousand-Robot Swarm." *Harvard School of Engineering and Applied Sciences*, August 14. http://www.seas.harvard.edu/news/2014/08/self-organizing-thousand-robot-swarm.

Peters, John Durham. 2010. "Introduction: Friedrich Kittler's Light Shows." In Kittler, *Optical Media*, 1–17.

Peters, John Durham. 1999. *Speaking into the Air: A History of the Idea of Communication*. Chicago: University of Chicago Press.

Peters, John Durham. 2013. *The Marvelous Clouds: Toward a Philosophy of Elemental Media*. Chicago: University of Chicago Press.

Peters, John Durham. 2015. *The Marvelous Clouds: Toward a Philosophy of Elemental Media.* Chicago: University of Chicago Press.

Pettegrew, John. 2015. *Light It Up: The Marine Eye for Battle in the War for Iraq.* Baltimore, MD: Johns Hopkins University Press.

Pinker, Steven. 2011. *The Better Angels of Our Nature: Why Violence Has Declined.* New York: Penguin.

Pinker, Steven. 2015. "Thinking Does Not Imply Subjugating." *The Edge.* https://www.edge.org/res.

Piore, Adam. 2014. "Rise of the Insect Drones." *Popular Science*, January 29. http://www.popsci.com/article/technology/rise-insect-drones.

"Politics." 2011. Lecture at the French Institute, London, November. http://www.bruno-latour.fr/sites/default/files/124-gaia-london-speap_0.pdf.

Popular Mechanics. 1956. "Pilotless Photo Drone Takes Aerial Pictures." 105 (6): 144.

Potter, Sean. 2011. "Retrospect: September 11, 2001: Attack on America." *Weatherwise.* http://www.weatherwise.org/Archives/Back%20Issues/2011/September-October%202011/retrospect-full.html.

Radio News. 1921. "French Claim Priority in Wireless Plane Guiding." *Radio News* 2 (12): 874.

Radloff, Bernhard. 2007. *Heidegger and the Question of National Socialism: Disclosure and Gestalt.* Toronto, ON: University of Toronto Press.

Raines, Rebecca. 1996. *Getting the Message Through: A Branch History of the U.S. Army Signal Corps.* Washington DC: Center of Military History United States Army. http://www.history.army.mil/books/30-17/Front.htm.

Rancière, Jacques. 2010. "The Final Enemy." In *Chronicles of Consensual Times*, 16–20. New York: Continuum.

Rattray, Gregory J. 2001. *Strategic Warfare in Cyberspace.* Cambridge, MA: MIT Press.

Raytheon. 2016. "Phalanx Close-In Weapon System: Last Line of Defense for Air, Land, and Sea." Raytheon.com, accessed April 10, 2019. http://www.raytheon.com/capabilities/products/phalanx/.

Redmond, Kent C., and Thomas M. Smith. 2000. *From Whirlwind to MITRE: The R&D Story of the SAGE Air Defense Computer.* Cambridge, MA: MIT Press.

Reeves, Joshua. 2016. "Automatic for the People: The Automation of Communicative Labor." *Communication and Critical/Cultural Studies* 13 (2): 150–65.

Reeves, Joshua. 2017. "Of Social Networks and Suicide Nets: Biopolitics and the Suicide Screen." *Television and New Media* 18 (6): 512–28.

Reeves, Joshua, and Matthew S. May. 2013. "The Peace Rhetoric of a War President: Barack Obama and the Just War Legacy." *Rhetoric & Public Affairs* 16 (4): 623–50.

Reilly, Thomas. 1997. "During World War I, Two Prolific Inventors Pursued Separate Quests to Develop America's First Guided Missile." *Military History* 14 (4): 24–29.

Richard, Marc. 2003. "E. Godfrey Burr and His Contributions to Canadian Wartime Research: A Profile." McGill University, Montreal, Quebec, accessed April 10, 2019. http://fontanus.mcgill.ca/article/viewFile/179/201.

Roach, Mary. 2016. *Grunt: The Curious Science of Humans at War.* New York: W. W. Norton.

Robertson, Linda Raine. 2003. *The Dream of Civilized Warfare: World War I Flying Aces and the American Imagination*. Minneapolis: University of Minnesota Press.

Robinson, Stanley Kim. 2012. *2312*. New York: Orbit.

Roff, Heather M., and Richard Moyes. 2016. "Meaningful Human Control, Artificial Intelligence, and Autonomous Weapons." Briefing Paper Prepared for the Meeting of Experts on Lethal Autonomous Weapons Systems, UN Convention on Certain Conventional Weapons, April. http://www.article36.org/wp-content/uploads/2016/04/MHC-AI-and-AWS-FINAL.pdf.

Rojas, Rafael. 2015. *Fighting over Fidel: The New York Intellectuals and the Cuban Revolution*. Translated by Carl Good. Princeton, NJ: Princeton University Press.

Roman, Gregory A. 1997. "The Command or Control Dilemma: When Technology and Organizational Orientation Collide." *Air War College Maxwell Paper No. 8*. Montgomery, AL: Maxwell Air Force Base.

Romero, Rene F. 2003. *The Origins of Centralized Control and Decentralized Execution*. Master's thesis, US Army Command and General Staff College.

Rose Shell, Hannah. 2012. *Hide and Seek: Camouflage, Photography, and the Media of Reconnaissance*. Cambridge MA: MIT Press.

Rozin, Igor, and Nikolai Litovkin. 2017. "Russia Joins World's Top Three for Military Spending." Russia Beyond the Headlines, April 24. https://www.rbth.com/defence/2017/04/24/russia-joins-worlds-top-3-for-military-spending_749453.

Rubinstein, Michael, and Wei-Min Shen. 2008. "A Scalable and Distributed Model for Self-Organization and Self-Healing." In *Proceedings of the 7th International Joint Conference on Autonomous Agents and Multiagent Systems*, 3:1179–82. Richland, SC: International Foundation for Autonomous Agents and Multiagent Systems.

Russill, Chris. 2013. "Earth-Observing Media." *Canadian Journal of Communication* 38 (3): 277–84.

Russill, Chris. 2016. "Earth Imaging: Photograph, Pixel, Program." In *Ecomedia: Key Issues*, edited by S. Rust, S. Monani, and S. Cubitt, 228–54. New York: Routledge.

Russill, Chris. 2017. "Is the Earth a Medium?: Situating the Planetary in Media Theory." *Ctrl-Z: New Media Philosophy* 7.

Santamarta, Rube. 2014. *A Wake-Up Call for SATCOM Security*. IOActive, accessed April 10, 2019. www.ioactive.com/pdfs/IOActive_SATCOM_Security_WhitePaper.pdf.

Santayana, George. 1922. *Soliloquies in England and Later Soliloquies*. New York: C. Scribner's Sons.

Sarker, Muhammad Omar Faruque, and Torbjørn S. Dahl. 2011. "Bio-Inspired Communication for Self-Regulated Multi-Robot Systems." In *Multi-Robot Systems: Trends and Development*, edited by Toshiyuki Yasuda, 367–92. London: Intech.

Saul, Heather. 2016. "Professor Stephen Hawking: Humanity Will Not Survive Another 1,000 Years if We Don't Escape Our Planet." *Independent*, November 15. http://www.independent.co.uk/news/people/professor-stephen-hawking-humanity-wont-survive-1000-years-on-earth-a7417366.html.

Savage, Charlie. 2016. "U.S. Releases Rules for Airstrike Killings of Terror Suspects." *New York Times*, August 6.

Savage, Charlie, and Eric Schmitt. 2017. "Trump Administration Is Said to Be Working to Loosen Counterterrorism Rules." *New York Times*, March 12.

Schaffel, Kenneth. 2004. *The Emerging Shield: The Air Force and the Evolution of Continental Air Defense, 1945–1960*. Honolulu, HI: University Press of the Pacific.

Scharre, Paul. 2014. *Robotics on the Battlefield*. Part I, *Range, Persistence, and Daring*. Washington, DC: Center for a New American Security.

Scharre, Paul. 2014. *Robotics on the Battlefield*. Part II, *The Coming Swarm*. Washington, DC: Center for a New American Security.

Scharre, Paul. 2018. *Army of None: Autonomous Weapons and the Future of War*. New York: W. W. Norton.

Schmitt, Carl. 1995. *The Concept of the Political*. Translated by George Schwab. Chicago: University of Chicago Press.

Schmitt, Carl. 2004. *The Theory of the Partisan: A Commentary/Remark on the Concept of the Political*. Translated by A. C. Goodson. East Lansing: Michigan State University Press.

Schrape, Niklas. 2014. "Gaia's Game." *Communication +1* 3 (5): http://scholarworks.umass.edu/cpo/vol3/iss1/5.

Schuster, Carl O. 2014. "Submarines." *Germany at War: 400 Years of Military History*. Edited by David T. Zabecki. Santa Barbara, CA: ABC CLIO.

Secor, H. Winfield. 1917. "Tesla's Views on Electricity and the War." *Electrical Experimenter*, August, 229–30, 270.

Serviss, Garrett Putman. 1898. *Edison's Conquest of Mars*. Serialized in *New York Journal*. Accessed April 10, 2019. http://freeread.com.au/@RGLibrary/GPServiss/EdisonsConquestOfMars.html#picPG21.

Shakespeare, William. 1599. *Julius Caesar*. New York: Dover.

Shannon, Claude, and Warren Weaver. 1949. *The Mathematical Theory of Communication*. Urbana: University of Illinois Press.

Sharkey, Amanda J. C., and Noel Sharkey. 2006. "The Application of Swarm Intelligence to Collective Robots." In *Advances in Applied Artificial Intelligence*, edited by John Fulcher, 157–85. Hershey, PA: IGI Global.

Sharma, Sarah. 2008. "Taxis as Media: A Temporal Materialist Reading of the Taxi-Cab." *Social Identities: Journal for the Study of Race, Nation, and Culture* 14: 457–64.

Shaw, Ian G. R. 2016. *Predator Empire: Drone Warfare and Full Spectrum Dominance*. Minneapolis: University of Minnesota Press.

Shea, John J. 2017. *Stone Tools in Human Evolution: Behavioral Differences among Technological Primates*. Cambridge: Cambridge University Press.

Sheehan, William. 1996. *The Planet Mars: A History of Observation and Discovery*. Tucson: University of Arizona Press.

Shelley, Mary. 1818. *Frankenstein; or, The Modern Prometheus*. London: Lackington, Hughes, Harding, Mavor & Jones.

Shermer, Michael. 2015. "When It Comes to AI, Think Protopia, Not Utopia or Dystopia." *The Edge*. https://www.edge.org/response-detail/26062.

Sherwood, Harriet. 2017. "Robot Priest Unveiled in Germany to Mark 500 Years since Reformation." *Guardian*, May 30.

Shiga, John. 2013. "Of Other Networks: Closed-World and Green-World Networks in the Work of John C. Lilly." Amodern 2: Network Archaeology, October. http://amodern.net/article/of-other-networks/.

Shiga, John. 2013. "Sonar: Empire, Media, and the Politics of Underwater Sound." *Canadian Journal of Communication*, 38 (3): 357–76.

Shome, Raka. 2016. "When Postcolonial Studies Meets Media Studies." *Critical Studies in Media Communication* 33 (3): 245–63.

Siegert, B. 2011. "The Map Is the Territory." *Radical Philosophy* 169:13–16.

Singh, Karanjit, and Shuchita Upadhyaya. 2012. "Outlier Detection: Applications and Techniques." *IJCSI: International Journal of Computer Sciences Issues* 9 (1): 307–23.

Sjoberg, Laura. 2013. *Gendering Global Conflict: Toward a Feminist Theory of War*. New York: Columbia University Press.

Skyttner, Lars. 2005. *General Systems Theory: Problems, Perspectives, Practice*. Singapore: World Scientific.

"Slaughtered: Milk Cows." 2010. Accessed September 21, 2017. http://rmhh.co.uk/files/Slaughter%20of%20the%20Milk%20Cows.pdf.

Sloterdijk, Peter. 1987. *Critique of Cynical Reason*. Translated by Michael Eldred. Minneapolis: University of Minnesota Press.

Sloterdijk, Peter. 2009. *Terror from the Air*. Translated by Amy Patton and Steve Corcoran. New York: Semiotexte.

Smalley, David. 2014. "The Future Is Now: Navy's Autonomous Swarmboats Can Overwhelm Adversaries." Office of Naval Research. http://www.onr.navy.mil/Media-Center/Press-Releases/2014/autonomous-swarm-boat-unmanned-caracas.aspx.

Solem, Johndale. 1994. "On the Motility of Military Microrobots." Los Alamos National Laboratory Report LA-12133.

Solem, Johndale. 1996. "The Application of Microrobotics in Warfare." Los Alamos National Laboratory Report LA-UR-96-3067.

Spangler, David. 1990. "The Meaning of Gaia: Is Gaia a Goddess, or Just a Good Idea?" *In Context: A Quarterly of Humane Sustainable Culture* 24 (1): 44–47.

Spanos, William V. 2003. "Heidegger, Foucault, and the 'Empire of the Gaze': Thinking the Territorialization of Knowledge." In *Foucault and Heidegger: Critical Encounters*, 235–75. Minneapolis: University of Minnesota Press.

Spark, Nick T. 2005. "Unmanned Precision Weapons Aren't New." *U.S. Naval Institute Proceedings* 131 (2): 66.

Stahl, Roger. 2018. *Through the Crosshairs: War, Visual Culture, and the Weaponized Gaze*. New Brunswick, NJ: Rutgers University Press.

Stein, Jeff. 2010. "CIA Mum on Lawsuit Alleging Drone Targeting Errors." *Washington Post*, October 4.

Sterling, Christopher H. 2008. *From Ancient Times to the 21st Century*. Santa Barbara, CA: ABC-CLIO.

Sterne, Jonathan. 2003. *The Audible Past: Cultural Origins of Sound Reproduction*. Durham, NC: Duke University Press.

Stiegler, Bernard. 1998. *Technics and Time, 1: The Fault of Epithemeus*. Translated by Richard Beardsworth and George Collins. Stanford, CA: Stanford University Press.

Stimson Center. 2014. *Recommendations and Report of the Task Force on U.S. Drone Policy.* Washington, DC: Stimson.

Stocker, Gerfried. 1998. "InfoWar." Information. Macht. Krieg-Theory [Part 02]. Ars Electronica. http://90.146.8.18/en/archives/festival_archive/festival_catalogs/festival_artikel.asp?iProjectID=8442.

Stockholm International Peace Research Institute. 2017. "World Military Spending: Increases in the USA and Europe, Decreases in Oil-Exporting Countries." SIPRI .org, April 24. https://www.sipri.org/media/press-release/2017/world-military-spending-increases-usa-and-europe.

Stoff, Joshua. 1996. *Picture History of Early Aviation, 1903–1913.* Mineola, NY: Dover Publications.

Suchman, Lucy. 2007. *Human-Machine Reconfigurations.* New York: Cambridge University Press.

Sullivan, Woodruff T. 2013. "Extraterrestrial Life as the Great Analogy, Two Centuries Ago and in Modern Astrobiology." In *Astrobiology, History, and Society: Life beyond Earth and the Impact of Discovery*, edited by Douglas A. Vakoch. New York: Springer.

Sun Tzu. 2000. *On the Art of War.* Leicester, UK: Allandale Online Publishing.

Sun Tzu. 2006. *The Art of War.* New York: Cosimo Classics.

Susskind, Richard, and Daniel Susskind. 2016. *The Future of the Professions: How Technology Will Transform the Work of Human Experts.* Oxford: Oxford University Press.

Tagg, John. 1993. *The Burden of Representation: Essays on Photographies and Histories.* Minneapolis: University of Minnesota Press.

Taylor, Travis S., and Bob Boan. 2011. *Alien Invasion: How to Defend Earth.* Wake Forest, NC: Baen.

Tesla, Nikola. 1898. "Tesla Describes His Efforts in Various Fields of Work." *The Electrical Review*, November 30, 344–45.

Tesla, Nikola. 1935. "A Machine to End War." *Liberty Magazine*, February 9, 5–7.

Thomas, James C. 2016. "The Secret Wheat Deal." This Land Press, December 12. http://thislandpress.com/2016/12/06/the-secret-wheat-deal/.

Thornton, Tamara Plakins. 1996. *Handwriting in America: A Cultural History.* New Haven, CT: Yale University Press.

Tse-tung, Mao. 1961. *Mao Tse-tung on Guerrilla Warfare.* Translated by Samuel B. Griffith. Washington, DC: US Marine Corps.

Tucker, Patrick. 2015. "How Wi-Fi Will Power Tomorrow's Battle Gear." Defense One, June 11. http://www.defenseone.com/technology/2015/06/how-wi-fi-will-power-tomorrows-battle-gear/115114/?oref=d-channelriver.

Tucker, Patrick. 2016. "Report: Weapons AI Increasingly Replacing, Not Augmenting, Human Decision Making." Defense One, September 26. http://www.defenseone.com/technology/2016/09/report-weapons-ai-increasingly-replacing-not-augmenting-human-decision-making/131826/?oref=d-channelriver.

Tucker, Patrick. 2016. "Special Operators Are Getting a New Autonomous Tactical Drone." Defense One, September 11. http://www.defenseone.com/technology/2016/09/special-operators-are-getting-new-autonomous-tactical-drone/131431/?oref=d-channelriver.

Tucker, Patrick. 2017. *The Future of Military Tech*. Defense One, June. http://www.defenseone.com/assets/future-military-tech/portal/.

Tucker, Patrick. 2017. "The Military Is Using Human Brain Waves to Teach Robots How to Shoot." Government Executive, May 5. http://www.govexec.com/technology/2017/05/military-using-human-brain-waves-teach-robots-how-shoot/137624/.

Turner, Fred. 2006. *From Counterculture to Cyberculture: Stewart Brand, the Whole Earth Network, and the Rise of Digital Utopianism*. Chicago: University of Chicago Press.

Ullman, Richard. 1983. "Redefining Security." *International Security* 8 (1): 129–53.

Uniform Code of Military Justice. Accessed April 10, 2019. http://www.ucmj.us/about-the-ucmj.

United States Air Force. 2011. *Air Force Basic Doctrine, Organization, and Command: Air Force Doctrine Document One*. Washington, DC: United States Air Force.

United States Air Force. 2014. "Dynamic Targeting and the Tasking Process." Curtis E. LeMay Center for Doctrine Development and Education, accessed April 10, 2019. https://doctrine.af.mil/download.jsp?filename=3-60-D17-Target-Dynamic-Task.pdf.

United States Department of Defense. 2009. *Unmanned Systems Integrated Roadmap, FY 2009–2034*. Accessed April 10, 2019. http://www.acq.osd.mil/psa/docs/UMSIntegratedRoadmap2009.pdf.

United States Department of Defense. 2011. *Unmanned Systems Integrated Roadmap, FY 2011–2036*. Accessed April 10, 2019. http://www.publicintelligence.net/dod-unmanned-systems-integrated-roadmapfy2011-2036.

United States Department of Defense. 2012. *Directive 3000.09*. Accessed April 10, 2019. www.dtic.mil/whs/directives/corres/pdf/300009p.pdf.

United States Department of Defense. 2013. *Unmanned Systems Integrated Roadmap: FY2013–2038*. Washington, DC: www.defense.gov/pubs/DoD-USRM-2013.pdf.

United States Department of Defense. 2014. *Climate Change Adaptation Roadmap*. Accessed April 10, 2019. http://www.acq.osd.mil/eie/Downloads/CCARprint_wForward_e.pdf.

United States Department of the Navy. 1946. *Radiological Safety at Operation Crossroads Atomic Bomb Tests 73862*. Film.

United States Department of the Navy. 1949. *Operation Crossroads AVA13712VNB1*. Film.

United States Office of Scientific Research and Development. National Defense Research Committee, issuing body. 1946. *Visibility Studies and Some Applications in the Field of Camouflage*. New York: Columbia University Press.

United States War Department. 1941. *Binaural Training Instruments, M1 and M2*. Washington, DC: US War Department.

United States War Department. 1944. *War Department Field Manual FM 100-20: Command and Employment of Air Power*. Washington, DC: Government Printing Office.

Unity Answers. 2014. "How to Detect Enemy in Effective Way." February 9. http://answers.unity3d.com/questions/635157/how-to-detect-enemy-in-effective-way.html.

Valdes, F., and Robert A. Freitas. 1980. "Comparison of Reproducing and Nonreproducing Starprobe Strategies for Galactic Exploration." *Journal of the British Interplanetary Society* 33 (5): 402–6.

van Creveld, Martin. 1985. *Command in War*. Cambridge, MA: Harvard University Press.

van Creveld, Martin. 1991. *The Transformation of War*. New York: The Free Press.

van Creveld, Martin. 2000. *The Art of War: War and Military Thought*. London: Cassell.

Vattimo, Gianni, and Santiago Zabala. 2011. *Hermeneutic Communism: From Heidegger to Marx*. New York: Columbia University Press.

Vego, Milan N. 2004. "Operational Command and Control in the Information Age." *Joint Force Quarterly* 35: 100–107.

Vinge, Vernor. 1993. "The Coming Technological Singularity: How to Survive in the Post-Human Era." VISION-21 Symposium sponsored by NASA Lewis Research Center and the Ohio Aerospace Institute, March 30–31. https://edoras.sdsu.edu/~vinge/misc/sigularity.html.

Virilio, Paul. 1989. *War and Cinema: The Logistics of Perception*. Translated by Patrick Camiller. London: Verso.

Virilio, Paul. 1994. *The Vision Machine*. Translated by Julie Rose. Bloomington: Indiana University Press.

Virilio, Paul. 2006. *Information Bomb*. Translated by Chris Turner. New York: Verso.

Virilio, Paul. 2007. *The Original Accident*. Translated by Julie Rose. Malden, MA: Polity.

Virilio, Paul, and John Armitage. 2001. "The Kosovo W@r Did Take Place." In *Virilio Live: Selected Interviews*, edited by John Armitage, 167–97. London: SAGE.

Virilio, Paul, and Friedrich Kittler. 2001. "The Information Bomb: A Conversation." In *Virilio Live: Selected Interviews*, edited by John Armitage, 97–109. London: SAGE.

Virilio, Paul, and Sylvere Lotringer. 1983/2008. *Pure War*. New York: Semiotexte.

von Neumann, John. 1966. *Theory of Self-Reproducing Automata*. Urbana: University of Illinois Press.

Vucetich, John, et al. 2012. "All about Wolves." Wolves and Moose of Isle Royale Project, Michigan Tech University, accessed April 10, 2019. http://www.isleroyalewolf.org/overview/overview/wolves.html.

The Wachowski Brothers. 1999. *The Matrix*. Village Roadshow Pictures.

Wade, Peter. 2003. "The Guardians of Power: Biodiversity and Multiculturality in Colombia." In *The Anthropology of Power: Empowerment and Disempowerment in Changing Structures*, edited by Angela Cheater, 71–86. New York: Routledge.

Wajcman, Judy. 1991. *Feminism Confronts Technology*. University Park: Pennsylvania State University Press.

Wajcman, Judy. 2004. *Technofeminism*. Malden, MA: Polity.

Wajcman, Judy. 2010. "Feminist Theories of Technology." *Cambridge Journal of Economics* 34 (1): 143–52.

Wall, Mike. 2016. "NASA Finds 1,284 Alien Planets, Biggest Haul Yet, with Kepler Space Telescope." Space.com, May 10. https://www.space.com/32850-nasa-kepler-telescope-finds-1284-alien-planets.html.

Wall, Mike. 2016. "Electronic E.T.: Intelligent Aliens Are Likely Machines." Space.com, November 14. https://www.space.com/34713-intelligent-aliens-machines-seti-search.html.

Wall, Tyler, and Torin Monahan. 2011. "Surveillance and Violence from Afar: The Politics of Drones and Liminal Security-Scapes." *Theoretical Criminology* 15 (3): 239–54.

Wallerstein, Immanuel. 2004. *World Systems Analysis: An Introduction.* Durham, NC: Duke University Press.

Ware, Willis. 1979. "Security Controls for Computer Systems: Report of Defense Science Board Task Force on Computer Security-Reissue." Santa Monica, CA: RAND.

Watkins, Ali. 2016. "The Numbers Game." Buzzfeed, February 28. https://www.buzzfeed.com/alimwatkins/syria-civilian-casualties-policy?utm_term=.yskDqZk5P#.ava5naybP.

Weisberger, Marcus. 2015. "Pentagon Wants to Pair Troops with Machines to Deter Russia, China." Defense One, November 8. http://www.defenseone.com/technology/2015/11/pentagon-wants-pair-troops-machines-deter-russia-china/123498/.

Wells, Herbert George. 1898. *The War of the Worlds.* Leipzig, Germany: Bernhard Tauchnitz.

White, Hayden V. 1973. *Metahistory: The Historical Imagination in Nineteenth-Century Europe.* Baltimore, MD: Johns Hopkins University Press.

Wild, Jennifer. 2005. "Brain Imaging Ready to Detect Terrorists, Say Neuroscientists." *Nature* 437 (September 22): 457.

Williams, Raymond. 1973. *Television: Technology and Cultural Form.* London: Fontana.

Williams, Richard. 1991. "Two Historic Storms Convinced the Japanese Divine That They Were Invincible in War." *Weatherwise* 44 (5): 11–14.

Williams, Rosalind. 1994. "The Political and Feminist Dimensions of Technological Determinism." In *Does Technology Drive History? The Dilemma of Technological Determinism,* edited by Merritt Roe Smith and Leo Marx, 217–35. Cambridge, MA: MIT Press.

Wilson, Heather. 2017. "Why I'm Directing the Air Force to Focus on Space." In *The Future of the Air Force,* 4–5. Washington, DC: Defense One.

Winegard, Timothy C. 2016. *The First World Oil War.* Toronto, ON: University of Toronto Press.

Winner, Langdon. 1977. *Autonomous Technology: Technics-Out-of-Control as a Theme in Political Thought.* Cambridge, MA: MIT Press.

Winner, Langdon. 1986. *The Whale and the Reactor: A Search for Limits in an Age of High Technology.* Chicago: University of Chicago Press.

Winthrop-Young, Geoffrey. 2002. "Drill and Distraction in the Yellow Submarine: On the Dominance of War in Friedrich Kittler's Media Theory." *Critical Inquiry* 28 (4): 825–54.

Winthrop-Young, Geoffrey. 2011. *Kittler and the Media.* Malden, MA: Polity.

Winthrop-Young, Geoffrey. 2012. "Hunting a Whale of a State: Kittler and His Terrorists." *Cultural Politics* 8 (3): 399–412.

Winthrop-Young, Geoffrey. 2015. "*De Bellis Germanicis*: Kittler, the Third Reich, and the German Wars." *Cultural Politics* 11 (3): 361–75.

Wirbel, Loring. 2004. *Star Wars: U.S. Tools of Space Supremacy.* London: Pluto Press.

Wolfe, Patrick. 2006. "Settler Colonialism and the Elimination of the Native." *Journal of Genocide Research* 8 (4): 387–409.

Wolff, Eric. 2016. "Mattis: Trump Cabinet's Lone Green Hope?" Politico, December 19. http://www.politico.com/story/2016/12/james-mattis-climate-change-trump-defense-232833.

Work, Robert O., and Shawn Brimley. 2014. *Preparing for War in the Robotic Age*. Washington, DC: Center for a New American Security.

Yale Quantum Institute. 2016. "US Lead in Quantum Computing 'Under Siege,' Says White House Cyber Adviser." Yale Quantum Institute, December 11. http://quantuminstitute.yale.edu/news/us-lead-quantum-computing-under-siege-says-white-house-cyber-adviser.

Yenne, Bill. 2004. *Attack of the Drones: A History of Unmanned Aerial Combat*. St. Paul, MN: Zenith Press.

Zaloga, Steven J. 2008. *Unmanned Aerial Vehicles: Robotic Air Warfare, 1917–2007*. Oxford: Osprey Publishing.

Zenko, Micah. 2017. "Obama's Final Drone Strike Data." Council on Foreign Relations, January 20. https://www.cfr.org/blog-post/obamas-final-drone-strike-data.

Zennie, Michael. 2013. "Death from a Swarm of Tiny Drones: U.S. Air Force Releases Terrifying Video of Tiny Flybots That Can Hover, Stalk, and Even Kill Targets." *Daily* Mail, February 19. http://www.dailymail.co.uk/news/article-2281403/U-S-Air-Force-developing-terrifying-swarms-tiny-unmanned-drones-hover-crawl-kill-targets.html.

Ziarek, Krzysztof. 2013. "A Vulnerable World: Heidegger on Humans and Finitude." *SubStance* 42 (3): 169–84.

Žižek, Slavoj. 2012. "Introduction: The Spectre of Ideology." In *Mapping Ideology*, edited by Slavoj Žižek, 1–33. London and Brooklyn: Verso.

Zylinska, Joanna. 2018. "A Feminist Counterapocalpyse." In *The End of Man: A Feminist Counterapocalypse*, 1–33. Minneapolis: University of Minnesota Press.

Index

absolute enmity, 138
Adami, Christoph, 98
Adelman, Rebecca, 13
aerial dominance, 53, 140, 148-51
agricultural monitoring, 82
aircraft: balloons, 124-25, 128; defense towers, 42-43; detection of, 38-39; energy sources and weaponry, 148-49; radiotelephones in, 49; registration of, 45; remote-controlled, 127-30; unidentified flying objects, 175-77; and weather, 72-73, 124; World War I autonomous, 125-26. *See also* drones, contemporary; unmanned aerial vehicles
Air Defense Systems Engineering Committee, 112
alien attack planning, 155, 189, 192, 196-97
alien intelligence, search for: analog versus digital imaging, 187; and artificial intelligence, 195; communication issues, 190, 193; data analysis problems, 193; and distance, 186, 192; enemies, as search for, 197; and enemy detection media, 188, 190-92; FOCAL, 187, *188*; historical overview of, 177-78; James Webb Space Telescope, 186-87; Keppler space telescope, 186; and light, 178, 185-86; "A Man Said to the Universe," 178-79; and media, 177; and military planning, 187; and NASA, 185-87; and new media, 186; probes, self-replicating, 191-92; SETI, 193; space observation and mapping, 178-83; and surveillance, 184-85; and telescopes, 185-86; and time, 178, 186, 192; Voyager spacecraft, 188-90
Allen, Booz, 199

Alliez, Eric, 105
analog computing, 169
anthropocentrism, 92-93, 100, 102-3, 196
anthropophobia: and automation, 17-18; in the military, 16-19; and UAVs, 130, 132-35
anti-satellite missiles, 189
Apocalypse Now, 201-2
apocalyptic imaginaries, 161-62
Arkin, Ronald, 136
Armageddon, 161-62
armed gaze, the, 130
armistice, 198
Arquilla, John, 153
Arrival, 192
artificial intelligence (AI): as adversarial, 171, 174; and alien attack planning, 155, 192, 197; and alien intelligence searches, 195; anthropocentric illusions of, 102-3; approximate rationality of, 98-99, 101; benevolence theories of, 92-93, 97; chaoplexic, 166-67; as conscientious objector, 209-11; decision-making of, 98-99; desertion potential, 207-9; discrimination, as supporting, 90-91; evolution of, 92-93, 97-98; as existential threat, 99, 106-7, 195, 213-14; future developments of, 92-93; and Gaia thesis, 86-87; humanist perspectives on, 91-94, 96, 100-101; and humans, 173-74; human values in, 102; and media escalation, 171; Michael Shermer on, 92-93, 97; and modernity, logics of, 106; versus natural intelligence, 93; and social shaping of technology theory, 93; Steven Pinker on, 92-93, 96-97, 100; utility functions, 98-100

artificial intelligence, fear of: anthropocentric critiques of, 92–93, 100; versus nonmilitary AI, 90–91; open letter on, 89–93; versus other technologies, 90; public forums on, 92; reasons for, 98–108
artificial intelligence, military: and anthropophobia, 18–19; applications of, 160; ban on, proposed, 89; command functions and response times, 16; as existential threat, 26, 108; versus the free market, 23; and Gaia thesis, 86; history of, 3–4; human accountability for, 101–2; humans, as replacing, 14–16, 18–19; learning capabilities of, 135; and media escalation, 26; and media technologies, 2–4; Target Image Discrimination (TID) systems, 14; targets, autonomous selection of, 14; as third revolution, 14, 89–90, 160; as tool, 101
Asimov, Isaac, 205–6, 211
Astrahan, Morton, 112
atomic weapons tests, 76–79, 82, 109
Aurora Flight Sciences, 149
automation: and anthropophobia, 17–18; of labor, 114; laissez faire capitalism as, 20; MAD necessitating, 121; and military production, 113; of nuclear deterrence, 113; self-engineered systems, 123. *See also* decentralized execution
autonomous operation, 124

Babich, Babette, 97
Ball, Patrick, 136
balloon warfare, 124–25, 128
Bates, Charles, 71
Becker, Jo, 137
Bertillon, Alphonse, 7
big data, 198
Block, the, 129
book overviews, 4, 26–27
Bostrom, Nick, 26, 99, 192, 195
Bousquet, Antoine, 60
bows and arrows, 143–44, 146
Braidotti, Rosi, 12
Brand, Stewart, 23
Brehm, Barbara, 67–68
Brimley, Shawn, 53
British military, 3, 37, 38, 127, 129, 145
Brown, Frederick, 212–13

Brown, Wendy, 20
Browne, Simone, 91
Buderi, Robert, 112
Burr, E. Godfrey, 41
Bush, George H. W., 139
Bush, Vannevar, 41–42

C4I: automation in, 10, 16, 19, 26; in the Cold War, 2; cyber attacks on, 152, 155; and popular media, 12; technologies enabling, 134. *See also* SAGE
Callicott, J. Baird, 61
capitalism, 19–20, 23, 105, 114
CARACaS system, 3–4
Carter, James Earl, 188–89
centralized control, 48–52
Chamayou, Grégoire, 137
chaos theory, 166–67
China, 79, 159, 164, 168
Chomsky, Noam, 89
Chow, Rey, 106
Christensen, Clayton, 152–53
Clausewitz, Carl von, 10, 58, 66–67
climate change: as existential threat, 195; Gaia approach to, 84–88; and media, 88; and the US military, 61
climate modeling, 82–83
Cockburn, Cynthia, 12
Cold War, the: and aircraft registration, 45; atomic weapons testing, 76–79, 81; drone programs during, 130; enemy detection media, 46; Ground Observer Corps, 115–17; and labor, 113–14, 117; Leviathan system, 123; media escalation, 6, 159; military-industrial-scientific complex, 113; military projects, characteristics of, 137; mutually assured destruction, 79, 87, 113; space observation, 184; as surveillance war, 130; technology in, 2, 114–15; as total war, 83; weather and climate data, 76, 79, 83. *See also* SAGE
command and control: of air power, 50–51; versus autonomy, 48; centralized, 51–52, 200; in cyber warfare, 53; decentralized, 58, 201; humans, removal from, 53; of submarines, 148. *See also* C4I; SAGE
communication: and alien intelligence, 190, 193; in command structures, 119; as mathematical problem, 10; and the

military-media complex, 9–11; satellite, 54–55; vulnerabilities in, 52–54; and warfare, 9–11. *See also* C4I
computing, methods of, 119, 167–69
conscientious objectors, 209–12
Context Institute, 84
Corn, Geoffrey, 101
Crandall, Jordan, 121
Crane, Stephen, 178–79
Crawford, Kate, 90–91
Crimean War, the, 48–49
crossbows, 143–45
cruise missiles, 59
C-SPAN navigation system, 54–55
cybernetics theory: and digital teleology, 166; and enemy ontology, 87; feedback in, 166–67; global epistemology, 86–87; and operational media, 121; and SAGE, 121–22; and weather and climatic data, 79, 83. *See also* Gaia thesis
cyberwar: advantages of, 152; and aerial supremacy, 154–55; and disruptive innovation, 152–55, 157; enemies, potential, 156; energy and information in, 152; and energy dominance, 141; versus guerrilla warfare, 153–54; history of, 152; and mapping, 151; netwar, 153; and oil dependency, 154; Stuxnet, 156–57

data collection, military, 198–99
Dean, Jodi, 22
death-worlds, 136
decentralized execution: definition of, 48; kill decisions, 55–56; swarms, 57–60; technologies enabling, 52–60; in US Air Force, 50–51
Deeds, E. A., 125
Defense Science Board, 11, 132–33, 160
DeLanda, Manuel, 18, 59–60, 113–14
Department of Defense (DoD): AI investments, 11, 54, 160; armistice definition, 198; authentication definition, ix; automation, need for, 55; autonomous operation definition, 124; centralized control definition, 48; *Climate Change Adaptation Roadmap*, 61; concept definitions, x; conscientious objectors, 209–10; decentralized execution definition, 48; deserter definition, 207; detachment definition, 200; and drone strike processes, 132, 134; drone strikes, Yemen, 137; escalation definition, 159; event matrix definition, 1; in extremis definition, 89; fuel consumption, 140, 150; hostile environment definition, 61; identification friend or foe definition, 29; intelligence, surveillance, and reconnaissance definition, 109; kill decision policy, 55–56; and National Security Council, 56; operation plan definition, v; Project Maven, 58; roadmaps, 4, 55, 59–61; SATCOM vulnerabilities, 54; Summer Study on Autonomy, 16, 160; and swarms, 59–60; unknowns, 177; *Unmanned Systems Integrated Roadmap*, 55, 59–60; vital ground definition, 139
depoliticization and liberalism, 19–23, 164
desertion, 207–9
detachments, 200–204
Dick, Philip K., 202
digital teleology, 164–70
digitization, 119–20, 166
direct energy weapons (DEWs), 155
discourse networks, 19
disruptive innovation, 152–55, 157
Division of Operational Energy Plans and Programs, 150
domestic struggles and warfare, 7
dominance: aerial, 53, 140, 148–51; cyber, 141, 150–54; disruptive innovation in, 151, 155, 157; and energy sources, 141–42, 148–49, 151, 156–57; Friedrich Kittler on, 142, 151; software, shift to, 153–54
dominance-dependence dynamic, 142, 156
drones, contemporary: accuracy of, 136; in Afghanistan war, 131; anthropophobic logics of, 132–35; civilian casualties, 136–37; costs of, 55; data security, 53–55; and decentralization, 53; DoD investment in, 134; enemy epistemologies of, 7, 137; energy sources, 149–50; ethical issues overview, 3; failed strikes, 132, 136; humans, as superior to, 132; information processing, 16; Ion Tiger, 149; in Iraq war, 131–32; Joint Air Tasking Cycle, 132–33; kill decisions, 55–56, 131; latency, 131–34; loitering, 132; versus manned aircraft, 53; media capacities of, 3; microdrones, 150–51; multiaircraft control, 53;

drones, contemporary: (cont.)
navigation technologies, 54; Obama administration, 136–37; operators of, 131–32, 135; in Pakistan war, 136; ScanEagle, 134; Stalkers, 149; and surveillance, 55; swarms, 57–60, 150; technological escalation of, 134; Trump administration, 137; US strikes, 131–32; in the War on Terror, 131–32, 136–37
drone strike policy, American, 56–57
Dubrofsky, Rachel, 12
Dyer-Witheford, Nick, 17
Dyson, George B., 113–14, 169

Earth: as enemy, 63, 87; human relationships to, 63, 65–66, 85–86; objectification of, 23–24, 62; photography of, 23, 79, 81; as resource, 105, 107. *See also* Gaia thesis
earth systems theory. *See* Gaia thesis
Edison's Conquest of Mars, 183–84, *185*
Edwards, Paul, 62, 68, 76, 109
Einstein, Albert, 187
Ellul, Jacques, 17
end of history: Fukuyama's thesis, 21, 162–65; Kittler's views, 165–67, 170–72; liberalism as causing, 21, 163; McLuhan's view, 164–65, 171–72; media escalation causing, 172; the third revolution causing, 160
enemy detection media: and alien intelligence searches, 188, 190–92; automated, 29–30, 36; Cold War, 46; as creating enemies, 188; data analysis problems, 193; Nikola Tesla's, 40; problems with, 47, 193; and September 11th attacks, 46–47; telescopes as, 181; in *The War of the Worlds*, 183. *See also* Identification Friend or Foe and media; radar; SAGE
enemy epistemologies: overviews of, 4–5, 8; automation of, 56; biometrics, 7–8; causal relationships, 6–7; of drones, 7, 137–38; of Earth, 86–87; of the human, 24; insider threats, 7–8; of liberalism, 20–22, 24; and media, 4–9; microbiology example, 5–6, 8; racialized, 7–8; SAGE example, 6; and soldiers, 8; of swarms, 59; and technological change, 8–9, 11–12;

and warfare, forms of, 8–9; in the War on Terror, 137–38
enemy identification. *See* Identification Friend or Foe
enemy ontology, 82, 87, 192
energy and weaponry: aircraft, 148–49; autonomous, 139–40; bows and arrows, 143–46; crossbows, 143–45; and culture, 144, 157–58; drones, 149–50; harpoons, 143, 145–46; renewable, 150; separation of, 146; spears, 142–43; submarines, 146–48
energy sources: and autonomy, 156; and conflict, 142; and cyberwar, 152; and dominance, 141–42, 148–49, 151, 156–57; dominance-dependence dynamic, 142, 156; and humans, 156–57; and logistics, 142, 156; and territory, 141–42, 150, 152
epistemological war, 13
escalation, 159. *See also* media escalation; military escalation
ethics: and conscientious objectors, 209–11; human, as limitation, 18; and inclusivity, 91; of military AI use, 3, 98, 136; and robots, treatment of, 206
Everett, Robert R., 121
evolution, 92–93, 97–99
existential threats, 26, 99, 106–7, 195–96, 213–14
in extremis, definition of, 89

Fahrney, Delmar, 129
feminism, post-human, 12
Finn, Peter, 57–58
Flammarion, Camille, 182
Floreano, Dario, 97–98
fog of war, the, 58–60
food shortages, 82
Foucault, Michel: on humanism, 24–26, 213; on liberalism, 19; on the military, 14–15
Freitas, Robert A., Jr., 191
friction, 66–67
Friedson, Idalia, 168
friend/enemy distinctions. *See* identification friend or foe
fuel. *See* energy
Fukuyama, Francis, 21, 162–65, 167
Fuller, John F., 71, 82

Gaber, Gustave, 127
Gaia thesis: and AI, 86–87; Bruno Latour on, 84–85; and climate science, 84–85; David Spangler on, 84; as enemy, 62, 83, 85–88; humans in, 85–87, 215; and US military planning, 86
Galison, Peter, 192
game theory, 120–21
Gane, Nicholas, 103
Gates, Robert, 53
Geneva Convention and robots, the, 101–2
German military: acoustic locator avoidance, 38, 120; aircraft defense towers, 42–43; and balloon attacks, 124; gas attacks, 74, 75; radar avoidance, 38; radio-controlled weapon systems, 127, 129; surveillance drones, 130; U-boats, 40, 72, 146, 150; zeppelin attacks, 73
Gerstenberger, Erhard, 63
global cybernetic epistemology, 86–87
global peace paradox, 196–97
global positioning system (GPS), 54, 111, 151
Gordon, Don, 83
Graham, Stephen, 2
Griffith, Samuel B., 153–54
Ground Observer Corps, 115–17
Grumman, Northrop, 54, 152
guerrilla tactics, 154–55

Hamilton, Clive, 85–86
Hansberry, Michael, 149
Hansen, Mark, 17
Haraway, Donna, 12, 104
harpoons, 143
Hawking, Stephen, 26, 89, 214
Hayles, Katherine, 2, 9, 20, 48
Heidegger, Martin: on anthropocentrism, 102; on capitalism, 105; epigraph quotes, 89; on modernity, 106; on modern war and humanity, 103–4; on technological threats, 106–7; on technology and nature, 214–15; world picture concept, 23–24
Herschel, William, 181–82
Hester, Helen, 12
high-tech industry labor, 114
Hollerith machines, 7, 70, 72
hostile environments, 61

human agency and technology, 94
human exceptionalism, 12
humanism: AI, approaches to, 91–94, 96, 100–101; complex systems in, 96; contradiction of, 24; of liberalism, 20, 24–25; project of, 100; technology in, 12, 102
human limitations: calculation times, 15–16; drone operators, 131–32; energy sources, 156; and MAD, 121; overcoming, methods for, 25; reaction times, 16; and submarines, 147–48; summary of, 18
humans: and AI, 173–74; AI replacing, 14–16, 18–19; as always already technological, 173–74; and automation, 17–18; conquest drive of, 213–14; drones, as inferior to, 132; Earth, relationship to, 63, 65–66, 85–86; essence of, 215; extinction of, 85, 215; in Gaia thesis, 85–87, 215; liberalism's inquiry into, 24–25; and media escalation, 170, 173; in the military, 107; and military anthropophobia, 16–19; and the military-media complex, 11; in military science, 14–15; as noise source, 10, 173; objectification of, 107; scientific drive of, 213; as scientific subjects, 25–26; soldiers, 14–15, 135; and technology, 12, 102–3, 107
Huygens, Christiaan, 181

IBM, 45, 110, 118, 121–22, 167
Identification Friend or Foe (IFF): aircraft defense towers, 42–43; Caesar and Brutus example, 31, 34; and camouflage, 40–42; dear enemy effect, 35; definition of, 29; enemy assessment, 30–31; the enemy detection process, 36; EnemyGraph, 30, 31; and evolution, 35; and friendships, 35; history of, 35; interplays and feedback loops in, 40–44; Johari windows, 47; nearness enabling, 30, 34; and physical closeness, 30–31, 32, 33, 36; and political existence, 5; reclassification problems, 30; SAGE, 44–45; September 11 attacks, 45–47; target identification, 44–45
Identification Friend or Foe and media: acoustic locators, 37–39; as aid in, 29–30; as already obsolete, 40, 47; in enemy detection, 36–40; false positives, 40; friend-enemy expansion, 34–35;

Identification Friend or Foe and media: (cont.)
versus human senses, 36; radar, 37–40, 42, 44–45; radio detection finders, 43–44; as range extension, 34; and second-order interpretation, 36–37, 39
Independence Day, 160–61
indigenous peoples, 79
Intel, 139–40
intelligence, surveillance, and reconnaissance (IRD), 109

Jacobs, John, 112
Jehovah Sabaoth, 63–65
Johnson, Gordon, 16, 132

Kahn, Herman, 199
Kaplan, Caren, 106, 140
Kaplan, Fred, 152
Kepler, Johannes, 183
kill chains, 58
kill decisions, 55–56, 60, 160
Kindervater, Katharine Hall, 56
Kittler, Friedrich: on American Empire, 140; artificial intelligence, 191; on communication problems, 10; on digital language, 119; digital teleology, 165–67; discourse networks concept, 19; on dominance and energy use, 142, 151; on end of history, 165–67, 170–72; on energy and resources, 142; versus McLuhan, 165, 169–70; on media, 9, 52, 62, 91, 102, 118, 158; on media, optical, 119, 178; on media escalation, 165, 171; on the media-military complex, 9; on military automation, 3, 18, 23; on power, 6; on recording technologies, 119; on SAGE, 109; on sensing technologies, 130; technocentrism of, 170; on technological escalations, 131, 159; on warfare, 10, 18, 141
Korean War, 115

labor: attacks on, 114; civilian, 115–18; cognitive, 113–14; Cold War organization of, 113–14, 117; epistemological, 118, 120, 122–23; as fallible, 117; Ground Observer Corps, 115–17; and the military-industrial complex, 114; and military production, 113; mnemonic, 118, 121–22; perceptive, 118–19; of surveillance, 118. *See also* SAGE and labor
laissez faire capitalism, 19–20, 23
language, digital, 119
Latour, Bruno, 62, 84–85
Lazzarato, Maurizio, 105
Lele, Ajey, 68
lethal autonomy, 160
liberalism: overview of, 19; and apocalyptic imaginaries, 161–62; and automation, 20; and depoliticization, 19–23, 164; discourse networks of, 19; enemy epistemologies of, 20–22, 24; Foucault's definition of, 19; humanism of, 24–25; laissez faire logics, 19–20, 23; and military escalation, 163–64; and robots, 100; and Shannon's information theory, 19; suicidal logic of, 22; utopianism of, 163–64; warfare of, 21
light, 178, 185–86
"line drawn in the sand" phrase, 139
loitering, 14, 60, 132
Lovelock, James, 83–85
lunar calendars, 179

machine autonomy and depoliticization, 19–23
Maconie, Robin, 200
Magnet, Shoshana, 12, 91
Mander, Jerry, 95
maps as instruments, 151
Marconi, Guglielmo, 52
Mars: *Edison's Conquest of Mars*, 183–84, 185; observation and mapping of, 179–83; Soviet probes on, 188; *The War of the Worlds*, 182–83
Massumi, Brian, 13
materialist xenofeminism, 12–13
Mattis, Jim "Mad Dog," 139
Mattiussi, Claudio, 97–98
Mbembe, Achille, 136
McLuhan, Marshall, 102, 119, 164, 169–70
media: as adversarial, 170; anthropocentric approaches to, 102–3; and centralized control, 48–52; and climate change, 88; enemies, as producing, 6–7; and enemy epistemology, 4–9; F-35 system, 2–3; humans, impact on, 102–4; and military strategy, 62; military technology, as

driving, 8–9, 12; and modernity, 106; operational, 121; optical logics, 104; peace with, 215; and the political, 5; reduction to calculability, 105; as situation-determining, 91, 94–95; smart weaponry, enabling, 2; space observation, 175, 177; telegraphy, 49, 134, 159; telescopes, 134, 181, 185–87; television, 129. *See also* enemy detection media; Identification Friend or Foe and media

media escalation: and AI, 26, 171; and AI, military, 19; and apocalyptic themes, 162; Cold War, 159; digital teloi of, 164–70; Friedrich Kittler on, 169; and humans, 170, 172–73; as human-technology struggle, 172–73; and liberalism, 19; media's adversaries in, 172; in media studies, 164–65; and microchips, 160; and military escalation, 26, 159–60; and nature, 170; polemocentric view of, 9, 169–72; and war, 165

Mehsud, Baitullah, 136

microdrones, 150–51

the military: Kettering project, 127; weather data, 70–71

military data collection, 198–99

military escalation: of AI, 160; and apocalyptic themes, 162; and media escalation, 26, 159–60; political logics of, 160; and quantum computing, 167–68; and technology, 162–63

military-media complex, the, 9–11

military planning: for alien attacks, 155, 189, 192, 196–97; and alien intelligence, search for, 187; and big data, 198–99; and Gaia thesis, 86; and history, 199; and speculative fiction, 199; war games, 18, 120–21, 199

military science, 14–15

military training, 14–15

Mindell, David A., 128–29

modernity, 105–6

Mouffe, Chantal, 22

Murray, John Courtney, 211

Murray, Matthew, 68

Musk, Elon, 26, 89, 108

mutiny: AI, 204–6; and *Bicentennial Man*, 206; danger of, 204; definition of, 204; in *The Matrix*, 206; risk factors, 204; and "The Three Laws of Robotics," 205–6

mutually assured destruction (MAD), 79, 87, 112–13, 121

national security, 83
Nebeker, Frederik, 71
Neumann, John von, 120, 191
Neumann, von, probes, 191
neural networks, 4, 171, 195
Nixon, Richard, 82
Noble, David, 113
Noble, Safiya, 91
noise: AI eliminating, 173; as camouflaging, 41, 120; in command and control, 119; and the digital telos, 167; humans as source of, 10, 173; liberalism's elimination of, 22–23; as mathematical problem, 10; reduction and vulnerability, 52

NORAD, 36
normalization and digitization, 119–20
nuclear energy, 95
nuclear submarines, 146–48
nuclear weapons tests, 76–79, 82, 109

oil, 140, 148–51
Omohundro, Steve, 98–99
Operation Popeye, 82
optical media, 104, 119, 178

Parks, Lisa, 9
Pearl Harbor attack, 111–12
Perry, William James, 134
Peters, John Durham, 91
Phalanx weapon system, 55–56
Pinker, Steven, 92–93, 96–97, 100
Plavchan, Peter, 193
polemocentrism and media escalation, 9, 169–72
Polk, Tim, 168
postdigital computing, 168–69, 168–69
predictive analytics, 198
Putin, Vladimir, 159

quantum computing, 167–68

radar: false positives, 112; human verification, need for, 115; in IFF, 37–40, 42, 44–45; and memory, 121–22; shortcomings of, 115; World War II, 37–40, 42, 112

radio: in airplanes, 49; and C4I, 119, 134; in enemy detection, 36, 43-44, 112; and media escalation, 159; vulnerability of, 52-53
radio-controlled weapons, 126-30
the radiographic episteme, 44-45
Rancière, Jacques, 161
RAND corporation, 58, 113, 120, 123, 148, 150, 152
Ranke, Leopold von, 25
remote control, 126-28
revolution in military affairs (RMA), 2, 68
Rigetti, Chad, 168
Rio Scale, 193, *194*
Roach, Mary, 15
robots: and alien attack planning, 155, 192, 197; and the Geneva Convention, 101-2; and liberalism, 100; religious, 210; rights of, 205-6
Roff, Heather, 14
Roman, Gregory A., 16, 134, *135*
Ronfeldt, David, 153
Rossi, Francesca, 26, 89
Rumsfeld, Donald, 199
Russell, Stuart J., 26, 98-99
Russian defense spending, 159, 164
Russill, Chris, 62, 74

SAGE (Semi-Automatic Ground Environment): overviews of, 6, 110, 118; aircraft registration, 45; as cybernetic system, 121-22; descendants of, 36, 110, 123; development of, 110, 120; display scope, interactive, 119; as enemy detection media, 36; failure of, perceived, 123; and human error, elimination of, 111-12; IBM promotions of, 118, 121-22; as media system, 119; memory technologies in, 121-22; as operational media, 121; organizational technology of, 113-14; Paul Edwards on, 109; purpose of, 110; and screening technologies, 110-11, 120; and surveillance, 45, 112, 120-21; target recognition, 44-45; technological predecessors, 36
SAGE and labor: overview of, 113; as attack on, 114; automation of, 110, 113, 118, 123; epistemological, 120, 122-23; mnemonic, 121-22; mutually assured destruction, 113; perceptive, 119; replacement of, 117-18

sand, 139-41, 151
Santayana, George, 212
satellite communications, 54-55
scenario-based planning, 82-83
Scharre, Paul, 57
Schiaparelli, Giovanni, 182
Schmitt, Carl, 5, 20-21, 138, 213-14
Schwartz, Norton, 135
science, 25-26
science fiction: *Animatrix*, 206, 208-9; "Answer," 212-13; *Arrival*, 192; *Bicentennial Man*, 206; *Edison's Conquest of Mars*, 183-84, *185*; *Her*, 207-9; *The Matrix*, 206; and military planning, 199; "Second Variety," 202-4; surveillance in, 182-84; "The Three Laws of Robotics," 205-6; *The War of the Worlds*, 182-83; *Weapon*, 211-12, *211-12*
screening technologies, 110-11
secrecy, 119-20
September 11 attacks, 45-47, 67
Serviss, Garrett Putnam, 183
Shakespeare, William, 29
Shane, Scott, 137
Shannon, Claude, 10, 19, 166
Shaw, Ian G. R., 17, 103, 137
Shermer, Michael, 92-93, 102
Shiga, John, 73, 76
Shostak, Seth, 195
Singer, Peter, 135
SKYNET program, 136
Sloterdijk, Peter, 23, 75, 96, 107
smart weapons, 1-2, 134
Snowden, Edward, 136-37
social shaping of technology (SST) theory, 93-95
soldiers, 14-15, 135
sonar, 73, 134
Soviet Union, the, 82, 109, 113, 188
space exploration, 214
space observation and mapping, 178-83
Spangler, David, 84
spears, 142-43
Sperry, Elmer, 125, 128
Squier, George Owen, 49
Sterne, Jonathan, 7
Stiegler, Bernard, 103, 173
Stocker, Gerfried, 10
storm gods, 63, 66

Suchman, Lucy, 12
Sullivan, Dan, 16
Sun Tzu, 29, 141, 200
surveillance: and alien intelligence searches, 184–85; of cell phone networks, 136; countering secrecy, 120; drones, 55, 130; global, 109–10; human error in, 111–12, 117; labor of, 118; and mutually assured destruction, 120; and norms, 44; and SAGE, 45, 112, 120–21; satellite, 190; in science fiction, 182–84; and war games, 120–21
swarms, 57–60, 150

Tang, Vincent, 166
Target Image Discrimination (TID) systems, 14
technology: anthropocentric approaches to, 102–3; and designer intention, 94; humans, influence on, 102–3; and humans, 12, 102–3, 107; large scale systems, 95–96; as ontological threat, 103–4, 106–7; repurposing of, 93–95; as situation-determining, 96; social shaping theory, 93–95; threat of, 94–95, 103–4, 106–8; war advancing, 162–63. *See also* media
technology, military: in the civilian sphere, 9, 95, 111; Heidegger on, 103–4, 106–7; and political agency, 96; purposes of, 95
telegraphy, 49, 134, 159
telescopes, 134, 181, 185–87
television, 129
territory and energy production, 141–42, 150, 152
territory and maps, 151
Tesla, Nikola, 1–2, 40, 126, *127*
third revolution, the, 14, 89–90, 160. *See also* artificial intelligence, military
Trump, Donald J., 56, 137, 163–64

U-boats, 40, 72, 146, 150
Ullman, Richard, 83
unidentified flying objects (UFOBs), 175–77
unmanned aerial vehicles (UAVs): aerial torpedoes, 125–26; ambivalence toward, 126–27; and anthropophobia, 130; autonomy versus human control, 128–29; balloons, 124–25, 128; Cold War surveillance drones, 130; domestication logics, 128, 130–31; early perspectives on, 128; enemy epistemologies of, 128; remotely controlled, 127–30; vision technologies, 129–30; World War I, 125–26. *See also* drones, contemporary
unmanned systems, 55, 59–60. *See also* drones; swarms
unmanned underwater vehicles (UUVs), 148
US Air Force (USAF): air superiority, 175; control and execution, 50–51; drone operators, 131; flexibility, need for, 51; and UFOBs, 175, *176*
the US military: AI investment, 11; air power doctrine, 50; Army Signal Corps, 69–70, *71*; and climate change, 61; Defense Science Board, 132–33; defense spending, 164; drone strike policy, 56–57; F-35 system, 2–3; Future Writing Warfare program, 199; and international military competition, 164; and postdigital computing, 168–69; and quantum computing, 168; the RMA, 2, 68; Russia analysis center, 159–60; Signal Corps, 130; smart weapons history, 2; soldier biometric data, 7; weather data collection, 68–70. *See also* Department of Defense
USS *Nautilus*, 146–47
USS *Triton*, 147

V2 rockets, 76, 79, *80–81*, 130
van Creveld, Martin, 15–16
van Leeuwenhoek, Antoine, 5, 8
Vattimo, Gianni, 25
Vego, Milan, 51–52
Vietnam War, 82, 130
Virilio, Paul: big optics concept, 79; on capitalism, 105; on enemy epistemology, 8; on escalation, 134; Kittler interview, 165–66; mentioned, 9, 13, 26, 119, 156, 205; on technology, 205
vital ground, 139
Voyager spacecraft, 188–90

Wajcman, Judy, 12, 90, 93–94
Wall, Mike, 186
Ware, Willis H., 152

warfare: communication problems, 9–11; and domestic struggles, 7; of liberalism, 21; and socio-political progress, 162–64; as special case, 13

war games, 18, 120–21, 199

War of the Worlds, The, 182–83

War on Terror, the, 131–32, 136–38

weather and climate: and airplanes, 72–73; Army Signal Corps, 69–70, 71; and atomic weapons, 76–79, 81, 87; and balloon warfare, 124; Carl von Clausewitz on, 66–67; climate modeling, 82–83; Cold War, 76, 79, 83; colonial era, 69; contemporary monitoring, 68–69; and cybernetics, 79, 83; discourse weather networks, 68–75, 87; and Earth-human relationships, 63, 65–66, 85–86; ENMOD, 81; food shortage prediction, 82; forecasting, early, 69–71; and friction concept, 66–68; and Gaia thesis, 84–85; and gas attacks, 72, 74–75; God/classic episteme, 62, 63–66, 87; in history, 66–67; and human extinction, 85; in mythologies, 66; nature/modern episteme, 62; and scenario-based planning, 82–83; and technology, 67–68; theaters, creating new, 87; as threat to soldiers, 69; and U-boats, 72–73; and V2 rockets, 79; Vietnam War, 82; weaponization of, 76, 81–82; weather fronts, 75–76; weather media, 62; World War I, 72–76; World War II, 76; and zeppelins, 73–74

Weaver, Warren, 10

Wells, H. G., 182–83

Wiener, Norbert, 79, 168

Williams, Rosalind, 12

Wilson, Charles E., 113

Wilson, Heather, 175

Winner, Langdon, 95–96

Winthrop-Young, Geoffrey, 142, 148, 159, 165

Work, Robert O., 2, 11, 52–53, 160

world picture, 23–24

World War I: autonomous aircraft, 125–26; gas attacks, 75; grenade-throwing crossbows, 145; radio-controlled torpedoes, 127; weather and climatic data, 72–76

World War II: acoustic locators, 37–39; aircraft, radio-controlled, 129–30; American air defenses, 43–44; American invasion of Oran, 49–50; British aircraft detection, 38–39; and digital computing, 119; Operation Torch, 49–50; postwar logics, dominant, 120–21; radar, 37–40, 42; submarines, 146; as total war, 83. *See also* German military

Worldwide Military Command and Control System, 109

Wozniak, Steve, 89

Wright, Jason T., 193, 195

Yehudi project, 41–42

Zabala, Santiago, 25

Zacharias, Greg, 135

Ziarek, Krzysztof, 105

Zurbuchen, Thomas, 196

Zworykin, Vladimir, 129

Zylinska, Joanna, 12